OPERATIONS AND MATERIALS

PLANNING AND CONTROL

Jean Nollet, Joseph Kelada, Mattio O. Diorio
with Isabelle Deschamps, Claude R. Duguay, Roger Handfield
and special contribution from Albert R. Wood

OPERATIONS AND MATERIALS

PLANNING AND CONTROL

morin

Montreal □ Paris □ Casablanca

Canadian Cataloguing in Publication Data

Nollet, Jean, 1952–

    Operations and materials planning and control

    Translation of: La gestion des opérations et de la production.

    Includes bibliographical references and index.

    ISBN 2-89105-595-0

    1. Production management. 2. Production management—Problems, exercises, etc. I. Kelada, Joseph, 1934– . II. Diorio, Mattio O., 1934– . III. Title.

HD33.N6513 1996   658.5   C95-941392-8

Montreal, Gaëtan Morin Éditeur ltée
171, de Mortagne Blvd., Boucherville, Quebec, Canada J4B 6G4, Tel.: (514) 449-2369

Paris, Gaëtan Morin Éditeur, Europe
20, rue des Grands Augustins, 75006 Paris, France, Tel.: 33 (1) 53.73.72.78

Casablanca, Gaëtan Morin Éditeur – Maghreb S.A.
Rond-point des sports, angle rue Point du jour, Racine, 20 000 Casablanca, Maroc, Tel.: 212 (2) 49.02.17

Translation: Terry Knowles
Copy editing: Pamela Ireland and Jane Broderick

Printed in Canada

La gestion des opérations et de la production, 2ᵉ édition (abridged translation)
© gaëtan morin éditeur ltée, 1994

Legal Deposit – Bibliothèque nationale du Québec – National Library of Canada, 1996

1 2 3 4 5 6 7 8 9 0   G M E 9 6   5 4 3 2 1 0 9 8 7 6

Operations and Materials Planning and Control
© gaëtan morin éditeur ltée, 1996

FOREWORD AND ACKNOWLEDGMENTS

This book is an updated and abridged version of *Production/Operations Management: A Systemic Approach* that takes into account the comments of teachers and students who have used the first book.

Whereas the first, 900-page volume was translated in its entirety from French, this second volume has been adapted to the needs of the largest percentage of users, who suggested that we emphasize inventory control and operations planning. Thus the change in title. Our approach in this regard was as follows:

1. The comments of teachers and students were taken into account when the French version was drafted.

2. Professor Albert R. Wood, of the University of Western Ontario, in co-operation with Jean Nollet, selected the texts dealing with inventory and operations planning.

3. The sections were combined to form a coherent whole, in particular for use in the Principles of Inventory and Operations Control course offered by the Purchasing Management Association of Canada.

4. A number of problems were added to help students better apply some of the concepts covered in the various chapters.

The authors wish to thank the following individuals, all of whom are responsible to varying degrees for making this book possible:

— Professor Albert R. Wood, for his astute comments, his meticulous attention to detail and his commitment to tailoring this book to the needs of its target audience;

— the teachers and students who used the English version of the first edition, in particular those from the Principles of Inventory and Operations Control course, for taking the time to send us their comments. Because of their input, we decided to take a different approach to the translation and to focus the English version on inventory and operations planning;

— the members of the National Professional Accreditation Committee and the Board of Directors of the Purchasing Management Association of Canada, for having believed in this book from the outset;

— the publishing staff at Gaëtan Morin, in particular Josée Charbonneau, Anne Rémillard, Christiane Desjardins, Veronica Schami, Céline Laprise and Gaëtan Morin, for their guidance and assistance;

— our translators, Terry Knowles and Pamela Ireland, for producing a high-quality translation, which is not always an easy job with a text of this nature, especially within such tight deadlines;

— the copy editor, Jane Broderick, and the proofreader, Nancy Barr.

We are pleased with the final product and are confident that, with your comments, the next edition will be even better.

Jean Nollet, Joseph Kelada, Mattio O. Diorio,
Isabelle Deschamps, Claude R. Duguay and Roger Handfield

Production and Operations Management Department
École des Hautes Études Commerciales

TABLE OF CONTENTS

CHAPTER 1

The Role of Production/Operations Management in the Company

JOSEPH KELADA
MATTIO O. DIORIO, *authors*

INTRODUCTION

1.1   Production/Operations Management in Changing Times

Much has happened since the first edition of this book was published. The world is divided by language, culture, ideology, religion, tradition and ethnicity, yet borders are disappearing, walls are crumbling, barriers are falling, nations are coming together and the world is becoming smaller all the time. Not so long ago, a novelist who dared to describe today's world would have been accused of having an overactive imagination, of carrying fiction too far. No more Berlin Wall? No more Iron Curtain? The USSR in tatters and the Cold War over? Impossible!

The world has been transformed in economic terms as well. The countries of the European Union (EU) are eliminating all obstacles to the free circulation of goods, capital and citizens. Other European countries have signed economic agreements with the EU, making Western Europe one huge integrated market, at least in theory. The 12 members of the EU have been joined by the seven members of the European Free Trade Association (EFTA) to create what is called the European Economic Area (EEA), representing 45% of international trade and the largest single market in the world, with some 380 million inhabitants. On this side of the Atlantic, free-trade agreements have already linked the countries of North America and may soon extend to South America. In the east, Southeast Asian countries have formed powerful economic alliances.

All these changes mean that business leaders must rethink their traditional approach to management. For example, senior management and those in charge of the Finance function stress profits, dividends and return on investment, whereas Marketing managers concentrate on markets and competition. Most managers work in relative isolation, practising *introverted management*, measuring their own performance against internal results directly related to their function: preparing financial statements, hiring or laying off staff, training and paying employees and managers, computerizing administrative activities, purchasing the goods and services necessary for production and the operation of the various departments, optimizing inventories of raw materials and finished goods, rationalizing space and internal resources, reducing operating costs or investments in facilities and equipment, and a hundred other concerns.

Companies are taking different approaches to management in an effort to remain competitive. They are tossing around terms such as *business re-engineering,*[4] redesigning the firm or simply reinventing it, as described by Naisbitt. Every senior, middle and front-line manager, every employee, whatever his or her position in the company, must keep in mind that the success of the company is founded on co-ordinated and constant efforts to satisfy all three components of the shareholder-customer-employee triangle.[6] Consequently, management is a three-part affair, with the added dimension of constant co-operation with external partners both up- and downstream, such as suppliers of goods, human resources and financial services, distributors and transporters.

This new approach leads to *extroverted management,* in which the company's performance is measured against shareholder and customer satisfaction—generally closely linked—instead of the performance of every department or sector of the company being evaluated in terms of internal results. Rather than the traditional product-out approach, the new concept is market-in; instead of thinking about products, the focus is on customers and shareholders, and not only in the Marketing and Finance functions, but throughout the company, at all times, at all levels and in all departments, as well as in dealings with external partners.

Companies are adopting global management approaches, such as *total quality*, that call for close co-operation among the heads of all departments. Operations plays a major role, especially if all aspects of procurement management are included in this function. Industrial companies, if they are to become and remain competitive, must be able to serve their customers better and faster, while keeping prices as low as possible.[1] They realize that proper management of Production/Operations is essential, and so are turning to a new management technology that aims for world-class production and elimination of waste,[1] based on a number of concepts, strategies, new approaches and techniques, such as WCM (world class manufacturing), MRP (material requirements planning), MRP-II (manufacturing resources planning), FMS (flexible manufacturing systems), QFD (quality function deployment), CIM (computer-integrated manufacturing), TPM (total productive maintenance),[9] TQM (total quality management), business re-engineering, concurrent engineering, just-in-time, SMED (single minute exchange of dies) and other, more conventional production planning and control techniques. Some of these tools are also used in the service sector, where they may be either adapted or applied unchanged.

In another connection, and in response to the globalization of markets, economies and competition, the International Organization for Standardization (ISO) is now bringing together representatives from some one hundred countries to draw up international standards for goods and services, in an attempt to simplify and encourage international trade. The goal, in other words, is to get businesses all over the world to "speak the same language." Aside from product standards, the best-known standards today are those in the ISO 9000 series, dealing with management systems that provide for quality control, by giving potential customers/buyers/users an *assurance* of product quality, even before the products are designed, manufactured and delivered. International standardization of quality assurance and management systems is a prerequisite to trade between companies wishing to do business in an increasingly global market.

Along with this political, economic and social revolution, we are witnessing a technological revolution without precedent in the history of mankind. The tragic events of the Gulf War clearly showed that battles are no longer fought as they were 20 or 30 years ago. Similarly, in the business world high technology is invading industries and services in both the public and private sectors. The fax machines, pocket cellular telephones, automated banking machines, telephone answering machines and automated telephone communication systems that surround us every day would have been regarded as mere science fiction just yesterday. This technological revolution has touched every aspect of our lives, from work to play, and even our eating habits. The development of microprocessors has given us a huge variety of programmable devices, including cameras, microwave ovens, telephones, television sets, VCRs and automobiles.

In addition to affecting the creation of new products and changes to existing ones, the technological revolution has had a great influence on the way in which these products are designed, developed and made. Computer-assisted design and manufacturing (CAD/CAM) is revolutionizing work methods throughout companies. Robots can now replace human workers in repetitive, monotonous or dangerous tasks or under conditions of excessive noise, heat or cold. In the services sector, a huge number of banking transactions are now made at automated banking machines, while plane tickets and life insurance can be purchased from electronic vending machines at airports. Cash is increasingly being replaced by "plastic"—credit cards that sometimes even have integrated microchips. At Digital, one of the largest computer manufacturers in the world, products change every six months; at Seiko, the famous Japanese watch manufacturer, a new model is created every shift![1]

Technological advances are not limited to consumer goods and services. They have generated large-scale changes to operating and management methods in all organizations. And while they affect all parts of the company, they have the greatest impact on the Production/Operations function. As a result, Production/Operations Management, or POM, has reclaimed its former importance in the organization, given its decisive role in the company's profitability and customer–satisfaction needs, for customer satisfaction is what determines medium and long-term profitability and competitiveness. The success of a large number of companies in Japan (like Toyota and Sony), in the U.S. (like Xerox and Motorola), and in Canada (like Northern Telecom and Bell Canada), is proof of this shift in emphasis.

Business publications such as the *Harvard Business Review, Fortune* and *Business Week* are devoting frequent articles to the different strategic and operations aspects of POM, whereas in the past they concentrated almost exclusively on the financial or marketing aspects of management. They are publishing studies on world-class manufacturing, operations management in the service sector, the application of POM techniques borrowed from Japanese industry and some U.S. companies, integrated quality management, and so on.

Today's focus on POM is amply justified when one considers the extent to which many North American industries have fallen behind their Asian, European and other competitors who have used POM to their advantage, combined with close and constant attention to their customers.

1.2 Objectives of the Production/Operations Management (POM) Function

Any company, or any for-profit or not-for-profit private or public organization, must offer its customers, on a given "public," goods and services to reach its strategic objectives and goals, be they economic or social. Creating these products and delivering them to users are the company's main activities.*

Since the turn of the century, the tertiary sector has gained considerably in relative economic importance in comparison with the secondary sector. More and more, service companies are successfully adapting and applying production management concepts and techniques drawn from industry. Since the term *production* is often

---

* We will use the term *company* to mean any for-profit or not-for-profit public or private organization in the manufacturing or service sector.

associated with the industrial world, it is generally replaced in service companies with the term *operations*, to mean everything involved in creating a product, be it a good or a service.

Note that there is a difference between manufacturing, operations or production, and POM. *Manufacturing* is limited to the transformation of materials, parts and sub-assemblies into finished products; *operations* or *production* concerns the acquisition and inventory of materials or inputs, their transformation into outputs (manufacturing) and the maintenance of production facilities and equipment. *POM* is defined as all the planning, organization, management and control activities, in addition to quality assurance activities, that go into production. Quality assurance consists of overall verification to ensure that the other four management activities are carried out properly and help the company reach its goals, or strategic objectives, through optimal use of the tangible and intangible resources at its disposal. In doing so, the people in charge of these activities must take account of various internal and external constraints.

To meet their strategic, economic (profits) or social objectives, companies and their Operations functions must reach *operational objectives* by supplying products of the required quality (Q) and quantity (or volume, V), while respecting manufacturing and delivery deadlines (on time, T), and delivering them to the agreed location (L), in the manner most economic (E) for the customer (Figure 1.1). In addition, the company and its representatives must maintain effective and courteous interrelations (I) with existing and potential customers, and establish efficient and error-free systems and methods of administration (A) for use by customers wishing to acquire the company's products (order-taking, billing, credit-checking, complaint handling, information and other systems). These are known as Q-V-A-L-I-T-E objectives.

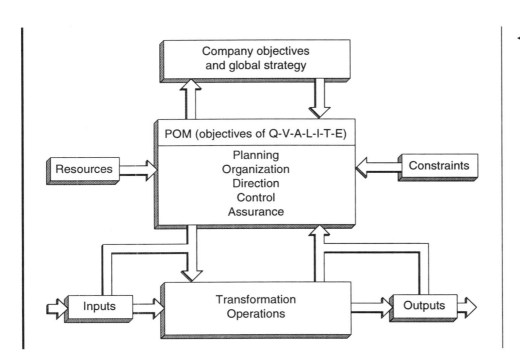

◄   **FIGURE 1.1
Production/
Operations
Management**

OPERATIONS MANAGEMENT AND THE SYSTEMS APPROACH

1.3   Operations Management and the Systems Approach

What is meant by *operations*? This term refers essentially to the process of acquiring, storing and transporting inputs, transforming them into useful outputs (goods or services) and maintaining the production system in good working order. Table 1.1 gives examples of inputs transformed into outputs.

TABLE 1.1 ▶
Examples of Inputs Transformed into Outputs

Inputs	Transformation (system)	Outputs
Various materials, parts	Factory	Automobiles, household appliances
Patients	Hospital	Healthy (recovered) people
Students	University	Managers, engineers
Passengers	Bus, subway	Transported to destination
Individuals, organizations	Insurance company	Insurance plans
Spectators	Theatre	Entertained audience

The *management* of these operations contributes to the company's reaching its objectives, and is sometimes considered a series of independent activities. The danger of this approach is that decisions may be taken without regard for the relations among them or with the other functions of the company. Many theoreticians and practitioners are convinced of the importance of overall, integrated management of this function. For this reason, we will be approaching the study of POM using a "systematic," or systems approach.

The *systems approach* provides an overall vision that is indispensable to sound, effective and comprehensive management. It is not possible to achieve effective POM without taking into consideration the relations among the Operations function, senior management and other company functions, as well as various components of the Operations function itself.

1.4   The Systems Approach: Concepts and Applications

The current trend in the business world is to adopt global, synthesizing or systems management approaches instead of the traditional analytical one, in which a complex problem is broken down into a number of smaller problems that can be easily solved.The overall solution to the problem is (sometimes wrongly) considered the sum of the solutions to these sub-problems. Division of work is one illustration of this analytical approach. In uncomplicated situations, in which each element is independent of the others, the analytical approach can be very useful. When there are complex relations among the elements or with other elements, however, it is not an effective technique. Solving just one part of an overall problem may lead to *sub-optimization*, in which one part is optimized at the expense of the whole.

To illustrate this point, consider the example of a company experiencing problems relating to quality, resulting in frequent returns and customer complaints. Senior management asks the operations manager to solve the problem as quickly as possible. The operations manager takes a number of steps, such as increasing the number of control points and inspectors, instituting more frequent maintenance of production equipment and reducing the production rate to keep a closer eye on product quality. The problem is finally solved. However, at the same time, costs have risen substantially and delivery deadlines are being missed. There are even more dissatisfied customers!

We cannot properly discuss the systems approach until we define the concept of system. A *system* is a series of interdependent elements organized to reach a goal. More specifically, a system includes interdependent and interrelated elements, objectives to be reached, and inputs acted upon by the elements to transform them into outputs. It also includes feedback as to whether the objectives have been reached. If they have not, corrective steps are taken. Furthermore, a system interacts with other systems, both inside (internal environment) and outside (external environment) the company (Figure 1.2). The main components of the internal environment of the system or the Production/Operations function are the Marketing, Finance and Human Resources systems (or functions). The external environment consists of political, economic, social, technological and ecological factors.

Note that system components are resources that transform, or are used to transform, inputs into outputs. Consequently, we do not consider labour an input to the system, as certain economic models do. Rather, we see labour as an element in the system that transforms the raw material (input) into a finished product (output). In addition, a number of intangible elements cannot be overlooked. Know-how, patents, experience and information contribute to the transformation, simplify the process or distinguish it from the processes used by competitors.

Essentially, the systems approach considers a system as a whole, one in which the parts are interdependent and interrelated. When analysing a complex situation in which crucial decisions may have to be made, one must have an overall vision of the

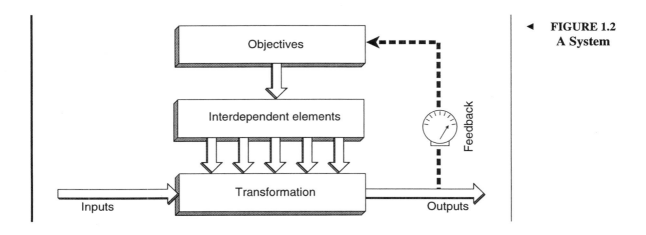

◄ **FIGURE 1.2
A System**

Analytical approach	Systems approach
– Division of the whole into parts, to facilitate analysis	– Division and integration; analysis and synthesis
– Study of parts	– Study of parts and their interrelationships
– Microscopic: focus on details	– Macroscopic: consideration of overall problem before individual details are examined
– Application if the parts are relatively independent	– Application if the parts are interdependent
– Risk of sub-optimization	– Possibility of optimization of the whole

system in which the situation applies (a global view) and interrelations between this system and others with which it interacts. Table 1.2 compares the analytical and systems approaches.

It should be pointed out that it is not always possible nor desirable to apply the systems approach. It may not be feasible to gather all the information required for a complete vision of a complex overall system, such as a company, or it may simply prove too time-consuming or costly. In such a case, it is best to use existing information, even if it is incomplete. On the other hand, the analysis may concern a relatively limited situation or problem in a sector, with few significant interrelations with other sectors of an organization, in which case the systems approach is neither necessary nor justified.

1.5   The POM Environment

POM managers do not work in a vacuum. Theirs is a dynamic internal and external environment that has an immediate or future influence on the working of the system as a whole. We will discuss three main aspects of this environment:[2]

- relations between the Production/Operations system and the other systems in the company;

- goals, power structure and other aspects of organizational culture;

- factors outside the company.

Figure 1.3 illustrates some of the relations between the environment and the Production/Operations system that managers must analyse and understand.

The *first aspect* of this environment is Marketing staff, who, through the Sales Department, obtain the orders to be filled; Finance staff provide the funds to acquire the necessary materials and equipment; and Human Resources recruits and hires workers. These activities are closely related to those of the Operations department, whose performance depends in part on the ability of its managers to properly coordinate its interactions with these other functions, and on how the managers of the other functions take account of the needs and constraints of the Production/ Operations system in designing and carrying out their respective activities.

This interdependence is key. While the Marketing manager must understand the impossibility of manufacturing a super-product that costs almost nothing and can be delivered in record time, the Production manager must understand that in order to keep customers or attract new ones it may be necessary to make changes to products and deliver them ahead of time, even if the production schedule suffers. In short, while each department has a particular role to fulfil, its manager must understand that all departments are bound together by the company's strategy. In addition to the skills required by that particular job, the Operations manager must develop and master the skills necessary to interface with other functions.

The *second aspect* of the environment brings together elements such as the power structure, goals and objectives of the company, and the organizational culture and history of the company. Every firm has its own particular organizational culture, a dominant system of values and beliefs. Some managers feel, for instance, that they have certain responsibilities as corporate citizens, while others think that their only responsibility is to protect and build on shareholders' assets. Some believe that management is always right, whereas others prefer a team approach. This second aspect of the environment might be termed the *rules of the game*. These rules depend on the company's strategy and influence the behaviour of production managers. If a company stresses its social responsibilities, for example, the POM manager will be sure to select equipment that minimizes pollution.

The *third aspect* of the environment consists of five factors external to the company: Political, Economic, Social, Technological and Ecological, which together make up the acronym PESTE. This PESTE environment creates challenges or opportunities, and must be taken into consideration in the company's overall strategy. The political environment refers to government legislation, growing political awareness among the general public, and the pressures brought to bear by lobbies and interest groups. The economic environment comprises everything that may affect the demand for products and the acquisition of resources—that is, market fluctuations, cost structure by industry, inflation, competition, and the supply of and demand for raw materials. The social environment includes values and attitudes, education, and changes in the age structure of the labour force. The technological environment includes existing and future technologies and the potential for developing them. Finally, the ecological environment concerns pollution control and the protection of natural resources.

The five elements of the PESTE environment are in fairly constant flux. They eventually result in changes in the management of the Operations system. Managers must decode their effects on the company. For example, the energy crisis (political), Japanese competition (economic), and antipollution legislation (ecological) have all had far-reaching effects on the automobile industry in the last 20 years. The industry has focussed its development efforts on designing and producing not only smaller vehicles, but also more fuel-efficient engines and more effective exhaust systems. Moreover, these changes have led to wage stability in the industry, increasingly participatory management, new technologies and new types of management systems. Aside from natural systems, all others, including those within a company, are created by humans, by managers. Faced with changes in the environment, managers must make whatever changes and corrections are necessary to reconcile contradictions and renew these systems.

POM managers must choose between the effects of the internal and the external environment if they are to ensure their company's survival and growth. They must make trade-offs by examining the pros and cons of each stimulus and the competitive factors facing the company.

▼ FIGURE 1.3
The Internal and External Environment of the Production/Operations System

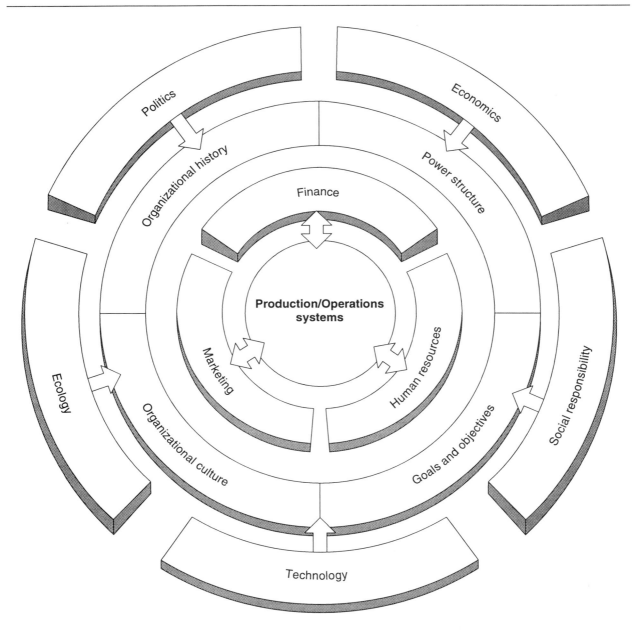

1.6   Competitive Factors

The successful company identifies the competitive factors that it expects to face in its market, for each product category. Working within its overall strategy, it then translates these factors into objectives, which the Production function must master particularly well. These factors can be reduced to four elements:[5]

- *cost*, which may be converted into price and efficiency. This factor requires that the production manager take particular care, with a view to the competition, to reduce costs and improve the efficiency of workers, capital and other resources—in short, to produce as economically as possible.

- *quality*, or a constant emphasis on product specifications and customer needs—or on producing a product with desirable characteristics lacking in those of the competition. To identify such characteristics, the company establishes and maintains effective and courteous relations with its customers.

- *certainty*, reliability, or the guarantee that the product will regularly be delivered on time, within the agreed deadlines, in the agreed volume and to the agreed location, and that any problems that arise will be corrected immediately.

- *flexibility*, or the ability to respond quickly to requests for changes in product design, quantity or delivery dates. Such quick response may even include innovation in products and services.

The relative importance to be assigned to each of these four factors is determined when the operations strategy is drawn up, and is based on the company's overall strategy. It is fairly rare, however (some would even say dangerous[10]), to aim for superior performance in all four areas, since it is impossible to develop an advantage in one without weakening the others, unless the system is unbalanced or slack. Others claim that a company trying to excel in all four will be "caught in the middle," with no real advantage in costs or quality.[8] Trade-offs of some kind must be made in determining the priority to assign each of the objectives resulting from these factors.

Not everyone agrees with this concept of trade-offs, however. How has Toyota managed to produce such high-quality cars at such reasonable cost, they ask, without getting "caught in the middle"?[7] According to Mintzberg,[9] it is possible to do so only if the organizational structure is such that it allows for the reconciliation of conflicts between individuals and functions, and even within individuals themselves, if the organizational culture is so strong that individuals are steeped in it. On the other hand, a recent study[3] has found that it is possible to improve competitive factors simultaneously, beginning with quality and continuing with certainty, flexibility and, finally, cost. Under the conditions described, the study suggests that these improvements would be long-lasting.

This theory of simultaneous improvement in competitive factors, albeit unproven, has plausible foundations and deserves more in-depth research. In fact, it is often noted in practice that efforts to improve quality generally lead to cost reductions, and that enhanced flexibility results in greater certainty. Any research in this field should also test the hypothesis that there would be a general increase in the minimal threshold for each factor.

Even if the priority given to one of these factors, or the simultaneous nature of the four competitive factors, is not entirely resolved for each of the resulting objectives, a series of criteria or performance measurements will be defined. For example, cost may be measured against such criteria as person/hours per product unit, or costs of materials or energy per unit; quality may be assessed in terms of internal and external standards, rework rates or return percentages; certainty may be evaluated according to the frequency of orders delivered by the agreed deadline; and flexibility may be measured in terms of the time necessary to manufacture a new or modified product, or the time required to change manufacturing rates. These factors and criteria allow managers to adjust their decision-making to the different problems they face.

1.7   Objectives of the Production/Operations Function and Related Problems

POM managers, along with the managers of other functions, help to identify the company's overall objectives. They must also identify the objectives of the Operations system. Where appropriate, they might then study the obstacles to reaching them.

The objectives of the Production/Operations system must contribute to the achievement of the company's overall objectives, which may be technical or technological, economic, commercial, social, environmental or political. To reach such objectives, every private or public organization in the manufacturing or service sector must offer its customers or users a line of products capable of meeting their needs. This is the aim of an overall strategy, which in turn leads to an operations strategy, or manufacturing strategy, as illustrated in Figure 1.4.

In a way, the Q-V-A-L-I-T-E requirements become the objectives of operations managers. Clearly, a company will not accord equal importance to all, but will focus its efforts on one or more of these objectives, usually on the one or more that it can more easily reach and on which its strengths and reputation are built. For instance, it may decide to be innovative and concentrate on product quality, or to stress its flexibility in meeting widely fluctuating demand, its reliability in respecting delivery deadlines, or its ability to offer quality products at the lowest cost to customers. This focus does not mean that a company can neglect the objectives it considers less important, but simply that it wishes to stand out from the competition in one particular area.

The POM system is closely linked with senior management and all the other systems. POM managers work with other managers in defining the company's overall objectives and its strategies and policies. These company strategies shape operations strategies, which in turn determine all actions in this sector.

Relations between Operations and Marketing are of prime importance. However, different functions have different goals. Marketing managers tend to seek great product diversity, in order to reach a wider clientele. Production/Operations managers tend to prefer a very limited range of products, ideally a single product. Marketing specialists also count on great flexibility, to respond to shifts in demand, in terms of both product quantity and variety. Operations managers seek stability, in order to simplify the task of planning procurement and manufacturing operations.

Managers and staff of the Technical function work in close co-operation with those of Production/Operations, for it is they who design and develop the products that Production staff are to produce, along with the processes for doing so. The POM manager is generally the most important client of the Finance and Human Resources functions, for most of the company's resources in those areas are devoted to operations.

▼ **FIGURE 1.4**
The Importance of Production Strategy in the Company's Overall Strategy

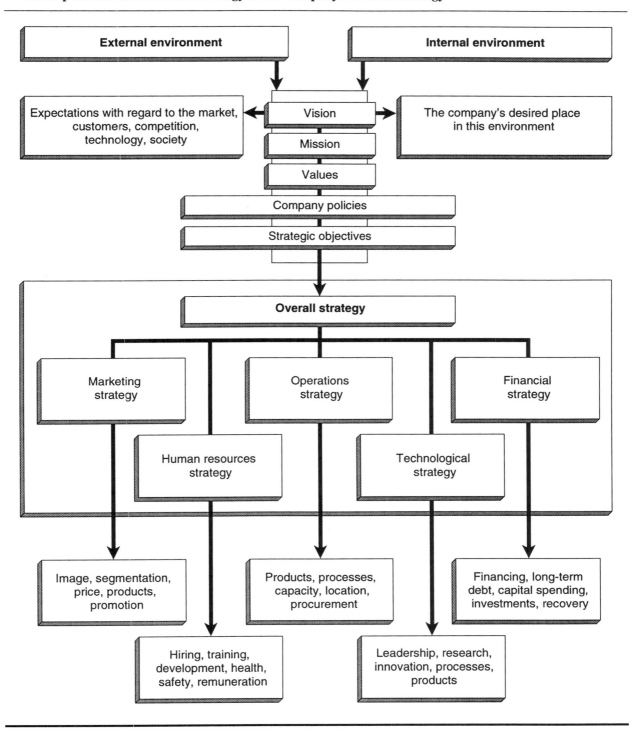

REVIEW QUESTIONS

1. What factors point to the growing strategic importance of the Operations function in manufacturing companies?

2. What are the benefits of using the systems approach to studying a given situation?

3. What are the objectives of the Operations function?

4. Describe the POM environment.

5. Name the four competitive factors in POM.

DISCUSSION QUESTIONS

1. Assuming that the global approach to studying a complex situation is more efficient, why is the systems approach not always used?

2. Consider an undergraduate program at a university as a system.

    a) Briefly define the main objectives of the system.

    b) Identify its inputs and outputs.

    c) What transformation takes place?

    d) Give two examples of feedback in this system.

3. The pulp and paper industry is undergoing a period of restructuring. Discuss the PESTE factors in this restructuring.

4. How are the internal and external environments of a company linked with the competitive factors that production managers must consider in their decision-making?

5. Discuss the opposing views concerning the trade-off in POM competitive factors, and compare these factors with trade-off of means.

6. What does a supermarket manager have to take into account when making trade-offs between the number of cashiers at the cash registers and the speed of service at the busiest times?

7. "Analysing trade-offs is simply an attempt to reach a compromise or perhaps a consensus among different managers." Comment.

8. "We need an efficient production system with high overall productivity, one that can provide customers with high-quality products and satisfactory service. We can obtain such a system with a plant equipped with modern machinery, up-to-date methods and procedures, skilled and well-allocated labour, a computerized information system and production managers familiar with scientific management methods."

    Would the system described here allow production managers to achieve the objectives generally assigned to the Production function?

9. Comment on the quote in question 8, using systems and trade-off concepts. Provide two specific examples.

10. Are the following decisions strategic, tactical, or operational? Explain.

    a) deciding how much to expand your educational institution

    b) setting the course calendar to be followed by teachers in the next two terms

    c) selecting student teachers to correct homework

REFERENCES

1. BUCAILLE, A., and C. DE BEAUREGARD BÉROLD, "Ariane contre la machine-outil," *Harvard-L'Expansion,* Summer, 1990, pp. 6-24.

2. ÉTIENNE, E.C., and M.O. DIORIO, "Le développement de la gestion de la production et des opérations," unpublished article, HEC, 1978.

3. FERDOWS, K., and A. DE MEYER, "Lasting Improvements in Manufacturing Performance: In Search of a New Theory," *Journal of Operations Management*, Vol. 9, No. 2, April 1990.

4. GULDEN, G.K., and R.H. RECK, *Combining Quality and Re-Engineering for Operational Superiority*, Vol. 8, No. 1, September-October 1991, (CSC Index Inc.).

5. HAYES, R.H., and S.C. WHEELWRIGHT, *Restoring Our Competitive Edge: Competing through Manufacturing*. New York: John Wiley & Sons, 1984, pp. 40-41.

6. KELADA, J., *Comprendre et réaliser la qualité totale*. Dorval: Éditions Quafec, 2nd ed., 1992.

7. PORTER, M.E., *Competitive Strategy: Techniques for Analysing Industries and Competitors*. New York: Free Press, 1980.

8. PRIMOR, Y., *TPM, La maintenance productive*. Paris: Masson, 1990.

9. MINTZBERG, H., "The Effective Organization: Forces and Forms," *Sloan Management Review*, Winter 1991, pp. 54-67.

10. SKINNER, W., *Manufacturing: The Formidable Competitive Weapon*. New York: John Wiley & Sons, 1985, pp. 139.

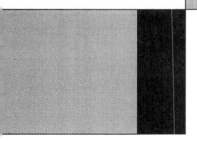

Product and Process Design

ISABELLE DESCHAMPS
MATTIO O. DIORIO
JEAN NOLLET, *authors*

INTRODUCTION

2.1   Nature and Objectives of Product and Process Design

Operations managers must constantly make and review two essential decisions: what product is to be produced, using what process? *Product* is defined as the combination of goods and services to be provided—in other words, the company's output. For example, in the company Lassonde Industries, the products are fruit juices (Oasis brand) and desserts (Fruité brand).[14] *Process* is all the operations and procedures by means of which the system creates or produces this output. At Lassonde Industries, once again, the process actually comprises many components, including the clarification of fruit juice, its storage, sterilization, packaging, mechanized quality control, etc.[26] Together, the product and the process make up the *heart of the operations system*. The process transforms the input into the output, or product, so the product and the process are closely linked (Figure 2.1a). The wood-processing and furniture-building industry, for instance, uses a great variety of processes to turn out many different products (Figure 2.1b). All these products and processes may be found in a single company or in a number of different companies that concentrate on a limited number of products and processes.

Products and processes are periodically replaced or changed. The company 3M, for example, adopted a policy in the 1980s requiring that 25% of annual sales revenues be derived from new products. In fact, according to Cooper and Kleinschmidt,[9] about 40% of all sales in the United States in 1986 were of new products, as compared with 33% in the previous year. In the automotive industry, the worldwide rate of introduction of new or modified products is impressive: over a five-year period, the U.S., Japanese and European giants brought out more than 231 new models[7] (Table 2.1).

▼ **FIGURE 2.1**
Interaction between the Product and the Transformation Process

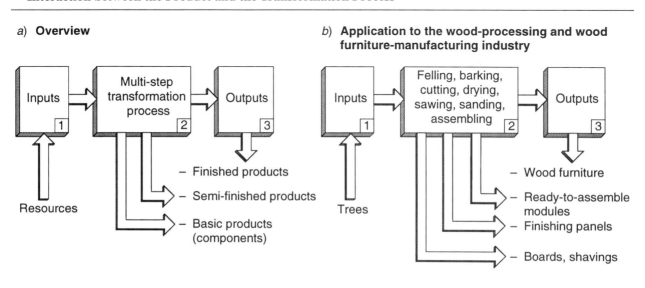

a) **Overview**

b) **Application to the wood-processing and wood furniture-manufacturing industry**

	United States	Europe	Japan
Average number of models	28	77	55
Number of new models	21	38	72
Average life span of a model	8.1 years	12.2 years	4.6 years
Source: Adapted from Clark and Fujimoto.			

◄ **TABLE 2.1 Changes in Automobile Models by Manufacturers in Three Major World Regions (1982–1987)**

In many industries, the variety of products and processes has grown as operations have become increasingly mechanized. Computerization has revolutionized the furniture-manufacturing industry in Canada, for example, where robots and programmable machines allow small companies to turn out original and varied product lines at lower cost and to compete with U.S. giants. Here we have a clear illustration of the two-way interaction between products and processes: first of all, the introduction of a new type of computerized equipment, such as numerically controlled machines (new process), leads to reduced machine setup time and operating time, increased precision and reduced waste and labour costs. Overall, according to a survey of the firms involved, these new machines reduce costs, increase capacity and quality, and make it possible for companies to manufacture new products in less time and to penetrate new markets. These trends will likely continue, since the strategy of Canadian furniture manufacturers is to produce a variety of styles and models at different prices,[36] which calls for greater process flexibility and productivity.

The above examples show how the complex interactivity between product and process can present challenges for the Operations manager. The initial design of the product or the process, and later additions, improvements or replacements, all call for specific methodologies. Furthermore, these methodologies and steps in product or process design must be adjusted to take account of various factors, including the age of the products or processes (corresponding to the life cycle), along with general conditions in the industry (competition) and the PESTE environment (regulations, economic cycle). In product and process design, the Operations manager must include and balance a variety of concerns when reviewing designs and promoting innovation. The main items that will influence these choices are summarized below:

First of all, *customer complaints* are important opportunities for review, since they point to customer dissatisfaction with the products and services offered. Hydro-Québec users, for example, were angry with the many lengthy blackouts in the late 1980s, and their complaints pushed the company to develop "intelligent" remote-monitoring devices to track each customer's energy consumption and warn of probable blackouts or overloads; the technology has actually resulted in reduced power bills and fewer blackouts for all customers. Manufacturers of children's products, such as Fisher-Price (toys, high chairs) and Pampers (diapers), regularly consult their customers with a view to improving the appearance, safety, convenience and efficiency of their products.

The discovery of *initial design errors* and resulting problems often leads to changes in products and processes. Some of these irregularities are hard to predict, meaning that products and processes must constantly be rethought. For example, after many years, it became apparent that microcomputer users were suffering from back pain, eye strain and other ailments. Based on these observations, manufacturers redesigned cathode ray screens, desks and office chairs. Other design errors stem from a lack of scientific knowledge about materials and their effects in the environment where they are used. The selection of different product components or processes is sometimes nothing more than a trial-and-error approach.

Competitive pressure can be an opportunity as well as a challenge. In the furniture industry, for example, furniture with an attractive highly lacquered finish may bring in customers and set its manufacturer apart from its competitors, yet call for complex (and potentially polluting) manufacturing processes.

Technological discoveries also lead to a review of existing products or processes, or to the design of new products. The development of a process based on enzyme engineering allowed the Eli Lilly pharmaceuticals company to design a new product, human insulin, to replace animal insulin.[13] Recent efforts to improve the waste-recycling process (mechanical separation, removal of impurities and paint, high-temperature heating under controlled conditions to reduce emissions and increase purity) have helped create products that are "ready to disassemble" or made from recycled materials, such as plastic garbage cans.[37]

Finally, technological discoveries often combine with *ecological and legislative trends* to force manufacturers to redesign a product, such as a lighter can, made of aluminum rather than tin, with thinner walls and manufactured from recycled materials. This, in turn, often leads to a redesigned process, such as the addition of steps to clean the metal and roll it into sheets.

In conclusion, product design and process design are two key decisions in POM, and both contribute to the *achievement of the multiple objectives of the company*.

1.   Together, product and process contribute to the attainment of *commercial and competitive objectives* regarding revenues, profit and the company's growth and competitiveness. A good example is the McDonald's restaurant chain, which has been able to create a competitive advantage and a distinctive name through a variety of products that can be prepared in advance. They are served as standard products, with an assembly-line cooking process and simplified work methods. This winning combination has allowed the company to serve customers twice as quickly as its competitors can.[30]

2.   The ultimate goal of product and process design is *customer satisfaction*, within the constraints of standards established by various authorities and intermediaries. Combining the design of product and process makes it simpler to deliver a product or service within quality, volume, time, location and cost constraints. For example, courier systems like Federal Express could not function without modern identification (bar codes), communication (cellular telephones) and transportation (short- and long-haul cargo aircraft) technologies. They allow the company to offer a variety of product and service options (two-hour delivery of letters and parcels 24 hours a day, etc.) and to satisfy a varied clientele spread around the world. A proper balance of process and product are essential in such competitive sectors, where success depends on winning the race against the clock, for late delivery or a wayward parcel could result in loss of customers.

3.   Product and process development has important *financial implications* for the company, for the necessary investments will have long-term positive (or

negative) repercussions. A poorly designed product can be costly, since most manufacturing costs (up to 70%) are determined at the design stage.[37] In addition, it could lead to complaints and perhaps even accidents, which can also prove expensive. The newer the product and the process, the greater the potential financial impact. For example, it cost GM nearly $5 billion to design its new Saturn models and build the plant to manufacture them. Nevertheless, the new cars produced by this division were so successful that GM managers had no choice but to invest even more to boost production capacity, even though the company was recording losses of more than US$500 million per year in 1992 and did not expect to climb back into the black until mid-decade.[34]

4. Decisions concerning product and process present a valuable opportunity for company managers *to ensure that their choices are compatible with the PESTE environment*. Over the last decade, mostly in response to new pollution-control standards, the automotive industry has had to alter exhaust systems, redesign certain types of engines, and reduce the size and weight of cars. These changes have required new materials and new processing and assembly techniques.

5. Product and process design determines how the POM function will be organized and used to *reach the company's overall objectives*. Even the tiniest change in product and process design must be studied with care, since it may have repercussions for other POM subsystems and for the entire company. For example, the design of a complete product line in modular form or with interchangeable parts presents an additional challenge, but on the other hand offers many benefits in terms of performance and operations management. Interchangeability means that inputs to the operations system must be strictly controlled, to ensure that all outputs are identical and can perform exactly the same functions.[34] For instance, it may be possible to use a number of different light bulbs in a given desk lamp without an adapter. The concept of modularity includes this notion of interchangeability but extends it even further:[34] a module is not only interchangeable, but can also be used in different ways. For instance, a timer may serve to turn lights on or off, or heat an oven, start a swimming pool pump or a sprinkler system. The concept of interchangeability applies to many finished products. Because modules can be used in so many products, the company handles a smaller variety of parts, components and intermediary products, and control activities (which we will discuss later)—and the operations system is simplified as a result. Scheduling, procurement, inventory management and quality management activities are all made easier. This succession of changes, from product design to the production process and POM techniques, culminates in reduced overall production costs, improved quality and simplified after-sales maintenance.

Many managers in POM and other company functions are involved in product and process design decisions and operations, and feel their repercussions. The term *design* refers to creation; invention; technical, strategic and financial analysis; integration; construction; and trials and comparisons. All these activities require the support of many disciplines and functions (e.g., Legal, Marketing), the integration of internal and external information sources (customer and supplier) and the participation of employees, managers and professionals at various levels. Traditionally, market needs and the products or services to be designed were determined by the Marketing function. Today, many excellent ideas come from the R&D (research and development) and Production/Operations functions. The same is true of processes: while innovations most often originate in the Production Engineering department, many also come from R&D, workers' committees, competitors and suppliers.

Since the mid-1980s, world leaders in the automotive, telecommunications, electronics and other industries have tended toward an integrated approach to product and process design. This implies that design decisions and activities are carried out simultaneously under the responsibility of multidisciplinary teams of Marketing, POM, Engineering, and R&D representatives, along with the designers. However, while perfectly synchronized product and process design sounds good, the administrative complexity involved has delayed its application in most companies. These new integrated approaches are most likely to be introduced in industries with complex products involving many assembly and sub-assembly processes (computers, automobiles, telecommunication systems, tools) and that therefore have many good reasons to design product and process simultaneously; every new product can then be manufactured in keeping with the limits imposed by existing manufacturing processes. For instance, in addition to aesthetic and functional considerations, the simplicity of the product, reduction of the number of parts, and ease of assembly must be taken into account. IBM, with its Proprinter III, is a good example of this trend.

Operations managers must be committed to the integration of product and process design. Their main objective—despite the tendency of experts to withdraw into their own worlds—is to arrive at an interactive product and process design process, in co-operation with the heads of other functions, with the goal of formulating company policy for products and processes, while always taking into account type of market, technologies, human resources, etc.

Above all, Operations managers must endeavour to strike *a balance between two extremes*:

1. *To provide what the market wants, regardless of the existing process.* In this case, market needs must be identified, the product created and, if necessary, the manufacturing process adapted to new products. This philosophy is unfortunately all too common, particularly in smaller companies that see themselves as "jacks of all trades." No order is ever refused, even if the company has to come up with new tools, lease equipment or hire temporary staff to fill it! This attitude is often found in car repair, home renovation, and management or engineering consulting firms, which have a limited core of resources and processes and depend on temporary means to satisfy unforeseen demands.

2. *To provide only what can be produced under the existing system.* At the other end of the spectrum, the company selects only products or services that are compatible with the existing process, and then tries to sell them. This approach, which is common in larger, more established companies with large-scale facilities, depends on the age and type of equipment, collective agreements, the existing network of subcontractors, investment plans and short- and long-term sales contracts. Firms as varied as steel mills, bakeries and oil companies fall into this category, as do many specialized firms, such as aircraft manufacturers, photocopier plants and banks.

PROCESS DESIGN: GOODS AND SERVICES

2.2   Process Definition and Design

The process used in manufacturing a product or delivering a service is the heart of the operations system, so much so that the terms *operating system*, *manufacturing process* and *transformation system* are virtually interchangeable. They refer to the part of an organization that transforms a set of inputs into a set of outputs by adding value, while respecting the constraints facing the company.

The inputs-transformation process-outputs triangle has already been briefly discussed and is illustrated in Figure 2.1. It should be noted that this chapter will not focus on the strictly technical considerations related to the transformation process (box 2, Figure 2.1*a*), but on the broader issue of manufacturing processes—that is, all the operations and management activities involved in identifying and assembling the inputs required (box 1, Figure 2.1*a*) and transforming them, through a series of steps (box 2, Figure 2.1*a*), to produce or make available the products (outputs) desired (box 3, Figure 2.1*a*). In other words, we will be dealing with all parts of the operations system that contribute to transforming inputs into outputs.

A *manufacturing process* (which we will call a *process*) is defined as *a collection, or set, of resources and tasks or operations, linked by a flow of materials, which transforms various inputs into useful outputs*. In addition, a process must make it possible to store not only materials, but also the information necessary to route these materials through the various transformation steps (box 2, Figure 2.1*b*).

Manufacturing processes are so complex that many specific planning, design, analysis and monitoring tools have been developed over the years. One of the basic tools is the *flow chart*, a schematic illustration of the flows of materials and information that occur during the process of creating a product, making it possible, through a series of special symbols, to visualize and analyse the steps in a process. A flow chart shows the routing not only of materials, but also of information (dotted lines).

The following example will help clarify this definition. Figure 2.2 shows a flow chart for the production of stretchers. A stretcher company procures materials and parts—that is, wood, canvas and staples, which it keeps in inventory. Each stretcher requires two wooden shafts, a piece of canvas and 24 staples, which are used to attach the canvas to the shafts. The first task is to cut the wood to the desired length. The second task is to carve a handle at each end of both shafts, with the help of a machine. The third is to cut the canvas to the specified dimensions. The fourth is to staple the canvas to the shafts, which is followed by quality control. Finally, the stretcher is rolled up and stored for eventual shipment to the customer. Value has been added at every step along the way.

The further along we move in the process, the closer we get to the finished product. In some cases the value added is in the form of human labour alone (manually rolling up the stretcher); in other cases it is added by a person and a tool (stapling the canvas to the shafts); finally, in some automated systems the value is added by a machine alone.

Throughout these processes, there are different kinds of flows.

▼ **FIGURE 2.2**
  Flow Chart

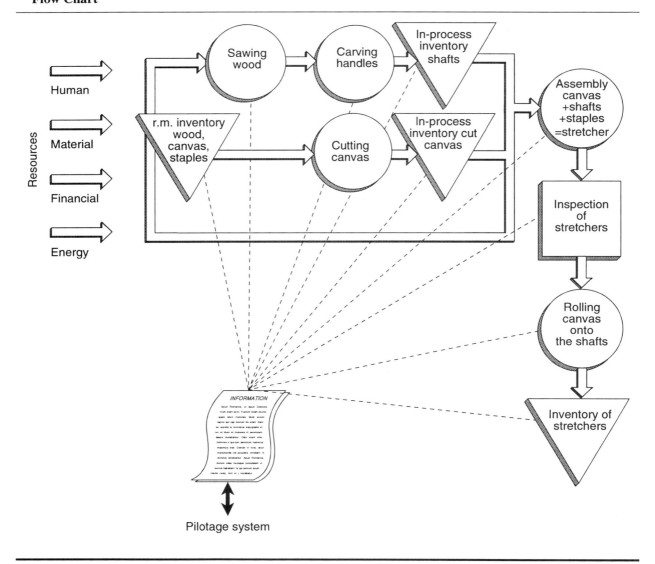

1. The *flow of materials* is the movement of materials from one location to another—i.e., from a storage room to a workstation, or vice versa, from one workstation to another, or to an inspection station. These movements call for handling, using machines, conveyors and so on. The value added at this step consists mainly of labour and energy.

2. These material flows may also involve the *movement of labour* from one activity to another. Sometimes the same person will operate a number of machines or perform various tasks, as in the case in systems that feature job enlargement or enrichment.

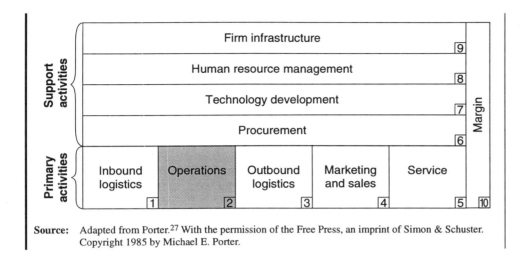

	Firm infrastructure				9	
	Human resource management				8	
	Technology development				7	Margin
	Procurement				6	
Inbound logistics	Operations	Outbound logistics	Marketing and sales	Service		
1	2	3	4	5	10	

◄ **FIGURE 2.3**
The Transformation Process in the Value Chain

Source: Adapted from Porter.[27] With the permission of the Free Press, an imprint of Simon & Schuster. Copyright 1985 by Michael E. Porter.

3. Another kind of flow, which is of vital importance, is the *flow of information*. As mentioned earlier, this information makes possible a link between the operations system and the control system, and it includes all the data necessary to control the system with regard to quality, volume, time, location and costs. Sometimes certain information follows the flow of raw materials, in which case we speak of a *batch sheet*, a document that lists each operation necessary for the production of a part, component or intermediate or final product, in an order designed to meet technical requirements.

The concept of value added is central to the definition of a process. Increasing the value added (rather than costs) by increasing efficiency remains key to designing or redesigning all or part of a process. The concept of a chain of value[28] is important here, since the transformation process is only one of the essential elements in what are considered the main activities: internal logistics, transformation, external logistics, distribution and after-sales service (respectively represented in boxes 1 to 5 in Figure 2.3). These main activities are accomplished with the assistance of support activities such as general administration (including planning), human resources management, technology development and procurement (boxes 6 to 9 in Figure 2.3). Together, if they are properly co-ordinated, these activities contribute to boosting the company's profits (box 10 in Figure 2.3). However, this kind of co-ordination requires proper knowledge of the general nature and detailed characteristics of the transformation process (box 2 in Figure 2.3).

2.3   Methods Study

Methods study is a branch of work study, which is based on a systematic process of identifying, analysing and solving problems related to a given job (Table 2.2). It helps managers to increase production by working smarter, not harder. Tools used in methods study are the operations flow chart, process flow chart, flow diagram (for materials), string diagram, multiple-activity chart, worker-machine activity chart, operator process chart, right-and-left-hand chart, and combined worker-machine and multiple-

TABLE 2.2 ▶
Methods Study
Procedure

Steps	Technique or approach	Action or result
Choice of the method (or problem) to be studied	Bottleneck, duplication of tasks, excessive reject rate, etc.	Identification of the object of the study
Collection of information on the current method	Charts or diagrams: operations process, process flow, worker-machine, multiple-activity, flow	Compilation of statistics, measurement of the time required for the current method, lead times, distances travelled, etc.
Information analysis (search for causes) "WWWWWH" (Who, What, When, Where, Why, How?)	Object of work: Why do it? Is it necessary? Where is it done? Why at this place? Time: Why is it done at that time? Person: Who does it and why that person? Means: Why is it done this way?	Evaluation of the current method and its results
Development of new methods (or a solution)	Can this operation be eliminated? Can it be simplified, can it be done more quickly elsewhere, by another person, at another time? Can it be done in another way?	Elimination of the operation. Combine it with other operations, elsewhere, give it to another worker Modify the method: automate if possible
Evaluation and choice of a new method (or solution)	Measurement of required time Profitability study Impact on the other operations, on all operations	Choice of the most profitable, fastest, least effort method that meets with the least resistance
Preparing for implementation	Preparation of instructions, standard times, required equipment	Updating of instructions, procedures manual
Final implementation and evaluation of the new method	Implementation and follow-up Measurement of results	New method introduced Actual results Modifications if necessary

activity chart. We will describe some of these charts and diagrams here. For more detail, the reader may refer to the specialized texts listed at the end of the chapter.

The *operations flow chart* shows the sequence of operations or activities identified by the symbols recommended by the American Society of Mechanical Engineers (ASME) (Table 2.3). This type of chart is useful for an overview of operations. In addition, it shows the order of entry of raw materials, from left to right, and the progress of the product through the process, from top to bottom. For instance, Figure 2.4 is an operations flow chart for a direct-mail campaign.

○	**Operation:** Modification, transformation, product assembly or information processing, preparation of a plan or an order.
□	**Inspection:** "An inspection occurs when an object is examined for identification or is verified for quality in any of its characteristics." [24]
⇨	**Transportation:** Movement of an object between operations or checkpoints, from or to warehouse, etc.
⊃	**Delay:** Delay in the flow of an item such as a delay between two operations (documents waiting for approval, items waiting to be counted, etc.).
▽	**Storage:** Arrival of an article into stores, or prolonged storage of raw materials or finished products in warehouse.
⊙	**Combined activity:** Operation combined with inspection.

◄   **TABLE 2.3**
Common Symbols in Process Charting

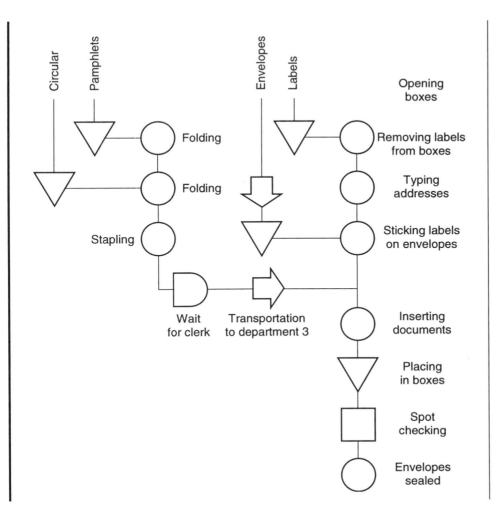

◄   **FIGURE 2.4**
Operations Flow Chart

The *flow diagram* (Figure 2.5) is a plan of the factory or work area in question, drawn to scale. It shows the exact location of machines and building details (columns, elevators, chutes, doors, etc.), along with the various points where activities such as movements of workers and materials occur. An inefficient layout and resulting unnecessary movements by workers can considerably increase the time it takes to complete a job. Moreover, it may affect the quality of finished products or of those in progress, if no protected storage areas are provided.

FIGURE 2.5 ►
Flow Diagram

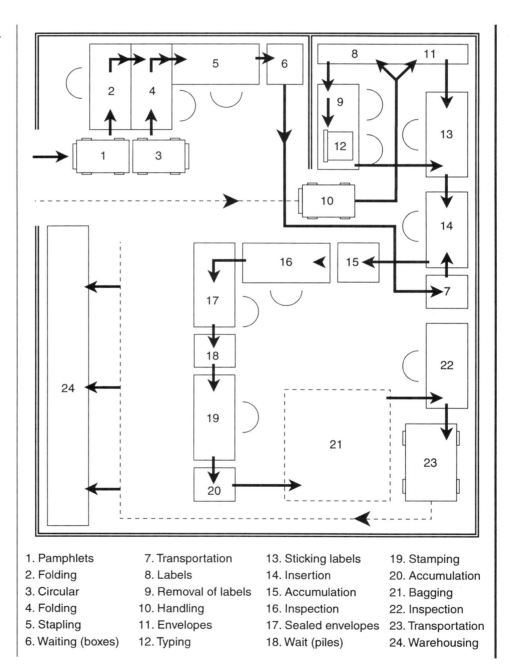

1. Pamphlets	7. Transportation	13. Sticking labels	19. Stamping
2. Folding	8. Labels	14. Insertion	20. Accumulation
3. Circular	9. Removal of labels	15. Accumulation	21. Bagging
4. Folding	10. Handling	16. Inspection	22. Inspection
5. Stapling	11. Envelopes	17. Sealed envelopes	23. Transportation
6. Waiting (boxes)	12. Typing	18. Wait (piles)	24. Warehousing

Improving layout is part of the job of work study experts.[18] Changes to a layout generally mean that many machines, materials and even wiring and ducts must be moved, and may even involve production shutdowns. Naturally, such changes will have to be approved by the plant manager and the engineers in charge of facilities.

These charts and diagrams make it possible to visualize and analyse a series of operations in order to improve work methods. With the information obtained, a new method can be designed, evaluated, tested and, finally, implemented.

2.4   Characteristics and Classification of the Manufacturing Process

Reducing the manufacturing process to its schematic form using a flow chart gives managers a better understanding of not only what is happening within the process, but also the characteristics of its design, planning and control. These characteristics concern level of technology, capacity, cycle time, flexibility, efficiency and effectiveness of the system.

The *level of technology* corresponds to the sophistication of operations—the process and techniques, and the methods and machines, used at each step in the system. It helps the manager grasp the relative importance of the use of labour or capital equipment, and whether it is possible over time to shift from one to the other. The choice of technology will also determine the links between each step in the process and the resources needed to transform inputs into outputs. Generally speaking, the technology selected has repercussions for the design, quantity and quality of the product to be manufactured, the type of material flow, and the very nature of the tasks to be performed. Technology will be covered in another chapter, but the example of automated banking machines, which we mentioned briefly earlier when discussing service companies, will help to explain this point. This system is more advanced technologically than the traditional arrangement of tellers serving customers at wickets. It allows for more transactions per unit of time, but can deliver only a limited range of products (e.g., it cannot provide foreign currency) and it depends on the customer's ability and readiness to try new tasks.

The *capacity* of the operations system determines the rate of production possible in a given system, in other words the quantity (weight, volume, number of units) that the process can transform per unit of time. The process must have the capacity to satisfy forecast demand (quantity/time). The flow diagram makes it possible to determine whether there are bottlenecks at specific points in the system, or insufficient capacity at certain steps, which could mean that the process will be unable to meet forecast demand.

Throughput time, which also relates to the concepts of capacity and bottlenecks, represents the total time required for all transformation activities. At a time when worldwide competition is focussed on speed, it is essential that this time be reduced.[4] Both small and large companies working in advanced sectors such as microelectronics, telecommunications, software and expert systems design, and specialized financial services face market requirements to stress the reduction of throughput time. For example, speed rapidity is the watchword at Virtual Prototypes,[35] which designs systems for the creation of products using artificial intelligence and real-time simulation technology. Products are built to customer specifications, and must be delivered with very short lead times. The same constraint applies at Eicon Technologies, which manufactures custom-made data communication cards for computers. Eicon has had to implement a process and a control system to meet customer demands within two weeks, whereas the industry standard is six weeks.[16] Even at service institutions such as the Montreal Stock Exchange processes are selected according to their throughput time. The new Montreal Exchange Registered Representative Order Routing System (MORRE), installed in 1990, can be used to record, allocate and automatically confirm market and limit orders. It minimizes the number of manual operations required, so orders can be filled faster and confirmed instantly, and also improves the MSE's processing capacity while enhancing reliability by reducing errors and ensuring data integrity.

Flexibility is doubtless the most complex characteristic for it has three dimensions: volume flexibility, product flexibility and lead-time flexibility.

Volume flexibility measures the system's adaptability to changes in product volume. For instance, can just 10 stretchers a day be manufactured, rather than the usual 1,000?

Product flexibility measures the system's ability to adapt to changes in the product itself or to the introduction of new products. For instance, can it adapt to manufacturing stretchers with aluminum shafts instead of wooden ones? Can it simultaneously produce stretchers and camping tents? In service companies such as banks, can the processes meet the needs of different kinds of clients? Automated banking machines, which were initially criticized because of their rigidity and the limited range of services they offered, have since been modified in many ways, with new transactions (e.g., inter-bank transfers) and operations (e.g., chequing-account balances), improved user-friendliness (better display, available in various languages) and a variety of options for handling transactions at different speeds, depending on the customer's choice (fast withdrawals of $20, $50 or $100), etc.[3]

Mix flexibility reflects the system's ability to cope with changes in demand for the product range. For example, automotive assembly lines are balanced to accommodate only small changes in the proportion of sedans, two-doors, hatchbacks and station wagons. Large changes in the demand mix for these models would cause significant problems.

Lead-time flexibility measures the time it takes for the system to react to a given delivery demand. If it normally takes 15 working days to manufacture a stretcher, can the system adapt to an urgent order and produce one in just five days?

Effectiveness and *efficiency* are often confused. They will be discussed later. For the moment, we will simply say that effectiveness indicates the ability to do something as planned or even to adjust to unforeseen changes so as to produce the output required by the customers and contribute to the company's profits. Efficiency refers to a more limited concept of performance. It consists of following instructions and policies established at each step, and ensuring conformity to guarantee maximum economy of inputs (of resources and time) to produce the predetermined outputs. For instance, at Virtual Prototypes, which was mentioned above, products are made to measure but must be delivered with a very short lead time. This calls for processes with low throughput times that minimize wasted time (efficiency), so that the company can constantly innovate and create new or modified products (effectiveness). These two objectives of efficiency and effectiveness are reconciled mainly through a proper fit of product and process, which calls for planning far in advance: as soon as an order is received, the company determines whether it is for a component or a complete system, whether the required product can be adapted to the needs of other customers (forecast batch size) and whether it is to be delivered alone or along with related services (user training). These questions, which come up every day, help orient product and process design.

The *cost structure*, which is the mix of fixed and variable costs, changes as process characteristics change. In general, increased automation and reduced direct labour lead to greater fixed and smaller variable costs. The resulting cost structures greatly influence the firm's competitiveness. For example, when variable costs are a high percentage of total costs, a company's ability to compete through price cuts is severely constrained. On the other hand, high fixed costs restrict the firm's *volume flexibility* and its ability to be profitable when demand is much lower than capacity.

This list of process characteristics shows that every process will differ in some way from the next. Nevertheless, processes can be grouped according to their degree of similarity—that is, whether they are used to manufacture products and serve markets for which requirements and competition are similar. These categories can be combined to produce a classification of manufacturing processes. The best-known and most useful classification, illustrated in Figure 2.6, is based on these characteristics: quantity of products manufactured at once (batch size), product variety, type of demand (indication of flexibility) and type of flow.

In *project*-type processes, a single complex good or service is produced. This may be a stadium, a prototype, or the entire Apollo space project. To complete the project successfully, a large number of operations and activities, using limited but varied resources, must be co-ordinated in a predetermined order specific to the service or product in question. Products are not only made to order, but are generally designed in close co-operation with the purchaser. This is the case at Virtual Prototypes.[20]

A *job-shop* process, in which items are produced to order, must be flexible to satisfy varying quality and quantity requirements. Products differ according to customer specifications; there is no such thing as a standard product. In the manufacturing process, the flow of materials is uneven; they are routed from one operation to the next as dictated by each order. Eicon Technologies, which produces communication cards, is a good example.[16] Throughput times are relatively long and work-in-process inventories are relatively high.

The *batch mass production* type of process handles a greater quantity of products of relatively smaller variety. This is the case in the food sector, for example, in the canning of vegetables, soups or jams. It is also the case in the manufacture of heavy equipment such as tractors or compactors. The process is designed so that the sequence of operations is almost identical no matter what the product. The operating flow is uneven, for although there is a dominant flow batches may be routed in different ways and undergo only a few operations. Lassonde Industries, the juice manufacturer, is an example of this type of process.[14, 26] Throughput times tend to be long, although when there is a single dominant flow they may be shortened.

In the *continuous mass production* type of process, production follows an established route through a long assembly line of specialized equipment. Most high-volume product assembly companies, turning out such goods as household appliances,

▼ **FIGURE 2.6**
Classification of Manufacturing Processes

TYPES OF PROCESS

Management variables	Project	Job shop	Batch mass production	Continuous mass production	Process
Product quantity	Single unit (or almost)	Low	Average	High	Very high
Product variety	Very large (unique product)	Large	Average	Reduced	Low (high standardization)
Types of order	Production to order				Production to stock
Operation flow	Fixed	Discontinuous	Discontinuous	Connected	Continuous
Example	Construction of a stadium	Mechanical job shop	Heavy equipment	Assembly (cars, TVs)	Sugar refining

Source: Adapted from Le Moal and Tarondeau.[21]

televisions and automobiles, function in this way. Products are assembled from standardized components. Although the flow is generally continuous, the system sometimes allows for special handling of certain products. The pace of this type of physical organization of production—the assembly line—may be determined by workers or by machines. GM's Saturn plant is a good example. Throughput times are short and work in process is low.

Finally, the *process* type is a perfect example of a clear, rigid and highly continuous flow. Volumes are high and generally only one highly standardized product is manufactured. Product and process are interdependent and inextricably linked, and the flow is rigid. This is the case for the oil refining, metal smelting and sugar refining industries.

The service sector has been the subject of few studies or efforts at standardization. The main classifications for this sector include the following criteria: degree of contact with customers, level of technology (ratio of operations performed by humans to those performed by machines); degree of standardization of operations (or, inversely, flexibility in response to customer demand and specific need); and potential for combining service delivery with promotion and sales operations (often measured by the type of training received by front-line employees). Figures 2.7 and 2.8 show two examples of service classifications based on these characteristics.

Competitive trends, which highlight the need for flexibility, fast response and personalized service in manufacturing and service companies, increase the number of characteristics that must be taken into account in process design.

A more strategic classification of processes would make it easier to identify effectiveness and efficiency characteristics, and to classify processes according to their ability to respond to various competing priorities. Table 2.4 shows this type of classification, based on the results of a study in the electronics industry.

Not every company uses a dominant type of process. Most firms use a combination of types—that is, a hybrid model designed to perform many different operations and to acquire many of the skills shown in Table 2.4, so as to respond to the specific nature of competition in the industry for each product line. Consequently, designing or redesigning a process involves integration of the various classifications we have discussed. For instance, McDonald's fast-food restaurants had to design an operations system incorporating many different skills (Table 2.4), since its objective was to offer customers fast and courteous service, a varied, inexpensive and innovative product line, and consistent quality. To do so, it divided its activities into two parts: with customer contact (counter) and without customer contact (cooking). The first part corresponds to type 4 in Figure 2.7—that is, a partially permeable system with average opportunity to promote products, products, described as "face-to-face, tight specs." These activities correspond to the "mass" type of service shown in Figure 2.8, where labour intensiveness is high but where there is little interaction between employees and customers. By contrast, the activities without customer contact correspond more to the "factory" type of service in Figure 2.8, where both labour intensiveness and extent of interaction are low. Such highly mechanized operations are essential if requirements in terms of speed, quality and cost are to be met simultaneously.

2.5   The Industrialization of Services

Levitt[24, 25] introduced the concept of industrialization of services, aimed at improving effectiveness and efficiency through a systematic, standardized, "industrial" approach to both design and delivery. He suggested that the conventional approach to services, which involved human variability and availability to customers, be replaced by rigid, flexible and hybrid technologies. *Rigid technology* consists of equipment that customers can use themselves, such as car washes, automated banking machines and fax machines, or that can be operated by a technician, such as medical and automotive diagnostic equipment. *Flexible technology* includes travel packages, income-tax preparation services and computer software. *Hybrid technology*, such as systems for controlling delivery-truck routes by radio, information technologies and debit-card technologies, involves a combination of the rigid and flexible varieties.

FIGURE 2.7 ▶
**Service-System
Design Matrix**

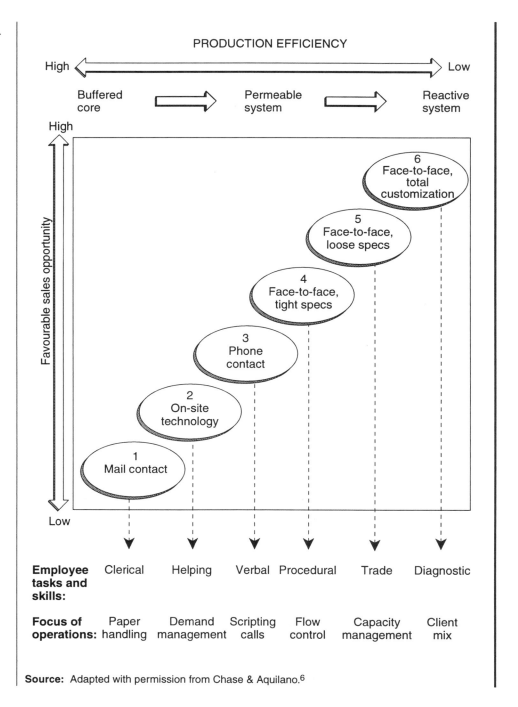

PRODUCTION EFFICIENCY

High ⟵────────────────────────────⟶ Low

Buffered core ⟹ Permeable system ⟹ Reactive system

High

Favourable sales opportunity

6
Face-to-face,
total
customization

5
Face-to-face,
loose specs

4
Face-to-face,
tight specs

3
Phone
contact

2
On-site
technology

1
Mail contact

Low

Employee tasks and skills:	Clerical	Helping	Verbal	Procedural	Trade	Diagnostic
Focus of operations:	Paper handling	Demand management	Scripting calls	Flow control	Capacity management	Client mix

Source: Adapted with permission from Chase & Aquilano.[6]

Industrialization of services often implies that low-volume services will be replaced by standardized services, with much higher outputs. Fast-food restaurant chains offer little flexibility, but rather speed, cleanliness and standard service everywhere, at all times, for a large number of customers. (On the other hand, there is still room for traditional restaurants, since they cater to a very different clientele.[2])

▼ **FIGURE 2.8**
Service Process Matrix

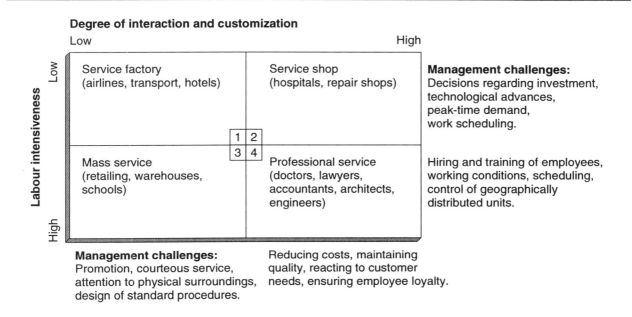

Degree of interaction and customization

	Low	High
Labour intensiveness Low	Service factory (airlines, transport, hotels)	Service shop (hospitals, repair shops)
	1 2 3 4	
High	Mass service (retailing, warehouses, schools)	Professional service (doctors, lawyers, accountants, architects, engineers)

Management challenges:
Decisions regarding investment, technological advances, peak-time demand, work scheduling.

Hiring and training of employees, working conditions, scheduling, control of geographically distributed units.

Management challenges:
Promotion, courteous service, attention to physical surroundings, design of standard procedures.

Reducing costs, maintaining quality, reacting to customer needs, ensuring employee loyalty.

Source: Adapted from Schmenner.[31]

Process characteristics	Sub-elements related to competitive priorities
Innovation	Skill in launching innovative products
	Skill in launching innovative technologies
Flexibility	Skill in making fast changes in volume
	Skill in coping with changes to specifications
	Skill in offering a varied range of products
Reliability	Skill in offering superior service
	Skill in delivering on time
	Skill in delivering quickly
Quality	Skill in offering products of consistent quality
	Skill in offering products of superior quality
Cost	Skill in minimizing costs
	Skill in offering low sales prices

◄ **TABLE 2.4**
Classification of Processes according to Strategic Scope: Characteristics of Production Processes according to Competitive Priorities

Source: Adapted from Dostaler.[12]

Standardization can be increased if the control of system characteristics and the definition of problems related to customers (income-tax returns) or their expectations (fast-food restaurants) allow appropriate planning. However, in other types of services, such as consultation services and most professional services, identifying problems and solutions may prove so complex that it requires a high level of skill and personal attention. Standardization is then much more difficult to achieve, even in cases where it is desirable.[17]

MANAGING TECHNOLOGY

2.6   Some Definitions and Types of Technologies

Technology has many dimensions, and experts in a good number of fields have attempted to come up with a definition of the term.

Economists have defined it as:

- a mixture of scientific know-how and empirical knowledge; and
- a series of codified and reproducible means of doing things, based on rational principles.[5]

Note that the term *technology* includes much more than equipment of hardware. Computer programs, methods of organization, and accounting and budgeting systems are all examples of technology.

Management specialists see technology as any system of related components and activities, since "any activity that creates value uses some technology to combine the means of production acquired and human resources to manufacture a product."[27]

The systems approach taken in this book is in accord with the above concepts. Technology is not limited to equipment, but is simultaneously a series of methods, processes, types of equipment and even approaches to providing a good or a service. Figure 2.9 shows types of technology and their applications. Here are some examples of applications.

1. *Technology applied to products*: a light and strong composite material, Duralcan, was developed in 1990; it is already used in industrial products, and other applications are expected to be found, such as in bicycles.[40]

2. *Technology applied to processes*: The introduction of an automated manufacturing cell in the DMS-100 division of Northern Telecom has allowed the company to reduce the number of in-process inventories by 82%.[33]

3. *Technology applied to information and communication systems*: Electronic data interchange systems between IBM and its suppliers have helped to reduce the design time for new microcomputer models to under 13 months.[8]

4. *Technology applied to management and control systems*: IBM and American Airlines have joined forces to automate the seat-planning system used by the Russian airline Aeroflot.[39]

Choice of technology has many ramifications throughout the company, especially on its operations system. Unfortunately, the word *technology* often summons up a vision of something best left to experts.[32] Yet technology is all around us, in many

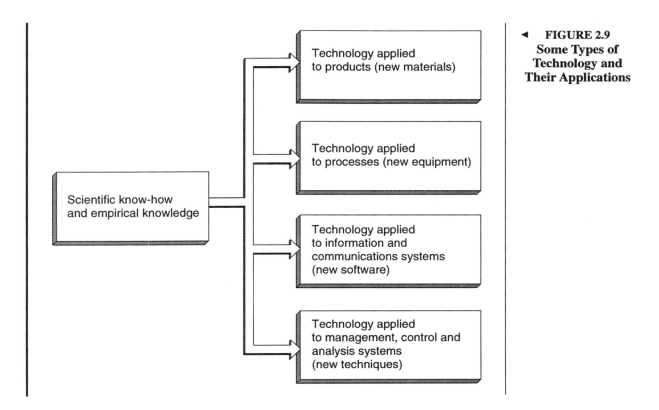

forms, not all of them incomprehensible to managers. Given the responsibilities of operations managers, they are mostly interested in process technologies (equipment, tools and procedures); control-system technologies (quality management, production planning and control, maintenance); and organizational technologies. Nevertheless, they are also concerned with product selection and must ensure that the management information system chosen will support operations and control activities. The operations manager, therefore, must ensure, in co-operation with colleagues from other functions, that all forms of technology in the company are appropriately chosen and managed properly. It is with this attitude of openness and co-operation that managers should approach the choice and implementation of any new technology.

2.7   Technological Sophistication of the Industry

The type of technological knowledge or skills required of an operations manager depends on the particular characteristics of his or her product and process technologies. These considerations are intimately linked to the industry itself and its economic environment. As Figure 2.10 shows, many features of the company's environment can influence the choice of product and process technologies. Taken together, these features illustrate what is called the *technological sophistication of the industry*, which varies according to the following factors.

▼ **FIGURE 2.10**
Technological Sophistication of the Industry: Sources and Impacts

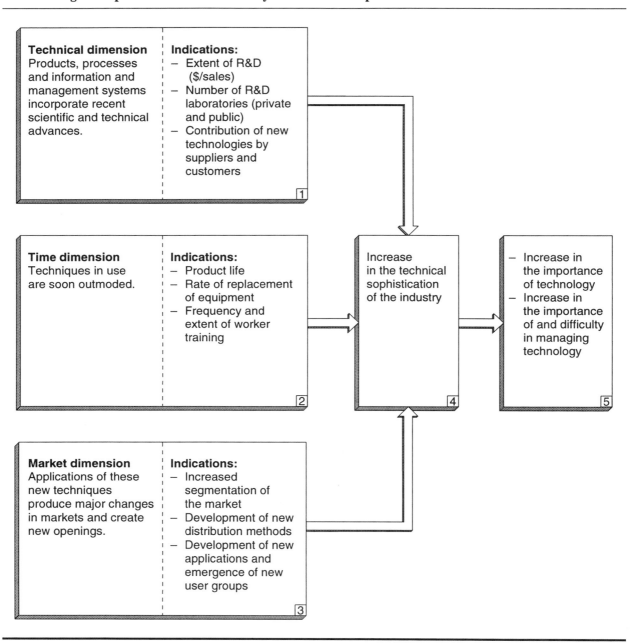

1. **Technical dimension:** products incorporate recent scientific and technical advances (box 1): indicated by the extent of R&D activities, the number of R&D laboratories, and new technologies contributed by the company's suppliers or customers.

2. **Time dimension:** the techniques in use soon become outmoded (box 2): measured in terms of the life cycle of products, the frequency of replacement of equipment, and worker training.

3. **Market dimension:** the applications of these techniques produce wholesale transformations in markets, and even create new openings (box 3): the more markets become segmented, the more distribution channels multiply or modernize; and the more user groups diversify, the greater the importance of this dimension and the greater the technological sophistication of the industry.

In short, the greater the extent of these three dimensions, the greater the technological sophistication of the industry, and the more difficult it becomes to manage technology. Today, very few industries, even long-standing ones, are not technologically sophisticated. Developments in biotechnology, electronics, microcomputing, multimedia communications and new materials mean that almost any company could be considered a high-technology firm. Any industry characterized by complex products and processes involving many materials (e.g., the automotive industry) must be well grounded in the art of combining many different technologies and expertise from various scientific fields.[19]

2.8   Strategic Management of Technology

In the interests of sound strategic management of technology, operations managers must consider all the various facets of a decision—and the inherent trade-offs. Strategic management of technology is linked to operations strategy, and consequently to overall company strategy. Like any strategy, it consists in following guidelines based on objectives set by management. Any company that wishes to compete on technological terms must be prepared to make significant trade-offs among very high process flexibility, product reliability and low production costs. For despite strict controls over product costs, it is mainly the first two, process flexibility and product reliability, that are most important in an organization attempting to seize or maintain technological leadership.

But what exactly is a technological strategy? How does one go about preparing or revising it? Figure 2.11 outlines the main steps and elements involved: combining the overall strategy (box 1) and the current and future technological forecast (box 2) to decide where the company now stands (box 3), and, from that information, preparing a technological strategy (box 4)—that is, a series of measures aimed at correcting weaknesses, increasing the technological lead, better balancing technological innovation efforts and risks, and clarifying the steps to be taken to achieve these goals—in short, how to acquire, implement and organize this technology.

A technological strategy starts with an analysis of the strategic and operations data provided by the POM manager and experts from other functions such as Marketing, R&D, Finance and Human Resources. Technological shortcomings often stem from a failure to adjust overall company strategy to existing functional constraints resulting in piecemeal decisions concerning technological strategy, usually on the basis of a single financial criterion.

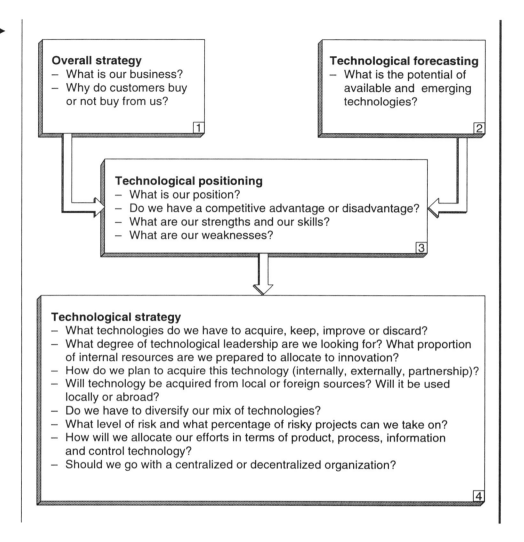

Overall strategy
- What is our business?
- Why do customers buy or not buy from us?

⌐1⌐

Technological forecasting
- What is the potential of available and emerging technologies?

⌐2⌐

Technological positioning
- What is our position?
- Do we have a competitive advantage or disadvantage?
- What are our strengths and our skills?
- What are our weaknesses?

⌐3⌐

Technological strategy
- What technologies do we have to acquire, keep, improve or discard?
- What degree of technological leadership are we looking for? What proportion of internal resources are we prepared to allocate to innovation?
- How do we plan to acquire this technology (internally, externally, partnership)?
- Will technology be acquired from local or foreign sources? Will it be used locally or abroad?
- Do we have to diversify our mix of technologies?
- What level of risk and what percentage of risky projects can we take on?
- How will we allocate our efforts in terms of product, process, information and control technology?
- Should we go with a centralized or decentralized organization?

⌐4⌐

Managers must also be cautious when confronted with diverse technologies. For example, they must avoid using widely differing technologies side by side, such as introducing pilot plants when products are at different steps in the life cycle of the whole product line, or when technologies represent management philosophies that cannot readily co-exist within the same plant. General Motors, for example, built an entirely separate complex in Spring Hill, Tennessee, to design, test and manufacture the Saturn, simply because the unique management philosophy and the new product and process technologies involved could not be integrated into GM's existing R&D centres or factories. Because of the risks discussed above, the company reduced technological innovation in its manufacturing processes, instead taking more conventional approaches.[36]

Experts[27] agree that technological strategy varies according to a company's approach to the market and the degree of technological leadership it seeks. A company like Hewlett-Packard, for example, which wants to be the first to reach the market with new products, obviously must do its best to remain at the leading edge of research. It takes huge risks, but with the possibility of enjoying equally impressive returns. On the other hand, a company such as Texas Instruments, which has a philosophy of minimizing costs, must devote considerable amounts to developing more efficient and more automated processes.

To conclude, a strategy must be based upon well-informed, systematic, step-by-step decision-making. Even so, the process will be complicated by the difficulty of determining exactly where technology strategy leaves off and operations concerns begin.

2.9   Operations Management and Technology Choices

Companies that make good use of technology opportunities have three characteristics:[15]

1. Managers have been with the company for a long time and have a good grasp of technical issues.

2. Managers allocate funding to projects on the basis of clearly defined criteria, to maintain the company's competitive advantage in certain areas.

3. Managers intentionally apply the systems approach, meaning that there is a close link between decision-making in technological areas and other areas.

These general principles are borne out by observations. A study by one of the authors of this book confirmed the importance of the systems approach. A comparative analysis of nearly 40 technological innovation projects, relating to products and processes, showed that the existence of strong links among researchers, technology designers and technology users (Marketing and POM) was the factor most closely associated with the success (or failure) of an innovation project.[10] This and other studies[22, 29] concluded that when there are direct, continuous and smooth links among designers, producers and sellers, innovation projects take less time, cost less, and lead to successful technological innovations with more advanced technical performance and design.

When the technological strategy is properly integrated with operations activities, and when each functional group plays a well-planned role in its development and implementation, there is a much greater chance that the process will meet with overall success (Figure 2.12). On the other hand, unbalanced strategic planning for development and implementation, coupled with a lack of co-ordination among players at the various steps, can prove very harmful. Neglecting operations, in particular, can be fatal. Placing too much emphasis on the initial steps of the innovation process (steps 1 and 2 in Figure 2.12) could result in senior management's withdrawing from the development, acquisition and implementation steps (steps 3, 4 and 5 in Figure 2.12), which are at the heart of the innovation process. This lack of interest and lack of encouragement can wear down the scientists, engineers, designers, market analysts, training and retraining experts, and others directly concerned. As a result, the technological strategy chosen by management can run out of steam, and the project may be aborted at steps 3 or 4, before it really gets underway. Or a weakness in the management of an operations aspect may lead to premature implementation (step 5) that will cause problems in the market or when the technology is applied. These two types of problems—abandonment and faulty implementation—will have long-term effects on the ability and willingness of managers to take part in the technological innovation process.[11]

The introduction of new process or product technologies most often occurs through projects or programs, each of which is intended to define, acquire and implement the technologies necessary for the company to meet a specific need—for instance, to improve or replace a product line or a manufacturing process. The operations units managing the technology may be divided by product, process, market or even main product component. In the automotive industry, for instance, different groups are assigned to the selection, technological development and manufacture of the engine, body, suspension and so on. However, there must also be means of integrating the individual efforts of these operations units if the company wishes to produce a workable systems and satisfactory products.

Every project or program intended to improve or change a technology or a group of technologies must proceed through each of the steps in boxes 2 to 8 in Figure 2.12. At each step, the operations manager will have to make decisions, based on information and decision-support tools.

DETERMINING PRODUCTION CAPACITY

2.10 Defining and Measuring Capacity

Decisions involving the company's capacity can have far-reaching effects. But what exactly is *capacity*? In everyday language, it means the quantity of a substance that a container can hold. In the context of production, however, we must specify exactly what we mean, for *capacity* has several different definitions: the floor surface, the volume of storage space, the production rate of a machine, the pace of an operation, the skill of an individual, and many other variants.

Capacity can be defined as the maximum theoretical quantity of products that can be turned out by a given operations system over a specific period of time, under established conditions.

This definition implies that capacity must be expressed as a production rate: the number of units of a good that can be produced over a given period—that is, quantity of outputs per unit time. The difficulty begins when it comes to defining the output. If a facility is designed to make a single product or several very similar (*homogeneous*) products, then the output can be adequately expressed by a single direct measurement. For instance, the capacity of a water purification plant is expressed in the number of litres treated per hour. On the other hand, if a facility is designed to produce a whole range of goods (e.g., a refinery transforms crude oil into a variety of products, such as naphtha, automobile fuel, airplane fuel, benzene, heating oil and paraffin), these *heterogeneous* outputs cannot be simply added up to express the capacity of the plant.There are at least two solutions to this problem: 1. Outputs are converted into common units, also called equivalent units (see Chapter 5). 2. Either the input or one of the key production resources is used to measure the plant's capacity. At the above-mentioned refinery, capacity is measured in terms of input—that is, the number of

▼ **FIGURE 2.12**
The Technological Innovation Process and Its Precursors

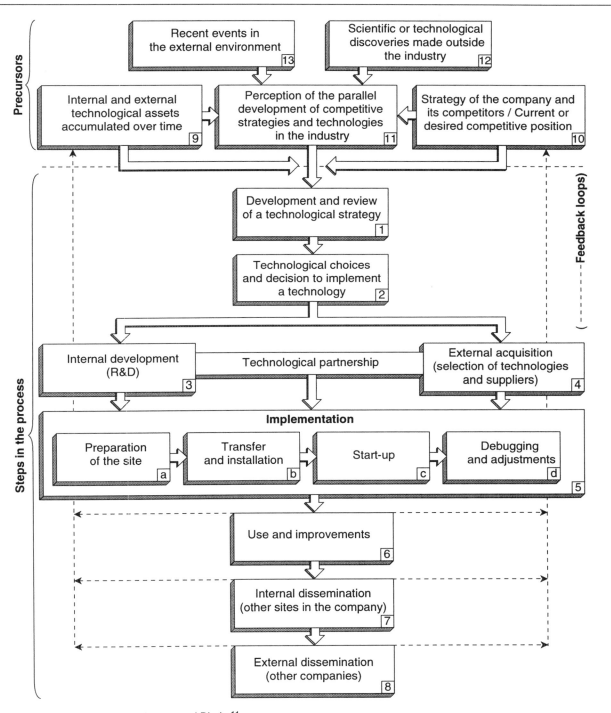

Source: Adapted from Deschamps and Diorio.[11]

TABLE 2.5   ▶
Some Examples of
Units for
Measuring
Capacity

Homogeneous Output		Heterogeneous Output	
Organization	Measure	Organization	Measure
Dairy	Litres of milk per day	Police department	Number of police officers
Iron mine	Tonnes of ore per year	Restaurant	Number of tables
Harbour commission	Number of containers loaded and unloaded per year	Hospital	Number of beds
Aeronautics plant	Number of airplanes per time period	Educational	Number of full-time equivalent students per year
Driver licensing office	Number of drivers' licenses issued per unit of time	Machine shop	Number of available machine-hours per unit of time
Automobile assembly plant	Number of cars assembled per day	Petroleum refinery	Barrels of crude per unit of time

barrels of crude oil transformed per day; in the case of a hotel, capacity is expressed in terms of a key resource, such as the number of rooms available per day.

In practice, every company in a given industrial sector measures capacity in the same way. The capacity of a stadium, for instance, is always expressed in terms of the number of seats. However, it is not a good idea to use units that can vary over time—measuring capacity in terms of production dollars should be avoided unless such amounts are adjusted, since inflation and fluctuating exchange rates can distort the real production value and plant capacity.

Table 2.5 offers examples of the measurement of capacity in which the output is either homogeneous or heterogeneous, for companies in the primary, secondary and tertiary sectors.

2.11 Concept of Capacity in the Service Sector

Capacity is measured in much the same way in the service sector, although some special features must be evaluated and considered: 1. Services cannot be stockpiled. 2. In general, they are not readily transportable. 3. They are partly or wholly intangible. 4. The customer is often present when the service is delivered.

The fact that *services cannot be stockpiled* removes an important variable in the control of delivery, for it becomes more difficult to meet cyclical and seasonal variations in demand. There must be sufficient capacity to reach the level of service identified in the company's strategy. Generally speaking, capacity will be closer to maximum than average demand. For instance, on Thursday night in a supermarket even 15 cash registers are barely enough to keep up, while on Tuesday morning two are sufficient. Since there is no way of stockpiling customer service on Thursday and pulling it out on Tuesday, and since a feature of services is that there are alternating periods of congestion and inactivity, the optimal number of cash registers will result in a balance of idle capacity (Tuesday) and long queues (Thursday).

Unlike physical goods, *services are not readily transportable*, which is why they should be located near the customer or the market. For example, there is no point in choosing between a single large McDonald's restaurant and several small ones, because they must generally be located close to customers. Some highly standardized services have become transportable, nevertheless, such as home delivery of pizza or other take-out food. In this case, capacity must be adjusted to customer location, and variations in strategy may be necessary.

The *intangibility of a service* and the *presence of the customer* in the system oblige managers to create as much flexibility as possible in their capacity. Customers can describe the features of the service they want, on site, and thereby influence the speed of delivery of the service and hence system capacity.

In determining capacity in services, managers must consider these specific factors and monitor the constantly shifting balance between customer contact requirements and the resources available to satisfy and sometimes limit customer demand.

2.12 Capacity Variables

A company's capacity to produce goods or provide services depends on a number of factors. Those discussed below are illustrated in Figure 2.13.

1. The *length of use* of a facility directly influences its capacity. The production capacity of a system designed to operate 80 hours a week is theoretically twice that of a system operating just 40 hours a week. The length of use of a system, in turn, depends on two criteria. Work can be distributed over several shifts, if management so wishes; this decision depends on the forecast demand for the product, and takes account of the economic and psychosocial aspects of longer working hours. Similarly, the decision may be based on technological imperatives that force managers to operate the facilities around the clock, such as in the chemical, petroleum and steel industries. A third factor is that some essential services must be offered 24 hours a day, such as in the case of hospitals, telephone companies and power companies.

2. *Product mix* also influences capacity. For instance, in the furniture industry, production capacity for manufacturing 1,000 chairs of the same type is less than that needed to make 200 chairs, 200 benches, 200 armchairs, 200 desks and 200 tables. Each type of product generally has different requirements in terms of setup time, labour, machines and space. Even if a plant has a limited product mix, the different setup times reduce capacity. The following example illustrates some effects that can be caused by a broad product mix.

FIGURE 2.13 ▶
**Factors Affecting
System Capacity**

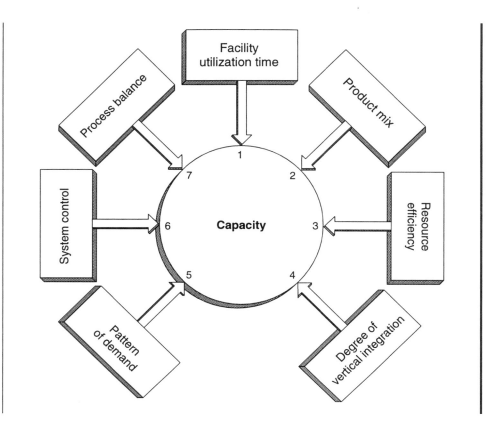

FIGURE 2.13 ▶
**Factors Affecting
System Capacity**

Example	A company wishes to fill one order for 100 identical products and 100 orders for one product, each slightly different. The setup time is 10 minutes and the operating time is one minute per unit in all cases. What is the average manufacturing time in the two cases?
Solution	One order for 100 units of a single product requires: 10 minutes + (100 units × 1 minute/unit) = 110 minutes or 1.1 minutes per unit, whereas 100 orders for one product require: (100 × 10 minutes) + 100 units × 1 minute/unit = 1100 minutes, or 11 minutes per unit.

This concept of product mix and its effects on capacity suggests that a factory cannot excel in everything. It must make choices corresponding to competitive objectives based on the company's strategy.

3. *Performance of production resources* also causes variations in a company's capacity. The term *under established conditions*, mentioned in the definition of capacity, presupposes fixed and uniform performance. Various elements, including worker motivation, can modify the performance rate and hence the production rate. Other elements include fatigue resulting from

working too rapidly or too long, physical conditions in the workplace, the use of space, the condition of machines and the quality of raw materials.

4. Capacity is influenced by the *degree of vertical integration* at a plant—in other words, the amount of subcontracting in the production of the good or the delivery of the service. A furniture manufacturer can design a complete manufacturing process from undried wood and plan various capacities for processing this wood. It can also begin the process with semi-processed wood, buying or subcontracting the manufacturing of components rather than producing them itself. This changes capacity requirements at various points in the process.

5. The pattern of demand for products has a substantial effect on both the size and the use of capacity. When demand fluctuates, should capacity be set according to maximum, minimum or average demand? What is the desired capacity, depending on whether demand for the product is growing, stable or shrinking?

6. New *control systems* can increase capacity considerably. Japanese firms, even though they invest less capital per vehicle than do their American counterparts, manage to use less labour in key manufacturing operations for small automobiles; for example, 17 hours of assembly are required in Japan as compared with 28 hours in the United States.[1] Proper operations management allows the Japanese to use only 60% (17/28) of the capacity required by American manufacturers for the same production volume.

7. *A balanced process*, or its counterpart, the *bottleneck*, is another factor that can cause variations in a plant's capacity. Production systems are generally broken up into subsystems or interdependent manufacturing steps designed so that a given step will not delay operations at the next step. A system is balanced when the output of each step provides exactly the input volume required by the following operation. This balance can be difficult to achieve, for at least two reasons: the design of a balanced multi-step system is a complex task; and operations variables lead to imbalances that cause bottlenecks. Like a chain and its weakest link, the capacity of the bottleneck determines the capacity of the entire system.

   It is often difficult, if not impossible, to achieve this perfect balance, since the capacity of the machines available for the different steps may vary. In the system operation, the variability of the products and demand for them, as well as changing operating conditions, all contribute to the creation of bottlenecks. The manager has a number of tools for correcting these imbalances, such as overusing or underusing equipment through overtime or idle time, subcontracting, safety stocks and other means that will be studied in Chapter 5.

Finally, it should be noted that many variables whose effects are difficult to measure accurately nevertheless have significant repercussions for the size, use and control of capacity. When it is time to determine or rethink the capacity of an operation, a manager studies the factors that make this decision important, revises the variables that influence it,and attempts to include various economies of scale or diversity and to avoid diseconomies and bottlenecks. It is essential that managers not consider these elements in isolation, but rather as integral parts of company strategy.

REVIEW QUESTIONS

1. How are product and process linked?

2. What are the various process types, and how are they associated with types of products?

3. What are the various ways in which technologies can be applied?

4. Define the "technical sophistication" of an industry. How is it measured?

5. What is meant by the strategic role of the capacity decision?

6. Is capacity measured differently in the primary, secondary and tertiary sectors?

7. Comment on the different factors that influence capacity.

DISCUSSION QUESTIONS

1. What is the role of services in manufacturing companies?

2. Give three examples of services that could be considered "industrialized" and three examples of services that would be difficult to "industrialize." Explain your answers.

3. Choose a service company and try to match its operations system to one of the classifications in Figures 2.7 and 2.8. Discuss its specific features, limits, critical points, etc.

4. How can the flexibility of a process give a company competitive advantages?

5. Why do many managers fear technology? What can and should be done to overcome this problem?

6. Give an example of one major and one minor technological choice in the tertiary sector.

7. "Overtime is the best means of increasing capacity." Do you agree? Explain your reasons.

8. The capacity of a production unit depends on several factors, including size of the unit, type of technology used, product mix, length of use, performance of resources, degree of vertical integration and balance in the process.

   Briefly describe the effects of each of these factors on the capacity of a production unit.

9. Given the following facilities:

   1. A steel mill
   2. A shoe factory
   3. A bottling plant
   4. A hospital
   5. A nightclub
   6. A hotel

   a) For each one, give a typical unit for measuring capacity.

   b) How do facilities 1, 2 and 3 differ from facilities 4, 5 and 6 in terms of the measurement of capacity?

10. Funco Inc. is a toy manufacturer. An analyst studies the assembly department, which is organized in a linear fashion. The following diagram shows the five workstations and their individual capacity in units per day for a given product.

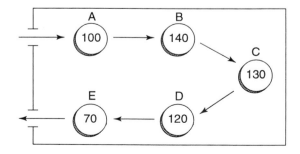

a) What is the daily capacity of the system? Explain.

b) When the system is working at full capacity, what is the percentage use of capacity of each of the workstations in the system?

c) If another operator were added at station E to double its capacity, how would your answers to a) and b) change?

d) What is the cycle time?

e) What is the throughput time?

11. Comment on the analogy between overcapacity and safety stock, and between undercapacity and stockout costs.

REFERENCES

1. ABERNATHY, W.J., K.B. CLARK and A.M. KANTROW, *Industrial Renaissance: Producing a Competitive Future for America.* New York: Basic Books, 1983.

2. BLOIS, K.J., "The Structure of Service Firms and Their Marketing Policies," *Strategic Management Journal*, Vol. 4, No. 3, 1983, pp. 251-261.

3. BOULEY, F., "Moyens de paiment et monétique," *Gestion des nouvelles communications*, 1990.

4. BOWER, J.L., and T.M. HOUT, "Cycle rapide et compétitivité," *Harvard-L'Expansion*, Fall 1989, pp. 33-49.

5. BROOKS, H., *The Government of Science.* Cambridge: MIT Press, 1968.

6. CHASE, R.B., and N.J. AQUILANO, *Production and Operations Management: A Life Cycle Approach*, 7th ed., Homewood, Illinois: R.D. Irwin, 1995, p. 113.

7. CLARK, K.B., and T. FUJIMOTO, *Product Development Performance: Strategy, Organization and Management in the World Auto Industry.* Boston: Harvard Business School Press, 1991.

8. COOK, B.M., "IBM Laptop: From Design to Product in 13 Months," *Industry Week*, August 5, 1991, p. 57.

9. COOPER, R.G., and E.J. KLEINSCHMIDT, *Developing Formal Processes for Managing New Products*, NCMRD Monograph Series. London, Ont.: University of Western Ontario, 1991.

10. DESCHAMPS, I., *Developing New Technologies in a De-Maturing Commodity Producer: An Empirical Study*, DBA Dissertation, Harvard Business School, March 1991.

11. DESCHAMPS, I., and M.O. DIORIO, "Stratégie technologique: Le rôle de la GOP," *Gestion*, Vol. 14, No. 3, 1989, pp. 94-104.

12. DOSTALER, I., "Stratégie d'opération et évaluation de la performance de l'unité de production," *Cahier de recherche No. 91-03,* Groupe de recherche en contrôle de gestion, Montreal, École des HEC, Summer 1991.

13. DURAND, T., and T. GONARD, "Stratégie et ruptures technologiques: Le cas de l'industrie de l'insuline," *Revue française de gestion*, November-December 1986.

14. DUROCHER, S., "Les rois de la pomme," *L'Actualité*, December 15, 1991, p. 41.

15. FROHMAN, A.L., "Technology as a Competitive Weapon," *Harvard Business Review*, January-February 1982, pp. 97-104.

16. GAUTHIER, P., "Corporation Technologies Eicon." Monograph prepared for the course "Séminaire: Environnement technologique," unpublished, Montreal, École des HEC, May 1991.

17. HAYWOOD-FARMER, J., and J. NOLLET, "Productivity in Professional Services," *Service Industries Journal*, Vol. 5, No. 2, July 1985, pp. 169-180.

18. INTERNATIONAL LABOUR OFFICE (ILO), *Introduction à l'étude du travail*. Geneva, 1970.

19. KODAMA, F., "Technology Fusion and the New R&D," *Harvard Business Review*, July-August 1992, p. 70.

20. LECONTE, C., "Virtual Prototypes: La passion de la création," *Commerce*, April 1991, pp. 46-47.

21. LE MOAL, P., and J.-C. TARONDEAU, "Un défi à la fonction Production," *Revue française de gestion*, January-February 1979.

22. LEONARD-BARTON, D., "Implementation and Mutual Adaptation of Technology and Organization," *Research Policy*, Vol. 17, 1988a, pp. 251-267.

23. LEVITT, T., "The Industrialization of Service," *Harvard Business Review*, Vol. 54, No. 5, September-October 1976, pp. 63-74.

24. LEVITT, T., "Production-Line Approach to Service," *Harvard Business Review*, Vol. 50, No. 5, September-October 1972, pp. 41-52.

25. MAYNARD, H.B., *Industrial Engineering Handbook*. New York: McGraw Hill, 1963.

26. NADEAU, J.B., "Les fruits de l'innovation," *Commerce,* February 1991, pp. 18-28.

27. PORTER, M.E., *Competitive Advantage: Creating and Sustaining Superior Performance*. New York: Free Press, 1985, Fig. 2.2, p. 37.

28. PORTER, M.E., *L'avantage concurrentiel: Comment devancer ses concurrents et maintenir son avance*. Paris: Inter-Édition, 1986.

29. PORTER, M.E., and V.E. MILLAR, "Pour battre vos concurrents... maîtrisez mieux l'information," *Harvard-L'Expansion*, Spring 1986, pp. 6-20.

30. SASSER, W.E., Jr., and D.C. RIKERT, *McDonald's*, case No. 9-681-044, Harvard Business School, Boston, 1991.

31. SCHMENNER, R.W., "How Can Service Businesses Survive and Prosper?" *Sloan Management Review*, Spring 1986, p. 25.

32. SKINNER, W., *Manufacturing in the Corporate Strategy*, 2nd ed. New York: John Wiley & Sons, 1984.

33. TAHERI, J., "Northern Telecom Tackles Successful Implementation of Cellular Manufacturing," *Industrial Engineer,* October 1990, pp. 38-43.

34. TARONDEAU, J.-C., *Produits et technologies: Choix politiques de l'entreprise industrielle*. Paris: Dalloz, 1982.

35. TOULOUSE, J.M., and R.A. BLAIS, *Les leçons de la réussite: 20 cas de PME technologiques à succès au Québec*. 1990.

36. TURCOTTE, A., Comité sectoriel d'adaptation de la main-d'oeuvre, Industrie du meuble et des articles d'ameublement, bilan situationnel. Monograph, March 1990.

37. WELTER, R.R., "Product Design Is About Possibilities," *Industry Week*, June 17, 1991, pp. 39-62.

38. WOODRUFF, D., "Saturn GM Finally Has a Winner, but Success Is Bringing a Fresh Batch of Problems," *Business Week*, August 17, 1992, pp. 85-91.

39. "IBM et American Airlines mettront sur pied le système de réservation d'Aéroflot," *Le Devoir*, April 27, 1992.

40. "Le Duralcan: Un modèle à suivre," *L'Ingénieur*, Vol. 4, No. 1, February 1991.

CHAPTER 3

Inventory Management and Independent Demand

CLAUDE R. DUGUAY, *main author*
JEAN NOLLET, *contributor*

INTRODUCTION

3.1   Strategic and Economic Importance of Inventory Management

An *inventory* is made up of a number of items, or stock, either in process or kept in reserve for later use. Finished products, components, raw materials, parts, etc., may be held in inventory to simplify production or to meet internal demand from the various departments of a company or external demand from customers. For purposes of inventory management, a distinction is made between two kinds of items: those subject to independent demand, such as finished products or spare parts, and those subject to dependent demand, which is determined by a company decision. In this chapter we will look at the basic concepts of inventory management and the systems that apply to independent demand items. Management of dependent demand items will be dealt with in Chapter 6, in the sections on planning material requirements.

Why do companies keep inventories? Items held in inventory are useful, but they may remain unused for some time after they are acquired. From an accounting point of view, inventories represent assets that will be realized at a later date. Most companies, despite valiant efforts to reduce inventories in the 1980s, still find that they are a major item on their balance sheets, particularly in the case of manufacturing and retail firms. The accumulation of such assets in inventory is justified by the important roles that inventory plays in a company. We will examine these roles later.

Some experts even question whether there is any need for inventory at all. In their eyes, assets held in inventory are wasted, since they are not being used. Proponents of the "just-in-time" approach, for example, feel that the best way of managing inventory is to eliminate it altogether. How can these two seemingly exclusive approaches be reconciled?

Items in inventory become useless once the purpose for which they were accumulated no longer applies or can be better met by other resources. But as long as such items still perform a useful purpose, it is worth managing them properly. For instance, a producer that reduces equipment setup time to a few minutes does not need to produce large quantities to offset its setup costs.

In this section we will first briefly review the types of inventory and their main purposes, then look at the nature and objectives of inventory management and present the ABC method of inventory analysis. In the next section we will discuss the basics of inventory management, the main costs and trade-offs involved. The third section will be devoted to the study of some basic inventory-management techniques. Finally, we will close with a brief description of three types of systems used for structured inventory management in which demand is independent.

3.2   Types of Inventory and Their Purposes

Manufacturers hold various *types of inventory*, intended to simplify production or meet demand. The three main types are *raw materials, components* and *supplies*; *work in process*; and *finished products*, at the plant or within the distribution network (distribution centre, regional warehouses, points of sale). Each type of inventory has a

▼ **FIGURE 3.1**
Role of Inventory in the Production System

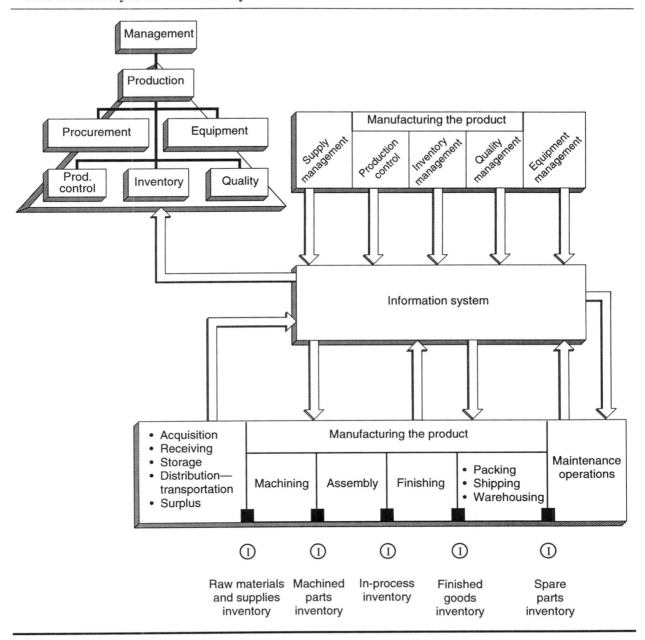

specific role in the production process. Figure 3.1 illustrates stockpoints and activities relating to their management in this process

   The relative importance of each type of inventory depends on the company's competitive position and its production process. Custom manufacturing calls for almost no finished-product inventory and little in the way of raw materials when they are specific to the products ordered. It is in-process inventories, corresponding to orders currently being filled, that must be managed most carefully. Continuous production firms have very different concerns, since their systems are designed to minimize in-process work. On the other hand, the standardization of their products and the volume of their operations often mean that they must stockpile finished products and maintain inventories of raw materials.[7]

Generally speaking, responsibility for inventory management is fairly decentralized. Procurement-system managers handle the acquisition of inputs, while those in charge of production planning and control (PPC) plan the production of finished products, based on orders received and forecast demand. When the finished product consists of various components from different sources, the PPC function also plans the various steps required for the production of assembled components. The PPC function often shares responsibility for production control with operations managers. In companies that rely on a large distribution network, inventories of finished products are frequently the responsibility of the PPC department. Companies with an integrated approach to operations combine inventory planning and control and purchasing in a single materials-management department.

There are five main inventory *functions*.[3]

1. *Pipeline* stock starts up the production system and keeps it running, through (a) the transportation of raw materials and components from the supplier to the production point, (b) work in process from one step to the next and (c) finished product through the distribution network to points of sale.

2. *Cycle* stock: the larger the lots produced, the more inventory accumulates. Stock resulting from decisions to increase lot sizes leads to reductions in the number of equipment adjustments or setups (internal) or orders (external) and their related costs. This type of inventory also makes it possible to take advantage of quantity discounts.

3. *Safety* stock offers the company some protection against random fluctuations in demand and delivery times.

4. *Buffer* stock, stored at different production points, allows the company to reduce the interdependence of operations and the dependence on suppliers, so that temporary problems at one point in the system do not bring the company's other production operations to a halt.

5. *Anticipation* stock plays a preventive role, allowing the company to deal with price increases and other market fluctuations, to avoid or minimize shortages due to strikes, and to manage seasonal variations in supply or demand.

In short, these five inventory functions give the production system greater flexibility and make for a more efficient and effective distribution system, since customers at the various points of sale are guaranteed that they can quickly obtain their goods as they need them. After all, what would consumers do if retailers did not keep goods on the shelves? They would have to place their orders and wait for the goods to be delivered, rather than purchasing the product they want just when they need it. The retailer would lose sales, especially impulse purchases. Moreover, it often proves costly for a company whose suppliers have high setup costs to order very small quantities of parts or raw materials. A furniture manufacturer would find it difficult to quickly adapt its production to demand fluctuations if it did not have the necessary wood on hand.

3.3   Inventory in Service Firms

Many service companies keep inventories of supplies or other items so that they can provide their services more quickly. Restaurants keep supplies of food on hand, hospitals have stocks of drugs, while garages keep inventories of spare parts.

Companies in the tertiary sector that use equipment to provide their services and that perform their own maintenance, including airlines, railways and trucking firms, must also keep stocks of spare parts and maintenance supplies on hand.

Most companies in the tertiary sector cannot stock the services they offer. If they are to meet demand from customers by a given deadline, their production capacity must correspond to the maximum demand they plan to meet.

As is the case with physical inventories, this capacity represents a resource that is often unused. In a restaurant, for example, unoccupied tables at a given time represent a sort of inventory; they allow the restaurant to meet demand by customers when they arrive. The same applies to an airline: seats left unsold for a given flight constitute unused capacity. At departure time, the inventory of available seats on the aircraft loses all value, in the way that the unoccupied tables in the restaurant lose value if no customers come to sit at them.

3.4   Systems Effects of Inventory Management

Few companies can escape the impact of economic cycles. Every year, unfortunately, the situation described below is played out thousands of times.

A company's cash flow is low. Sales are flat. All the company's managers are concerned about excess inventory, and urge the vice-president of operations to reduce the overall holdings of raw materials and work in process by 10% per month over the next three months. The vice-president is faced with a number of options.

- Delay certain purchases. Unfortunately, the purchases of raw materials required for the best-selling finished products are the ones that will suffer the most, since the company makes greater quantities of these products, or at least makes them more often, than slower-moving products.

- Reduce the amount and value of work in process, by reducing lot sizes or improving the production process. The effects of this kind of improvement are rarely felt in the very short term, however, and such an initiative may also increase the inventory of finished products for which sales do not rise proportionally.

- Reduce the book value of all items that are partly obsolete. This will not improve the current situation, but will at least help to reduce the book value of inventory where it is appropriate to do so.

- Order items in small lots rather than immediately purchasing the economic order quantity (section 3.10). Unit costs will rise, but the total value of inventory will decline, since there are fewer of each item in inventory.

- Perform preventive maintenance on equipment while depleting inventory. Maintenance time reduces production time.

If all these measures are applied haphazardly, the company will probably be unable to meet demand and therefore its sales will drop. It will have only its less-popular goods for sale, since reductions in purchases of raw materials will make it impossible to manufacture its best-selling products on time and in sufficient quantities to meet demand.

Inventory is not a homogenous group of items that can be increased or decreased indiscriminately. Consequently, when it becomes necessary to reduce inventory, it is essential to determine which specific stocks can best be reduced. Sound inventory management also takes account of the needs of the Production/Operations function and other functions. Operations managers are thoroughly familiar with the trade-offs inherent in different kinds of inventory and their functions. They should make decisions in the best interests of the firm as a whole, setting objectives for the inventory system based on the company's overall strategy and, in particular, its financial capacity.

Inventory represents a necessary investment for a company, but one that competes with other worthwhile investments. Every item held in inventory represents an investment decision. Operations managers have a vested interest in adopting a strategy that will allow them to maintain stocks at the lowest acceptable level, keeping in mind the capacity of their production system. Without necessarily aiming to eliminate inventory, as many managers who favour just-in-time and zero-stock strategies do, they should regularly review the usefulness of various kinds of inventory and just as regularly evaluate the quantities of items produced or ordered.

3.5   Nature and Objectives of Inventory Management

Inventory management consists mainly in determining when an item should be restocked, and in what quantity. It comes down to two questions: when to order, and how much ? The answers to these questions are fairly simple for each of the thousands of products, components and materials used by a manufacturer or retailer. Taken together, this multitude of answers determines the service level and the total inventory shown on the balance sheet. Their cumulative effect is of strategic importance for the company, and the entire inventory is naturally more difficult to manage than stocks of a single item.

The primary objective of inventory management is to avoid stockouts, and therefore to offer good service. The simple solution would be to order large quantities well ahead of time, but this approach runs counter to the second objective, minimizing costs. The solution to this second objective, of course, is to order items as they are needed; if materials arrive shortly before they are to be used, their carrying cost will be almost nil, and the company's cash flow will benefit.

Given the enormous number of items kept in inventory, most manufacturers and retailers rely on inventory-management systems to make the above decisions. These systems have operating rules for handling the various trade-offs among all the objectives to be considered. The most common inventory management systems will be described later in this chapter.

The traditional approach to inventory management is to strike a balance between the various costs of maintaining inventory and the costs of shortages, or stockouts. The first trade-off concerns the balance between stockout costs and inventory-management costs. Figure 3.2 illustrates this balance, although it should be noted that it is impossible to reach it in practice because many costs, particularly stockout costs, cannot be determined precisely.

To overcome this problem, managers often set a certain target service level and focus on making trade-offs between a high service level and low inventory-management costs. We will examine this approach in greater detail in section 3.9, which covers service levels.

The other particularly important balance to be attained in inventory management concerns the trade-off between carrying costs and ordering costs (or setup costs, if appropriate). The greater the number of orders, the smaller the inventory, and vice versa. Frequent orders result in frequent receipt of small lots, just enough to meet needs until the next lot arrives. Taken to the extreme, a company could place an order whenever an item is needed—or place only one order every year or two. The first approach minimizes inventory building costs, the second ordering costs. The goal is to find a position between very frequent ordering, resulting in low inventory and very infrequent ordering, resulting in high inventory. An example with calculations is included in section 3.10.

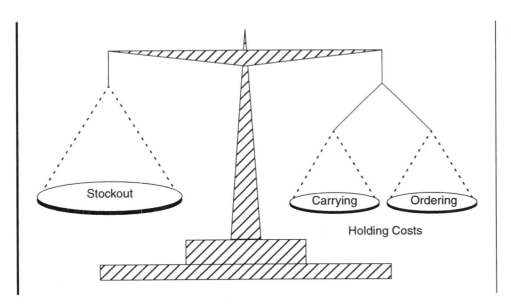

◄ **FIGURE 3.2
Inventory Cost
Trade-offs**

The inventory turnover rate, which is calculated by dividing the cost of sales by the average value of inventory, is a commonly employed performance measure in inventory management. A company that can maintain a higher turnover rate than its competitors, while at the same time satisfying its customers, is more successful at managing its investment in inventory. Similarly, frequent setups for smaller lots in a flexible production system is preferable to longer setup times.

Britney[1] notes that a lower turnover rate can also be the result of different objectives. Since carrying costs can vary widely from one company to the next, and even more from one country to the next, comparisons of inventory turnover ratios can be misleading. He suggests a different measurement, the *k-turn*, which also takes carrying costs into account. This measurement justifies a company carrying a larger inventory when its carrying costs are lower than those of the competition.

Items are not equally important. A basic principle is to devote more management attention to the most important ones, and the ABC method can be used to do so.

3.6   ABC Method of Inventory Analysis

The ABC method, which is illustrated in Figure 3.4, is as simple as it sounds. It can be applied to customers, accounts receivable, etc., as well as inventory. The underlying principle is to focus on the most important items, without neglecting the less important ones. The method consists in classifying items A, B or C, the most costly, most important items under A and the least costly, least important under C.

There is no hard and fast rule for determining the class to which an item belongs. The most commonly used criterion in inventory management is the volume of annual use of each item. Another criterion is the average value of items held in inventory, assuming that it is preferable to devote more attention to goods of greater value, whereas the volume of use gives more weight to items for which there is strong internal or external demand.

Class A items require the best demand forecasting and inventory-management methods. It is logical that more time be spent studying costs and the market for these than for items in the other two classes. Similarly, the costs inherent in inventories of class A raw materials must be more clearly identified. Finally, the company must generally keep an accurate perpetual inventory record of class A items.

Since class A items are worth more than the others, the company will exercise stricter control over them—for example, by erecting a fence to protect valuable finished products or raw materials. In fact, part of the cost of storing goods is attributed to theft. Costly products that are tempting to thieves (cameras or cars, for instance) may even justify the installation of a closed-circuit camera. Generally speaking, control of raw materials and finished products comes under stores management, the specific objectives of which must fit with those of inventory management. Once again, some trade-offs are necessary, particularly between the costs and benefits of controls.

Class C comprises those items that managers consider the least important. When items are classified by cost, some important but inexpensive items may fall into this class. Given their lower value, a greater margin of error can be tolerated in demand forecasting, as well as looser controls over the quantities carried. For particularly important class C items, a safety stock sufficient to reduce or eliminate stockouts can be maintained relatively inexpensively.Some computer software programs can order class C items directly, with minimal human intervention, although the procurement manager will have to set minimum and maximum quantities per order. Even if the quantity differs from the amount a buyer would have purchased in the same circumstances, where class C items are concerned the consequences are less serious.

One method sometimes used to control class C items is the *two-bin* system. As the name suggests, inventory items are placed in two bins (Figure 3.3). Stock is taken from the first bin as needed; once it is empty, and before any stock is taken from the second bin, the clerk quickly sends off an order form, which has already been completed and placed on top of the second bin, to the purchasing department. This system is effective only if it is strictly observed, which is not always possible in emergencies. For instance, the clerk may forget to send off the form on time if he is not authorized to open the second bin, and this could lead to a stockout. In addition, this technique does not always give the manager immediate information on the quantities in stock and the frequency of use of items. Its main advantage is its simplicity.

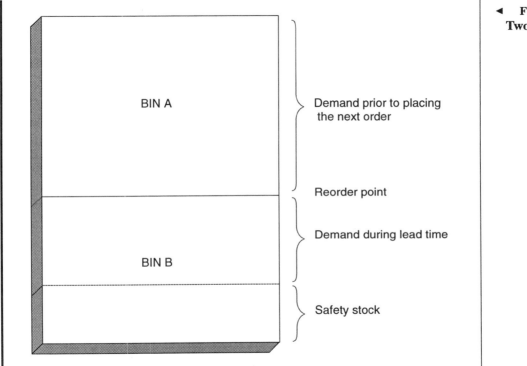

◄   **FIGURE 3.3**
Two-Bin System

More often than not, class B comprises items that are not critical or valuable enough to be included in class A but are still more important than those in class C. The techniques and controls applied fall somewhere between those for A and those for C.

How are stocks divided into the various classes? Suppose a company chooses annual use of items as the main criterion. The manager will then proceed as follows:

   – prepare a list of all the items used in the previous year;

   – classify items by decreasing order of annual use;

   – calculate the cumulative percentage of values and of the number of items;

   – assign the items to classes. Although descriptions of the method normally refer to three classes (A, B and C), it is equally possible to divide stocks into five classes, or even more. It is all a question of judgement, just as it is in deciding the boundaries for the various classes. Typically, using cost-based ABC analysis, A units constitute 20% of the items in stock and 75% of the value, B units 30% of the items and 20% of the value and C units 50% of the items and 5% of the value.

We will now illustrate these classes using an example.

Example ■

As the basis for the ABC classification, the manager chooses the quantities of raw materials used the previous year. The company for which he works uses 10 raw materials. The following are the dollar values, rounded off to the nearest thousand:

A = 20	F = 80
B = 30	G = 16
C = 3	H = 95
D = 1	I = 32
E = 0	J = 23

Do the ABC analysis.

Solution

A glance at the four classification steps already mentioned shows they can be combined in one step, in the following chart.

Item	Rank	Usage (in '000s of $)	Cumulative value (%)	Number of items (%)	Class
H	1	95	31.7	10	A
F	2	80	58.4	20	
I	3	32	69.1	30	
B	4	30	79.1	40	B
J	5	23	86.8	50	
A	6	20	93.4	60	
G	7	16	98.7	70	
C	8	3	99.7	80	C
D	9	1	100.0	90	
E	10	0	100.0	100	

According to Figure 3.4, the ABC curve has a regular shape; it does not join all of the top portions of the frequencies of the histogram. Class A consists of 20% of the raw materials and represents 58.4% of the total value. Class B consists of 40% of the raw materials and represents 35% of the annual dollar usage. Class C consists of 40% of the raw materials and represents 6.6% of the total dollar usage.

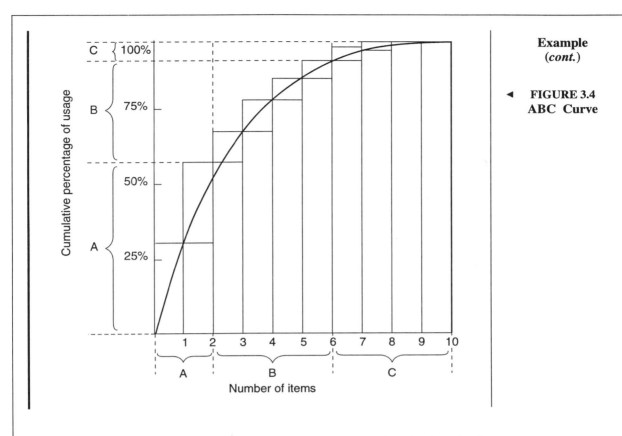

Example
(*cont.*)

◄   **FIGURE 3.4**
ABC Curve

The manager must devote the most attention to the raw materials in class A; the amount of effort will depend on whether demand for these items is dependent or independent.

In the next part of this chapter we will review the two main factors in inventory management: costs and service levels. In the last part, we will consider techniques for reaching the desired balance between objectives—that is, economic order quantities and safety stocks.

MAIN FACTORS IN INVENTORY MANAGEMENT

With a just-in-time approach, eliminating inventory is almost an end in itself, since all stocks are considered a waste. With traditional inventory-management approaches, the main objective is to reduce inventory-related costs. The most important costs to be considered are stockout costs, carrying and ordering (or setup) costs and purchase price. We will examine these costs in the following sections. However, we should begin with two fundamental questions: when is it worth managing inventory, and what costs should be considered?

Contrary to what one might think, economic trade-offs among the various types of costs are not considered for each transaction. In practice, many situations are not analysed. Trade-offs are made intuitively or on the basis of routine procedures, without any explicit analysis. In such cases, the techniques presented below will probably prove useful.

Under what circumstances is it worth determining the different inventory-related costs? It is appropriate in the following situations:

- when some items are very costly or very important;
- when managers are devoting extensive human and material resources to improving inventory management;
- when arbitrary rules exist, not based on valid considerations (e.g., never purchase items that will not be required in the two weeks after they are received; place an order when there are 10 items left).

In such situations as these, the costs of determining inventory-related costs will most likely be lower than the potential saving of not doing so.

What costs should be considered? The allocation of carrying costs is often approximate, since it is difficult to assign an accurate proportion of costs for energy, handling and property taxes, for example, to each item. Nevertheless, it is possible to arrive at a reasonable estimate of these costs.

The inclusion of overhead in these costs increases both the ordering cost and the size of lots ordered. The higher the ordering cost, the greater the temptation to space the orders more widely. In addition, overhead as a consideration is a result of past decisions and may therefore distort the decision as to the maximum number of items to be carried in inventory. Decisions concerning overhead may be questioned from time to time, but should have no effect on later decisions. Overhead costs are usually past costs, which makes them irrelevant. Vollmann *et al.*[9] suggest that managers ask themselves two questions about each cost to determine which should be included in computing inventory-related costs: Is it an expense rather than an investment? Does the cost vary in relation to the inventory decision made?

If the answer to both questions is yes, the cost in question should be included, since the decision may entail additional costs. For instance, the cost of building a new warehouse is not charged to inventory, because it is an investment. On the other hand, the cost of insurance on inventory is not a fixed cost, since it varies according to the value of stock on hand. Note that the first question raises that eternal accounting dilemma: should overhead be allocated to each individual product, or considered as a whole? If overhead is not charged to each product, carrying costs may be understated, leading to excess inventory. Unjustified charges, on the other hand, undermine sound inventory management.

3.7   Stockout Costs

Stockout costs are primarily the result of a shortage of items ordered, and the resulting foregone profit. They represent a significant opportunity cost. The main costs of internal and external stockouts are shown in Table 3.1. Internal stockouts occur when there are insufficient raw materials or work in process to meet production needs. In some circumstances, this kind of shortage can lead to an external stockout as well.

Internal stockout	External stockout	
– Idle worker	– Temporary or permanent damage to reputation	◄ TABLE 3.1 **Internal and External Stockout Costs**
– Machinery downtime		
– Higher price paid to speed up delivery of required items	– Loss of current and future orders because customers have lost confidence in the promised delivery schedule; this situation can result in lost customers	
– Possible loss of quantity discount if the order placed reduces the quantity of future orders to the point of changing price break interval		
– Overtime at work centres preceding those where there is a risk of stockout, to compensate for insufficient quantities	– Subcontracting becomes necessary in order to deliver on time, the profit on the order going in part to the subcontractor and in part to the original supplier	
– Negative impact on employee morale	– Overtime not paid by the customer	
– Changes to scheduling resulting in more frequent setups	– Quicker and more expensive transportation used to reduce shipping delays	
– Information changes in the data files and particularly to the master production schedule		
– Creation of bottleneck		
– Loss of production capacity		
– Increase in the number of expediters		

An external stockout occurs when the company has insufficient stocks of a finished product to make a delivery to the customer. In cases where the company is manufacturing items for stock, this shortage occurs when the customer orders. Some of the related costs are difficult to evaluate but are no less real: for instance, the damage to the company's reputation or the opportunity for a competitor to seize a share of the market. Other costs are easier to quantify, such as the loss of profit on items that cannot be sold because they are unavailable.

Despite the difficulty of measuring stockout costs, the fact remains that they are considerable. Consequently, operations managers do their best to produce sufficient quantities of all items and endeavour to satisfy customers.

Managers come under more criticism for stockouts than for excess inventory, and are probably more severely penalized for them. After all, a stockout translates into customer dissatisfaction, with potentially serious and lasting consequences, and it gives competitors an ideal opportunity to penetrate the market. Excess inventory is less clearcut and has a less obvious cumulative effect. This reason and those discussed earlier explain why, until the early 1980s, most companies preferred to pay inventory carrying costs rather than risk stockouts. However, the very strong pressures of international competition produced a change in this attitude.

3.8   Ordering and Carrying Costs

Ordering and carrying costs are sometimes referred to as the cost of possessing inventory. Ordering costs are all the costs inherent in preparing, processing and paying orders, and may vary substantially depending on the items concerned, from a few dollars to several hundred, or even thousands of dollars for specialized equipment parts.

When a company requires an item or a raw material, it places an external or internal order. In the first case, there is an ordering cost attached; in the second case, there are preparation costs, representing all the costs of setting up the equipment used to produce the required good. Table 3.2 lists ordering and setup costs. Much of the drive to reduce stocks has been concentrated on reducing ordering and setup costs. We will concentrate on ordering costs, although the discussion applies equally to setup costs.

Since it is sometimes difficult to distinguish between fixed and variable ordering costs, and although ordering or preparation costs vary from one situation to the next, some companies use the following ratio to arrive at an approximate cost:

$$\text{Unit ordering cost } = \frac{\text{Total annual ordering cost}}{\text{Annual number of orders}}$$

Where there is a great variety of ordering costs, items are classified according to the ordering cost to be applied. The level of detail is a matter of judgement.

In practice, the unit ordering cost is calculated by closely monitoring a number of orders for which the portion of variable costs listed in Table 3.2 is determined. We recommend this approach, as it gives more accurate results than does the ratio above. Since the unit ordering cost varies from one year to the next, the effect on the economic order quantity for different items must be verified regularly. Computerization has greatly simplified this task, for all the information required is placed on file and a change to the ordering cost of an item is automatically taken into account when the economic order cost is calculated, as we will see in section 3.10 and the successive sections. The widespread introduction of electronic data interchange (EDI) has considerably reduced many of these costs.

TABLE 3.2 ▶
**Ordering and
Setup Costs**

Ordering cost	Setup cost
– Preparation of requisition	– Preparation of requisition
– Preparation of purchase order	– Processing of other internal documents, such as the production order
– Data processing	
– Postage	– Machine setup time
– Follow-up	– Employee training for change in manufacturing from one type of article to another
– Authorization and payment of invoice	
– Receipt of merchandise	
– Handling	– Defective parts produced during setup
– Inspection	

Opportunity costs	– Cost on borrowed capital or	**Breakdown of**
	– Rate of return on investments other than inventory	**Inventory**
Storage costs	– Property taxes	
	– Insurance on warehouse and stores	
	– Energy	
	– Handling	
	– Repairs to warehouse	
Holding costs	– Insurance on inventories	
	– Obsolescence	
	– Deterioration	
	– Packaging	
	– Fire, theft, damage	

Carrying costs comprise three categories: opportunity costs, storage costs and costs related to inventory losses. These are listed in Table 3.3.

Carrying costs are substantial, accounting for up to 50% of the annual purchase or production costs. Many researchers and managers agree that the carrying cost of an item represents from 30% to 40% of the initial cost. Rhodes,[6] however, considers these figures double what they should be, for two reasons: a 40% rate normally includes overhead; and the advantages of carrying inventory are overlooked, although these may be difficult to evaluate—for example, a car dealer would certainly sell fewer cars if the showroom were empty.

Carrying costs do not usually increase linearly, and fluctuations make it difficult to calculate the exact carrying cost for a given quantity. In practice, however, carrying costs are often considered to be linear, on the assumption that the resulting error may be less expensive than the trouble of obtaining data that are more detailed.

Since transportation costs frequently represent from 10% to 15% of the cost of a good, Vollmann *et al.*[9] suggest they be included in trade-offs concerning ordering and carrying costs. Consequently, it is the total cost of these three factors that should be minimized. Note that the selection of a means of transport itself represents an important trade-off, with repercussions for customer satisfaction. The cost of transportation will be lower if a manager can reduce transportation time and uncertainty, but carrying costs may rise. Tables 3.2 and 3.3 offer more information on the breakdown of the main types of costs.

3.9   Service Levels

When demand is deterministic, i.e., when there is no uncertainty—forecasts are guaranteed and there are generally no shortages. But if there are random fluctuations in demand and/or lead times, the company must take steps to reduce the risk of stockouts.

Given the distribution of demand and of lead times, and considering the relationship between stockout and carrying costs, the company must decide what level of service it wishes to offer, in other words what frequency of stockouts it is willing to tolerate. A service level of 95% means that 95% of demand will be satisfied.

"Satisfying demand" has different meanings, of course, depending on the position of the company in the market. It may mean having the item requested in inventory, or it may mean being able to deliver it within 24 hours. A company's competitiveness depends heavily on the level of service it offers; indeed, this criterion shapes its image. If there are frequent stockouts, for instance, customers will look to other suppliers.

Although the service level refers to the entire period, risk of a stockout occurs only when stocks of the item are about to run out.[4] The more the company orders in large quantities, the less often it will face a risk of stockouts. For instance, if 100 units of an item are used daily, and it is ordered in lots of 3,000, the risk of a stockout occurs only once a month, when the lot of 3,000 is nearly used up. If the company prefers to order in lots of 200, there will be a risk of a stockout every two days. We will examine this point in greater detail in our discussion of safety stocks (section 3.14). Figure 3.5 illustrates the trade-offs involved.

The risks related to a stockout because of a fluctuation in demand have different consequences from those of a risk related to a variation in delivery lead times. Rising demand represents a risk of a stockout only if the stock is about to run out and must be reordered. The rest of the time, upward fluctuations are offset by downward fluctuations.

Delivery delays may be caused by a number of factors: the time required to obtain authorization for an order or send it to the supplier, mechanical problems, absenteeism or other internal problems faced by the supplier, or transportation delays. Although there is an element of uncertainty to all delays, they are not usually random occurrences. The main cause of manufacturing delays is order backlogs. These orders can be filled at a particular workstation, but will then overload this station, and so cause further delays (in other orders). Such backlogs can result in lower than expected service levels unless scheduling is improved. This issue is discussed in Chapter 7. As can be seen, service levels, scheduling and inventory are closely tied.

INVENTORY MANAGEMENT TECHNIQUES

3.10   Economic Order Quantity: Basic Model

This is the first of several sections in which we will discuss the quantitative aspects of inventory management. We will begin with the number of units to be ordered or produced. Then we will look at the optimal time for ordering, mainly in the sections dealing with fixed-quantity and fixed-period reorder systems.

The economic order quantity (EOQ) method is a quick means of calculation that will minimize total ordering and carrying costs. Purchase price is not considered, since it is assumed to be constant. The basic model comprises seven assumptions altogether, the most important of which is that demand for the item is deterministic and constant. These assumptions are listed in Table 3.4. Note that none of them stipulates

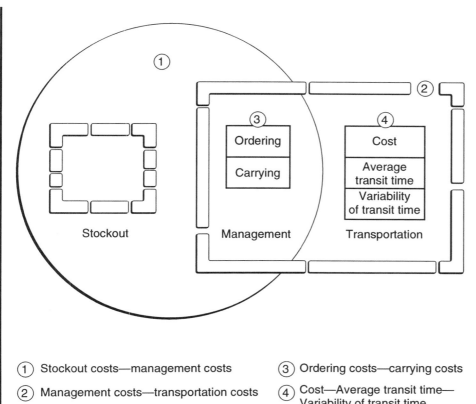

◄   **FIGURE 3.5**
Summary of Four
Trade-offs:
Stockout—
Ordering—
Transportation—
Carrying

① Stockout costs—management costs

② Management costs—transportation costs

③ Ordering costs—carrying costs

④ Cost—Average transit time—
Variability of transit time

1. Deterministic and constant demand (use)
2. Immediate delivery (production), in a single lot, of quantities ordered
3. Constant ordering (setup) cost
4. Constant purchase price; no quantity discount
5. Unit and linear inventory carrying cost
6. No stockouts accepted
7. Infinite planning horizon

◄   **TABLE 3.4**
Underlying
Assumptions of the
Basic Economic
Order Quantity
Model

that the EOQ model applies solely to cases of independent demand. Nevertheless, it is easy to see that if the EOQ approach were used in certain cases of dependent demand, when usage is determined by management decision, the quantities ordered or manufactured would not be depleted at a constant rate, as the model assumes.

Suppose, for instance, that the assembly of 50 specially designed chairs takes 50 backs and 200 casters, among other parts. Applying the EOQ approach would suggest that the backs be produced in lots of 125 and the casters in lots of 1,000. What would be done with the remaining units, if there were no other demand for these parts in the following three months? In any case, this example violates the assumption that demand is constant. Despite the apparent contradiction between the assumptions underlying EOQ calculations and the reality of dependent demand, this method can sometimes be used to advantage in such situations. Chapter 6 contains more details on models used for making decisions regarding dependent demand.

In the basic model, ordering and carrying costs are the only pertinent costs. The total ordering cost (C_{to}) depends on the unit order preparation cost (C_o) and the number of orders placed during the year, which in turn depends on the annual demand (D) and the quantity ordered each time (Q). Therefore, the total annual ordering cost is:

$$C_{to} = C_o \times \frac{D}{Q} \tag{1}$$

The total carrying cost (C_{tc}) depends on the unit carrying cost per year (C_c) and the annual average quantity in inventory. This varies linearly from the maximum quantity (Q) to the minimum quantity, zero, as illustrated in Figure 3.6. Since the assumptions governing the model specify that there are no stockouts and that demand is constant, the average inventory is $(Q + 0)/2 = Q/2$. Accordingly, total annual carrying cost is:

$$C_{tc} = C_c \times \frac{Q}{2} \tag{2}$$

The total annual inventory holding cost C_t corresponds to the sum of these two costs. This gives the following formula, which is used to determine the value of Q such that the inventory holding cost is minimized:

$$C_t = C_{tc} + C_{to}$$
$$= C_o \times \frac{D}{Q} + C_c \times \frac{Q}{2} \tag{3}$$

FIGURE 3.6 ▶
Average Quantity in Inventory

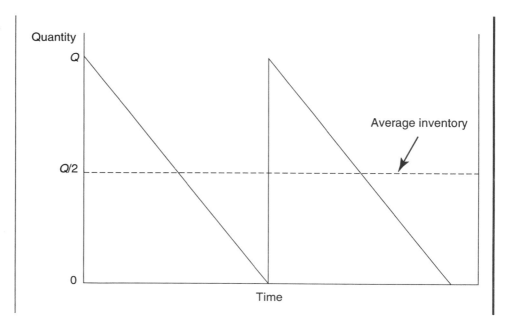

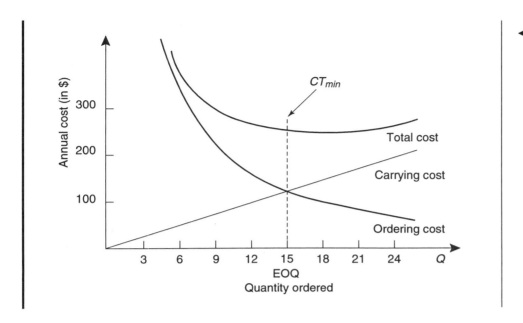

Figure 3.7 illustrates the inventory holding cost C_t as a function of the quantity ordered Q.

The EOQ can be determined using differential calculus. A more straightforward way is to consider the trade-offs involved. According to Figure 3.7, the minimum total cost CT_{min} is reached at the intersection of curve C_{to} and line C_{tc}. Any quantity less than the EOQ has a declining marginal ordering cost greater than the increase in the corresponding carrying cost. The inverse is true for quantities greater than the EOQ.

The optimal quantity can also be calculated using the following formulas, assuming that at the optimal quantity, annual carrying costs and ordering costs must be equal.

Therefore:

$$C_{to} = C_{tc} \tag{4}$$

By substituting the value of C_{to} given by (1) and the value of C_{tc} given by (2), we obtain:

$$C_{to} \times \frac{D}{Q} = C_c \times \frac{Q}{2} \tag{5}$$

$$2C_o \times D = C_c \times Q^2$$

thus:

$$Q^2 = 2C_o \times \frac{D}{C_c}$$

$$EOQ = \sqrt{2D \times \frac{C_o}{C_c}} \tag{6}$$

The total ordering and carrying cost (CT_{min}) corresponding to the EOQ is obtained using the following formula (we will not show the calculations here):

$$CT_{min} = \sqrt{2D \times C_o \times C_c}$$

Now we will look at an application of the basic EOQ model, in which an iterative process is used to calculate the total cost.

Example
■

Ms. Green is responsible for purchasing all kinds of paper and office supplies. She has just received an order from the computer services department for four boxes of a special variety of perforated paper. Upon reviewing the most recent similar orders, Ms. Green finds that the department needs four boxes every week. Since she knows that the ordering cost is $9, the annual carrying cost $16 (per box) and the unit purchase price $40, should she change the weekly frequency of orders?

Solution

The objective here is to minimize the total cost CT, consisting of the ordering cost C_{to} and the carrying cost C_{tc}. Given that four boxes are needed weekly and that 200 boxes are ordered annually (assuming 50 working weeks), she draws up the following table:

(1) Quantity ordered (Q) per order	(2) Carrying cost based on average inventory $C_{tc} = Q/2 \times \$16$	(3) Ordering cost based on annual number of orders $C_{to} = (200/Q) \times \$9$	(4) Total annual cost (2) + (3) CT
1	$ 8	$1,800	$1,808
2	16	900	916
3	24	600	624
4	32	450	482
5	40	360	400
10	80	180	260
12	96	150	246
13	104	138.46	242.46
14	112	128.57	240.57
15	120	120	240
16	128	112.50	240.50
17	136	105.88	241.88
18	144	100	244
19	152	94.74	246.74
20	160	90	250
25	200	72	272

Example
(cont.)

The lowest annual cost CT_{min} is $240, or an order of 15 boxes at a time. The savings over ordering four boxes weekly are $482 - 240 = \$242$. Figure 3.7 shows how carrying and ordering costs change as the amounts ordered increase.

What would happen if Ms. Green used the EOQ formula rather than an iterative process? The formula for the basic model is:

$$EOQ = \sqrt{\frac{2DC_o}{C_c}}$$

where D = demand for a given period,

$\quad C_o$ = unit ordering cost,

$\quad C_c$ = unit carrying cost over the period.

If we insert the data from the problem, we obtain:

$$EOQ = \sqrt{\frac{2 \times 200 \times 9}{16}} = \sqrt{\frac{3600}{16}} = 15 \text{ boxes per order,}$$

or the same answer.

Using the data from this example, we can prove that at the optimal cost the annual ordering cost is equal to the carrying cost, or $120.

Quantity ordered	Annual carrying cost	Annual ordering cost	Variance with previous quantity		
			C_c	C_p	Net marginal cost (saving)
13	$104	$138.46	$8	($11.54)	($3.54)
14	112	128.57	8	(9.89)	(1.89)
15	120	120.00	8	(8.57)	(0.57)
16	128	112.50	8	(7.50)	0.50
17	136	105.88	8	(6.62)	1.38

In addition, there is no benefit to ordering quantities greater than 15, as this will result in a net cost rather than a net saving.

Similarly, the total ordering and carrying cost CT_{min} that corresponds to the EOQ increases. It can be obtained with the following formula:

$$CT_{min} = \sqrt{2DC_o C_c}$$

Using the data from the previous example, we arrive at the following total cost:

$$CT_{min} = \sqrt{2 \times 200 \times 9 \times 16} = \sqrt{57,600} = \$240$$

which corresponds exactly to the result in the table.

The answer obtained using the EOQ formula should not be applied blindly. Rather it is a guideline that suggests the EOQ formula be used and keeps managers from ordering quantities that are much too high or too low. They still have a great deal of room to manoeuvre, as shown by the sensitivity analysis in the following section.

Other constraints may also play a role. Factors such as transportation costs, shortage of funds or limited storage space may justify some departure from the EOQ. In any case, it is obviously not in the company's interest to determine the quantities to be ordered without taking these other factors into account.

3.11   Sensitivity Analysis

It has been mentioned that costs, and particularly stockout costs, could be difficult to determine accurately. What, then, are the consequences of an error in determining or estimating these costs? In fact, under- or overestimating demand by 20% of the carrying or ordering cost leads to a difference of only 5% of the total obtained using the EOQ model.[5]

Figure 3.7 clearly illustrates that the curve for the total ordering and carrying cost varies little in EOQ. Ordering 80% to 125% of the EOQ rather than the exact quantity translates into a financial penalty of less than 3%. In the above example, quantities of 12 and 19 boxes (80% and 125%, respectively, of the EOQ) cost $246 and $246.74, whereas the total minimum cost was $240. A number of other important lessons can be drawn from this observation and from Figure 3.7.

First of all, when in doubt, it is better to order more than less. The total cost curve shows that costs increase much less quickly toward the right than toward the left. Consequently, for the same absolute difference from the EOQ, the additional cost of ordering too much is less than the additional cost of ordering too little. We will return to the previous example to illustrate this point. If Ms. Green had ordered 10 boxes rather than 15, this difference of five boxes per order would have cost $260 in total annual ordering and carrying costs. On the other hand, had she ordered 20 boxes, or five more than the EOQ, it would have cost only $250.

Second, it is not essential that figures be completely accurate. Calculations can be done with reasonable approximations, for the resulting margin of error is low. Despite appearances, the model is fairly flexible and does not demand absolute precision and accuracy.

Third, even when factors push the company to order quantities as much as 20% more or less than the EOQ, the financial consequences due to ordering and carrying costs are not great.

Sound inventory management is based on a systems approach. Trade-offs are necessary, and the EOQ is one of the factors to be taken into account. But sometimes many items must be ordered at the same time, some of them in quantities that differ from the EOQ. In practice, managers must often rely on judgement and experience in deciding how much to order. Or the decision may be coloured by the funds available. The EOQ method remains potentially useful, although many managers reject the model and its variations, claiming that all its assumptions can never be met at one time.

Sensitivity analysis has shown that the model is flexible and can be a useful tool, but before using it managers should ask themselves whether actual conditions are so far removed from the underlying assumptions as to invalidate the results obtained with the model. For example, if demand for the period is not constant, is it close enough to linear demand for the EOQ model to apply just the same? There is also some question as to whether the EOQ model can apply under inflationary conditions. Jesse *et al.*[2] have examined this issue and shown that it is flexible enough to cope with inflation.

Various authors have studied the basic model not only with stockouts, but also with quantity discounts and with phased production or delivery. These two models are discussed in the following sections.

3.12 EOQ with Quantity Discounts

A manufacturer can often save money by producing long runs, because of increased worker efficiency. For this and other reasons, producers generally offer discounts on large purchases, in which case buyers may benefit from purchasing quantities greater than those recommended by the basic EOQ model. The model is intended to help calculate the minimum total cost, on the basis of ordering and carrying costs. As we have seen, if a quantity in excess of the EOQ is ordered, the higher carrying cost is not offset by the saving resulting from a smaller number of orders. However, this net additional cost is unimportant if the discount offered by the supplier more than makes up for the difference. The EOQ model with quantity discounts can be used to determine the minimum cost, taking into account not only the ordering and carrying costs but also any discounts offered.

This variant of the model may be used when discounts are offered on quantities greater than *or* less than those suggested by the basic model. Figure 3.8 clearly illustrates these two situations, and the discontinuity in the total cost curve is readily apparent.

If the EOQ determined with the basic model occurs *before the first quantity discount interval*, only the lower figure of the quantity discount interval should be considered. Any quantity greater than the EOQ has a marginal carrying cost greater than the savings in ordering costs. Only the discount can offset this increase. Any quantity other than the lower limit of a discount interval cannot correspond to a better total cost. Consequently, there is no benefit to ordering a quantity different from the EOQ as determined with the basic model or the lower limit of the quantity discount intervals. We will illustrate this point with an example.

Where the EOQ calculated using the basic model lies *within a discount interval*, the method of calculating the EOQ is similar to the method shown earlier, albeit somewhat lengthier.

The EOQ model with quantity discounts cannot be used if the discount is simply a temporary dip in suppliers' prices, but Tersine and Price[8] show that the model can be modified to take account of such temporary discounts. One of the important conclusions of their study is that in many situations a temporary discount may justify ordering much higher quantities.

FIGURE 3.8 ▶
Two Possibilities of
the Economic
Order Quantity
Model with
Quantity Discounts

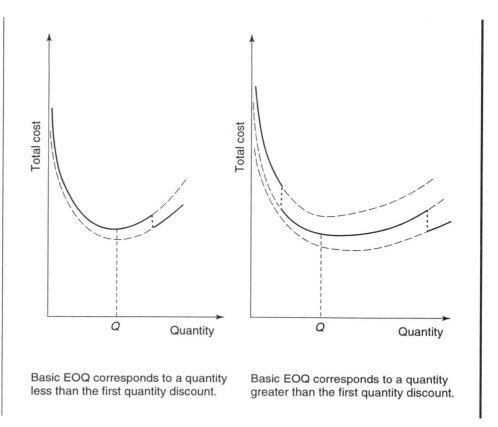

Basic EOQ corresponds to a quantity less than the first quantity discount.

Basic EOQ corresponds to a quantity greater than the first quantity discount.

Example
■

The supplier who sells Ms. Green boxes of paper offers the following quantity discounts:

0 to 19 boxes = no discount

20 to 29 boxes = 5% discount

30 or more boxes = 10% discount.

Is it in Ms. Green's interest to purchase more than 15 boxes—i.e., the EOQ calculated using the basic model?

Solution

In this case, neither the ordering cost of $9, the carrying cost of $16 nor the annual demand of 200 boxes is changed by the discounts. However, the discounts lower the $40 basic price to $38 and $36, respectively. Ms. Green decides to compare the three quantities she is interested in ordering—that is, 15, 20 and 30, and the increase in costs that would result from purchasing an amount greater than the lower discount limit:

Quantity purchased	Annual ordering cost	Annual carrying cost	Annual purchase price	Total annual cost	Example (*cont.*)
15	$120	$120	$8,000	$8,240	
20	90	160	7,600	7,850	
30	60	240	7,200	7,500	
31	58.06	248	7,200	7,506.06	

The EOQ as calculated using the basic model would be 15, but the significant discounts largely offset the increase in carrying costs. The lowest total annual cost corresponds to an order of 30 boxes, so this is the minimum quantity that Ms. Green should order. If the carrying cost were expressed as a percentage of the purchase price (rather than set at $16), the total annual cost would be less, given the lower purchase price.

3.13   EOQ with Phased Production or Delivery

The EOQ model described in this section may apply when the characteristics of deliveries spread out over time are sufficiently similar to the assumptions for the model. For instance, assume that a supplier regularly makes 15 or 20 shipments per week to a customer. Note that the characteristics of small lots and frequent shipments are fundamental aspects of the just-in-time philosophy we will be discussing in Chapter 9.

Demand may be considered constant at a daily rate (d). The daily quantity produced or delivered (p) must exceed the daily demand, in order to satisfy that demand. Inventories of the manufactured item will accumulate at a daily rate of $(p - d)$ units. After a certain number of days (t), production of this item will be halted and other categories of items manufactured. This is termed *phased* rather than *immediate* production, and is one of the assumptions underlying the EOQ model. Figure 3.9 shows what happens in this model.

Setup costs are not altered by phased production, in contrast to carrying costs. It can be shown that the average quantity in inventory is:

$$\frac{t\,(p-d)}{2}$$

since the maximum quantity is $t\,(p-d)$ and the minimum quantity is 0. To find the equilibrium point between ordering costs and carrying costs, we use:

$$\frac{D}{Q} \times C_o = \frac{t\,(p-d)}{2} \times C_c \tag{1}$$

Since the quantity produced (Q) corresponds to the daily production rate (p) multiplied by the number of periods (t), we can substitute Q/p for t, so that equation (1) becomes:

$$\frac{D}{Q} \times C_o = \frac{Q\,(p-d)}{2p} \times C_{c'} \tag{2}$$

FIGURE 3.9 ▶
EOQ with Phased
Production

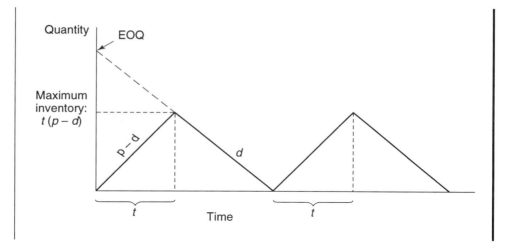

Where p and Q are not nil, this is equivalent to:

$$2pDC_o = Q^2 (p - d) C_c \qquad (3)$$

If we solve (3) for Q, we obtain:

$$Q^2 = \frac{2pDC_o}{C_c (p - d)} = \frac{2DC_o}{C_c} \times \frac{p}{(p - d)} \qquad (4)$$

Therefore:

$$Q = \sqrt{\frac{2DC_o}{C_c} \times \frac{p}{p - d}} \qquad (5)$$

$$= \sqrt{\frac{2DC_o}{C_c \frac{p - d}{p}}} \qquad (6)$$

To better compare this model with the basic model, it can be expressed as follows:

$$Q = \sqrt{\frac{2DC_o}{C_c \left(1 - \frac{d}{p}\right)}}$$

This comparison shows that the EOQ increases more and more rapidly as the *d/p* ratio grows. In other words, the closer the rate of use is to the production rate, the longer the production period. For example, on an assembly line the goal is to obtain a rate of use equal to the rate of production, for all stations. If this goal can be reached, the result is a perfectly balanced assembly line on which production is never interrupted. However, increased production leads to stockouts, whereas the reverse situation leads to excess inventory and occasionally requires a halt in production. We will now consider an example of the EOQ with phased production.

Thus far we have studied the EOQ model and some of its variants. These models give the managers technical tools to answer the question of how much to order. In

One workstation, where holes are drilled in bookshelf supports of various sizes, feeds a slower workstation, where workers paint and pack the supports at a rate of 360 supports per hour. Over the same hour, the drill can turn out 1,200 supports. Since the product is in high demand, the slower workstation spends 10 hours per day, five days a week, on it. The setup cost for the drill is $8 and the annual carrying cost is $0.50 per unit. If there are 240 work days per year, what is the most economic lot size to be drilled?

The EOQ is:

$$Q = EOQ = \sqrt{\frac{2 \times (240 \times 360 \times 10) \times 8}{0.50\left(1 - \frac{360}{1,200}\right)}} = \sqrt{39,497,143}$$

$$= 6,284.68 \approx 6,285.$$

It is recommended that 6,285 supports be drilled before the workstation begins drilling other models. The drill will work for a little more than five hours, or, to be exact, 5.24 hours. This figure is obtained by dividing 6,285 by 1,200 supports per hour.

At the end of this period, there will be 4,402 supports on hand (5.24 (1,200 – 360)). This quantity will be sufficient for nearly 12.23 hours (4,402 / 360).

The drilling operation will take only 30% of the time, or (5.24 / (12.23 = 5.24)) hours, leaving the drill free for other work the rest of the time.

the next section we will look at useful statistical techniques for answering the other major question in inventory management: when to order.

3.14   Safety Stock

Safety stock is a quantity of items kept on hand to avoid stockouts resulting from fluctuating demand and/or delivery lead times.

The risk of a stockout occurs only when the product must be delivered and demand is subject to random fluctuations. If there is no delivery lead time for a product, a stockout is theoretically impossible.

When there is a lead time for a product for which demand is not random, a stockout can occur only if the product is not ordered early enough. For instance, if the lead time for a product is three weeks and the demand for the product is 100 per week, then one need only place an order before the stock falls below 300 units. On the other hand, if the demand is 300 on average but fluctuates between 250 and 350 from one week to the next, a stockout may occur. If there are 300 units on hand when the order is placed, there will be a shortage if demand exceeds the average for the following three weeks. There is an even greater risk if the lead time also fluctuates. The supplier, for example, may sometimes take four weeks to deliver instead of three. Thus the company must protect itself against two main sources of uncertainty and stockouts by means of safety stock. The four possible situations are as follows:

		Lead time	
		Deterministic	Variable
Demand	Deterministic	No risk	Safety lead time
	Variable	Safety stock	Combination

In this section we will look at a simple case in which demand varies during the lead time, and discuss some results and techniques for more complex cases.

Where demand is variable and the lead time is deterministic, the risk of a stock-out is equal to the probability that demand during the lead time will exceed the stock available when the reorder was placed. In such cases it is enough to have fairly high inventory on hand. One must know the distribution of the probability of demand during the lead time before using probability calculations to determine the stock level necessary in order to minimize or eliminate the risk of a stockout. The following example will illustrate.

Example
∎

In Mr. Bowler's company, daily average demand for item B58 is 20, with a standard deviation of four units. The lead time is constant at three days. What safety stock must Mr. Bowler carry to satisfy demand 99% of the time?

Solution

According to his friend Mr. Dahan, a statistician, the distribution of demand during the lead time can be estimated using the sum of demand during each of the three days, since, as Mr. Dahan points out, it can be assumed that demand is independent for each day. In this case, the risk of a stockout corresponds to the probability that a normal variable with a mean of 60 and a standard deviation of $4\sqrt{3}$ will exceed the quantity of stock available to cover needs during the lead time.

Since the required lead time is three days, the average demand during this period is:

3 days at 20 units per day = 60 units.

The standard deviation for the demand occurring during the lead time (σ_{dd}) is calculated with the following formula:

$$\sigma_{dd} = \sqrt{n \times \sigma_{d^2}}$$

where n = number of days of lead time,

σ_d = standard deviation of demand per day.

Using the data from the example, we obtain:

$$\sigma_{dd} = \sqrt{3 \times (4)^2} = 4\sqrt{3}$$

Example
(cont.)

The coefficient from the normal distribution table is 2.33 for a probability of 99%. See Table I.

A quantity of:

$$60 + 2.33\,(4\sqrt{3}) \;=\; 60 + 16.14 \;=\; 76.14 \text{ units}$$

thus makes it possible to meet demand during the lead time in 99% of cases. If an order is placed when the stock reaches 76 units, the probability of a stockout during the lead time will be 1%.

The minimum quantity to be held before placing an order is generally called the *order point* (or *reorder point—Rop*). On average, when the order is received, only this additional quantity will be on hand, since it must be kept to meet variable demand. This quantity is called the *(SS)*. In the above example the safety stock is 16 units.

Generally speaking, the safety stock can be calculated using the following formula:

$$SS \;=\; Rop - E\,(DL)$$

where DL = average demand during the lead time,

       $E\,(DL)$ = expected value of DL.

Where both demand and the lead time are variable, the same reasoning applies, but the demand probability distribution during the lead time is more difficult to calculate. In specific instances where the following conditions apply:

   –   lead time is normally distributed;

   –   quantities required from one day to the next are independent;

   –   daily demand is normally distributed $[N\,(\mu, \sigma)]$;

then demand during the lead time has a mean normal probability distribution equal to $E\,(n) \times \mu$, and the formula for determining the standard variation in demand during the lead time is as follows:

$$\sigma_{dd} \;=\; \sqrt{E\,(N) \times \sigma^2} \;=\; \sqrt{E\,(N)}$$

where N = number of days of lead time (random),

      $E\,(N)$ = expected number of days of lead time.

Computer simulations are generally used when mathematical distributions cannot produce a valid approximation. Simulations can be used to vary the values of certain parameters so as to quickly see the effect of such variations on the service level.

A high level of flexibility in production reduces manufacturing lead times and their variability, making it possible to reduce safety stocks substantially and respond quickly to demand.

The basic EOQ model and its variants are a "scientific" response to the question of how much to order. Safety stock quantities are also based on strict statistical analysis and represent an important part of the answer to the other basic question in inventory management, when to order. However, they do not provide a complete answer.

Moreover, thus far we have examined only situations involving one item at a time. In the next section we will round out our examination by looking at inventory-management systems.

INVENTORY MANAGEMENT SYSTEMS

An inventory management system is a set of rules and procedures that allows managers to arrive at systematic and complete answers to the two basic questions in inventory management: how much to order, and when. These rules and procedures are defined for every item and are first applied separately to each item. Managers then introduce scheduling considerations that may affect the decisions generated by the system. Rarely will inventory be managed without human intervention.

In the following sections, we will discuss three types of systems, that correspond to the most common practices:

- fixed-quantity/variable-period systems;
- fixed-period/variable-quantity systems;
- time-phased planning systems.

The first two types are *reactive* systems; they simply respond to something that has already happened. The third type comprises *proactive* systems, which respond to forecast demand for the approaching periods.

3.15   Fixed-Quantity/Variable-Period Reordering Systems

When using a fixed-quantity/variable-period reorder system, the manager places an order once stocks reach an established level called, as we have seen, the *order point* (or *reorder point—Rop*). These systems are also called *order-point systems*. The amount ordered is fixed, normally based on EOQ calculations. Since variations in sales influence the rate at which stocks run out, the interval between orders also varies.

The *Rop* depends on the lead time, and corresponds to the stocks required to cover usage during the lead time. This quantity is equal to average demand during the lead time *(DL)* plus a safety stock corresponding to the desired service level. Thus $Rop = DL + SS$.

To calculate the *Rop*, the manager must first calculate the safety stock, as explained in Section 3.14. It is important to distinguish between the desired service level and the probability of a stockout during the lead time, which is used in calculating the safety stock. This probability is always higher than the service level, since there is no risk of a stockout until the inventory level reaches the *Rop* (Section 3.9).

Figure 3.10 illustrates such a situation, using the same data that was used in the example of Mr. Bowler and his B58s. We will assume that demand varies daily but that the lead time of three days remains stable. The *Rop* corresponds to the sum of the average demand during the delivery lead time *(DL)* and the safety stock *(SS)*:

$Rop = DL + SS$

In Mr. Bowler's case, this number corresponds to the quantity determined earlier:

$Rop = 3$ days $(20$ units$) + 16 = 76$ units

The *Rop* is seldom reached precisely at the end of the day. This is why the points in Figure 3.10 do not exactly match the whole numbers on the Y axis. If daily demand were not variable but constant, the 16 items of safety stock would not be necessary and the *Rop* would drop to 60.

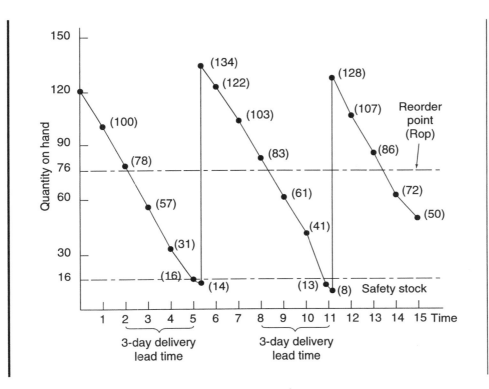

◄   **FIGURE 3.10**
Fixed-Quantity
Reordering

Example
■

The demand for Mr. Bowler's B58s is as follows for the first 15 days of June:

1 = 20	6 = 14	11 = 28
2 = 22	7 = 19	12 = 26
3 = 21	8 = 20	13 = 21
4 = 26	9 = 22	14 = 14
5 = 15	10 = 20	15 = 22

Orders are received exactly 72 hours after they are placed. Daily average demand is 20 units with a standard deviation of four, and the EOQ is 120 units.

When should Mr. Bowler place an order?

Solution

In the previous example we saw that if Mr. Bowler held 76 units at the beginning of the three-day lead time, the probability of a stockout during that period was 1%. This gives a service level of 99% during the lead time and an overall service level of 99.4%, or $(1 - 0.01 \times 76/120)\%$. The *Rop*, therefore, is 76 units, and when this point is reached Mr. Bowler will order 120 units.

Four factors influence the *Rop*:
-    lead time;
-    average daily demand;
-    variability in demand and in lead time; and
-    target service level.

In the order-point system, except with the specific case of the two-bin system, an exact perpetual inventory is required at all times. On the other hand, the system offers some flexibility for coping with unforeseen changes in demand. When demand rises, the system adapts by placing orders more frequently. If demand drops, orders are placed less often. These fluctuations affect the risk of stockouts only during the lead time.

3.16   Fixed-Period/Variable-Quantity Reordering Systems

Rather than placing orders based on inventory levels, managers can place regular orders, at fixed intervals—for instance, every week or at the beginning of each month. If inventories are taken regularly—monthly, for example—such fixed-period/variable-quantity reorder systems can be advantageous.

This method is undoubtedly the one used most frequently by retailers, since they cannot continuously place numerous small orders with the same suppliers, particularly if they deal with a large number of suppliers. In order to obtain quantity discounts and to plan purchases of a variety of items from the same wholesaler, many retailers order on a regular basis (fixed period) rather than waiting for stocks to reach the *Rop* (fixed quantity).

In fixed-period/variable-quantity reorder systems, the order point is determined mainly by the period selected and when it begins. The quantity ordered (Q) corresponds to the quantity necessary to cover needs during the period (M), depending on the target service level and the available stock (S). This gives us the following formulas:

$$Q = M - S$$
$$M = d \times l + SS$$

where l = number of days in the period,

     d = average daily demand,

   SS = safety stock.

The quantity ordered Q corresponds to the quantity sold during the period just ended, and so is variable. If, for instance, Mr. Bowler places an order at the beginning of every month, he will order a quantity M that is sufficient to cover his needs for one month. This quantity M will be equal to the average demand, plus a safety stock. The quantity ordered will be equal to the amount sold in the month just ended.

If the lead time of Mr. Bowler's supplier is one week, this quantity M will have to cover demand not only for the month, but also for the week it takes to receive the order, supposing that Mr. Bowler orders at the beginning of the month and receives the goods one week later. The above formula then becomes:

$$M = d \times (l + L) + SS$$

where L = delivery lead time in days.

Note that the safety stock is calculated for the entire period, not just the lead time. Assuming equal variability in demand, it will be higher than before.

In administrative terms, this system is the simplest, since it requires no perpetual inventory, but simply stocktaking when the order is placed. However, it does call for a larger safety stock, and it reacts more slowly to changes.

Example
■

Mr. Bowler wants to know the effects of ordering at fixed intervals as opposed to ordering fixed quantities. He also wants to determine when he should place orders. The initial inventory is 120 units, and the lead time is three days. Based on the data from the preceding example and assuming that he decides to place an order at the end of the third day, what should he do?

Solution

Since the EOQ discussed earlier is 120 units and the average daily demand is 20 units, Mr. Bowler can place an order every six days. In addition, since the reordering period is fixed, the variability of demand must be taken into consideration for these six days, along with the three-day lead time. If he orders less than he needs, the error cannot be corrected until the next order is received, nine days later. Thus his safety stock level must be:

$$2.33 \left(4 \sqrt{6 + 3} \right) = 28 \text{ units.}$$

Given that this quantity ensures a service level of 99%, he must have a maximum *(M)* of:

$$M = (9 \text{ days} \times 20 \text{ units per day}) + 28 \text{ units}$$
$$= 208 \text{ units on hand.}$$

So when he places his order, Mr. Bowler will subtract the quantity on hand from this number. He must also make sure to take account of the quantity that will be used during the lead time. Since at the end of the third day the quantity on hand is:

$$\text{Inventory} = 120 - 20 - 22 - 21 = 57 \text{ units,}$$

the quantity to be ordered is:

$$Q = M - 57 = 208 - 57 = 151 \text{ units.}$$

Therefore he must order 151 units on the third day.

At the end of the ninth day, the quantity to be ordered is:

$$Q = 208 - 92 = 116 \text{ units}$$

So he must order 116 units on the ninth day.

This example is illustrated in Figure 3.11.

The worst-case scenario is low demand for six consecutive days, then high demand for the next nine days (order period and lead time). For Mr. Bowler, this would mean:

$$\text{Quantity ordered on the 21st day} = 208 - 98 = 110 \text{ units.}$$

Example
(*cont.*) Demand could then be 24 units per day on average for nine days, or 216 units, but Mr. Bowler would have only 208 units (98 + 110) to meet this demand. Once again, it must be remembered that one of the underlying assumptions is that demand is distributed normally. Consequently, it is highly unlikely that demand will reach 216 units over a nine-day period.

FIGURE 3.11 ▶
Fixed-Period Reordering

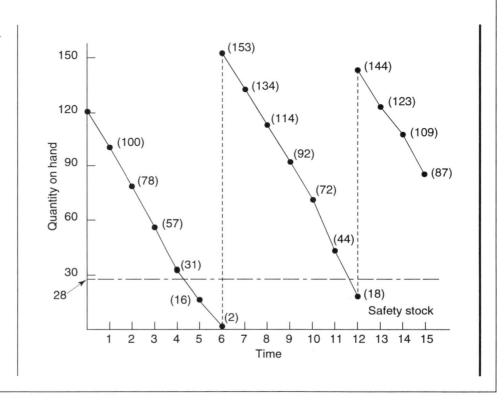

The two inventory-management systems we have just examined are reactive systems, since they respond to mainly past events. Forecasts are used only to calculate certain parameters such as average annual demand or the lead time, for order-point systems, and average demand over the period for fixed-period systems. The proactive systems we will be examining in the following sections respond to forecasts of future events.

3.17   Time-Phased Planning Systems

In time-phased planning systems, the order point is determined by calculating how long it will take the forecast available inventory to run out. These systems can be considered order-point systems, since an order is triggered when the inventory level reaches an established point. However, in this case the point is determined by the forecast inventory during the coming periods, rather than the existing inventory.[10]

The decision as to when to order is based on expected trends in available inventory, and so requires a forecast of anticipated needs for the coming periods. To begin, the forecasts of needs per period are entered in a planning grid, as shown in the example below.

Then the trends in inventory over the periods in question are forecast. Finally, starting with the period when the forecast inventory reaches the safety level, an order is placed, allowing for the lead time.

The order may be a fixed quantity or may vary to reflect anticipated needs for periods following its receipt, depending on the company's lot-sizing policy.

Example

Forecast demand for Mr. Bowler's B58s is as follows for the next eight periods:

1st period: 20	4th period: 26	7th period: 39
2nd period: 22	5th period: 35	8th period: 20
3rd period: 21	6th period: 34	

The supplier's lead time is three periods after the order is placed. The EOQ is 120 units and the initial inventory is 68 units. When should Mr. Bowler place an order?

Solution

We will enter the problem data in the planning grid and then forecast inventory trends.

	Periods							
	1	2	3	4	5	6	7	8
Needs	20	22	21	26	35	34	39	20
Forecast available inventory		68	48	26	5	−21		
Orders planned								

Note that a stockout is anticipated in the fourth period. To avoid it, Mr. Bowler must place an order in period 1, since the lead time is three periods. By continuing in this way to the end of the planning horizon, we obtain the following grid, which represents the anticipated situation and shows when orders should be placed.

	Periods							
	1	2	3	4	5	6	7	8
Needs	20	22	21	26	35	34	39	20
Forecast available inventory: 68	48	26	5	99	64	30	111	91
Orders planned	120			120				

If sales during periods 2 and 3 exceed forecasts by more than five units, a stock-out will result. To avoid this risk, we can establish a safety stock, applying the rule that there must be a safety stock of more than 10 units at all times. In the above example, this means that we must place an order one period earlier.

Proactive systems are much more adaptable than reactive systems. In administrative terms, however, this type of system involves a great deal more work than reactive systems, since the company must make up detailed forecasts for every period and study expected trends in available stock. Computerization has made such systems available on a large scale. Once they have been designed and perfected, they are relatively simple for managers to use, although they require somewhat more training than reactive systems do.

Which system is best? There is no one answer. Every company must use the basics explained here to select the solution that best meets its needs. In the following section we will summarize all the information we have seen on inventory management systems, which may help readers to make a choice.

3.18   Inventory Management Systems: Summary

The overall situation is straightforward. In deciding whether to select a proactive system or a reactive fixed-period or fixed-quantity reorder system, companies must consider their situation, the resources at their disposal for managing inventory, and the relative importance of stocks as established with ABC analysis. Management's strategic planning must also be considered. If managers understand the impact of inventory on their firm's competitive position, and even on internal working conditions, they will allocate the necessary resources to ensure a sound system. If demand or lead times are variable, safety stock must be carried.

In fixed-quantity systems, the basic EOQ model and its variants for quantity discounts or phased production are used to determine what quantity to order. From a technical point of view, fixed-quantity reordering allows the company to determine the safety stock and the appropriate order point. Fixed-period reordering triggers the order process regularly and determines the quantity to be ordered on the basis of quantities still on hand and the safety stock corresponding to the target service level. If reordering periods are relatively long, these are the simplest systems to use.

Proactive systems come with a heavier administrative cost but offer better performance. They are also more sensitive to departures from assumptions, since they rely more heavily on accurate data and forecasts. Their success depends to a large extent on the skills of the people using them. An ideal system would be as follows: use a proactive system for class A items, an order-point system for class B items and a fixed-period system for class C items. Then this initial arrangement could be adjusted to take account of practical considerations specific to the company in question.

One of the main criticisms of the EOQ model is that it does not correspond to the way in which things actually operate in a company. It can be argued that no model corresponds exactly to reality. Because the main purpose of a model is to facilitate decision-making, it is basically a representation of reality. Consequently, it is essential that one examine the actual conditions in a company and then compare the reality to the underlying assumptions of the model in order to determine to what extent it applies. Managers should bear this in mind when using the EOQ model, although its flexibility does offer an advantage when it is used appropriately.

Even if the system design is planned for a 99% service level, errors in data processing and scheduling changes could lead to a lower service level in reality. Consequently, even when this model is used, the appropriate design and use of the production system remain vital factors in achieving the company's objectives.

REVIEW QUESTIONS

1. What is inventory?

2. List and explain the five main inventory functions.

3. What managers are responsible for inventory?

4. Is it really possible to talk about inventory in service firms?

5. When comparing the inventory turnover rates of different companies, why is it necessary to take their capital costs into consideration?

6. What are the main types of costs inherent in inventory?

7. How are items classified into the appropriate A, B or C classes? Can some items move from one class to another in a given year? Why?

8. "The annual stockout risk related to the variability of delivery lead times is attributable not only to the distribution of demand and lead times, but also to the frequency of orders." Comment.

9. In what circumstances is it preferable to use the fixed-period / variable-quantity reorder method?

DISCUSSION QUESTIONS

1. Is it easier to manage raw-materials, work-in-process or finished-product inventories? Justify your answer by explaining the problems inherent in managing each of these kinds of inventory.

2. How do you choose which items to cut back when a decision is taken to reduce inventory value by 20%?

3. What are the risks of quickly reducing inventory by approximately 20%?

4. Based on a situation of your choice, explain the procedure for estimating stockout costs.

5. "The EOQ model has fallen into disfavour these days because it is based on too many unrealistic assumptions." Comment.

6. How can you determine and calculate the service level at a lottery ticket sales outlet?

7. When is it best for a company to assign responsibility for managing inventory to more than one person?

8. A consulting firm makes the following recommendations to the purchasing department of a large company:

   – For inexpensive items, increase inventory levels.

   – For costly items, which represent only 15% of the parts purchased by the company, but 85% of its costs, adopt a more sophisticated inventory-management system.

   a) Why did the consultants recommend an increase in inventory levels for inexpensive items?

   b) What system could be used, and why?

PROBLEMS AND CASE STUDIES

1. For each of the following cases, state whether the use of one of the methods for calculating the EOQ is valid. Justify your answer. If your answer is affirmative, what method should be used?

   a) A retailer of custom-made furniture receives almost all its completed orders the week after placing them. Orders arrive on Wednesday at 9:30 a.m. Sales for the three most popular products are as follows:

      – Product 1: steady demand of 25 tables per week.

      – Product 2: normally distributed steady demand with a mean of 30 and a standard deviation of 5.

      – Product 3: irregular demand varying between 40 and 50 units per week.

   b) A printer orders paper on average twice a week. If it orders more than 100,000 sheets per week, it benefits from a 5% discount. If it pays in less than 10 days, it receives an additional discount of 2%.

2. Using the EOQ model, Micron orders an item 12 times a year. The company uses an average of six units daily, and the delivery lead time is 24 days. The transportation and storage costs of one unit are $5 annually and the stockout cost is $25.

Quantity used during the delivery lead time	Probability
108	0.15
120	0.10
132	0.15
144	0.20
156	0.10
168	0.20
180	0.10

What should the reorder point (*Rop*) be?

3. Magnetron is a manufacturing company that produces microwave ovens. To assemble its products, the company needs component 2104, which it manufactures itself.

   The production cost of the component is $50. The annual handling and storage costs are $18. The setup cost is estimated at $200. Next year the company plans to produce 20,000 units.

   Each work day, the shop produces 160 units of component 2104, and the assembly department uses 80 units.

   a) Calculate the EOQ.

   b) Determine how many production runs will be required next year.

   c) If component 2104 were purchased from another firm and the costs were the same, calculate the quantity that Magnetron would have to order.

   d) If the component were purchased from another firm and the delivery lead time were 10 days and Magnetron maintained a safety stock of 500 units, what would the *Rop* be?

4. An inventory-management consulting firm is faced with an interesting situation. Rather than applying the concept of economic order quantities (EOQs), its client, Cegedil Ltd., has always relied on the following policy:

   – if the setup cost is $100 or less, manufacture a lot sufficient to meet two months' needs;

   – if it is from $100 to $200, manufacture a lot sufficient to meet four months' needs;

   – if it is from $201 to $300, manufacture a lot sufficient to meet six months' needs.

   To compare the costs of this method and those obtained with the EOQ method, Cegedil has selected a part, *alpha*, which represents 40% of the company's total inventory.

   It is known that inventory costs are 25% of the manufacturing cost, and that it costs $75 to manufacture each *alpha* part. Given that the setup cost for *alpha* is $150, the company manufactures lots of 2,700, since it needs 8,100 units a year. In all the above cases, the units are manufactured almost instantaneously.

a)   Is there any benefit to replacing the company's current policy with the EOQ method?

b)   What are the basic assumptions of the EOQ model that the consultant should explain to the client?

c)   What EOQ model would be required if the rate of use while the part is being manufactured were not negligible?

d)   If the *alpha* part represented only 1% of the total value of manufactured products, would Cegedil be justified in using an EOQ model, or would it be better off continuing with its current method?

5.   For many years the Marshall company has been purchasing loudspeakers from the same supplier, to be used in one of the television models it produces. It has the appropriate equipment and technology to make the loudspeakers itself, but has always found the supplier's prices more attractive. The supplier has just sent the company its price list for the coming year, and some of the prices have risen considerably. Its prices are now as follows:

Quantity (units)	Unit price
0–999 units	$20.00
1,000–1,999	$19.50
2,000 or more	$19.00

Marshall estimates that it will sell 10,000 televisions in the coming year. Its ordering costs are $50 per order, while annual carrying costs represent 20% of the value of the loudspeakers in inventory.

Because of this substantial price increase, the company manager at Marshall is thinking of manufacturing the loudspeakers internally rather than purchasing them. Pre-production tests show that:

–   the unit manufacturing cost would be $19.25 per loudspeaker;

–   the setup cost would be $311.85 per production run;

–   the carrying cost would remain at 20% of the inventory value;

–   the production rate would be 80 loudspeakers per working day (250 working days per year).

a)   What would be the EOQ and the total cost if Marshall continued to purchase loudspeakers from its supplier?

b)   What would be the optimal production run and the total cost if the company decided to manufacture the loudspeakers itself?

c)   What should Marshall do?

6.   The Goodbuy department store estimates demand for its garden shears at 600 units next year. The supplier charges $20 per unit, and ordering costs are $12. The annual storage and handling costs are always 20% of the purchase price before any discounts.

a)   What is the EOQ?

b)   Goodbuy currently places orders of 100 units. How much could it save by ordering the EOQ?

c)   Draw a chart to show how the two total cost curves (including the purchase price) would change if the supplier offered Goodbuy the following discounts:

Quantity	Discount
1–49	0%
50–99	10%
100–299	20%
300 or more	30%

7.   The daily demand for product B, carried by XYZ wholesalers, is distributed normally with a mean of 200 units and a standard deviation of 50. In the past, the company has aimed for a service level of 90%, but now the company realizes that it is losing customers because of frequent

stockouts of product B. Management wants to increase the service level to 95%.

The company uses a fixed-quantity/variable-period inventory-management system. The delivery lead time is three weeks.

a) Calculate the current reorder point (Rop) for product B and the Rop for a 95% service level.

b) Determine the increase in safety stocks required to reach a 95% service level.

c) What additional information would be needed to determine the economic value of this change in the service level?

8. Monidas,[*] the largest maker of emery wheels in Ontario, has asked two of its regular suppliers, Alpha and Delta, to submit tenders for special emery wheels that it does not manufacture but that it wants to use in its sanding machines next year. It has specified that it will need a total of 500,000 hours worth of this type of emery wheel.

Upon opening the tenders, Mr. Dalton, the Purchasing manager, notes that the suppliers have indeed quoted on the requested type of emery wheels. However, Alpha specifies that its emery wheels have a life of 80 hours each and quotes the following prices:

Lot ordered	Unit price
0–399 wheels	$20
400–999 wheels	$18
1,000 or more wheels	$17

The other supplier, Delta, sells emery wheels with a longer life, 100 hours each, but at a higher cost:

Lot ordered	Unit price
0–499 wheels	$25
500 or more wheels	$24

Mr. Dalton expects the annual carrying costs for the next year to total 30% of the value of the items on hand and ordering costs to be $100 per order. It is understood that, whichever supplier is selected, a new order will have to be placed for each lot ordered. Moreover, both suppliers promise to deliver the lots ordered very quickly so that production at Monidas will not suffer due to a shortage of emery wheels.

a) Mr. Dalton must make his recommendations to the firm's management committee this afternoon, with the following information:

- the supplier selected;
- the quantity of emery wheels ordered, and the lot sizes chosen;
- the following costs and their total:
  - annual ordering costs
  - annual carrying costs
  - annual purchase price;
- annual savings, depending on the supplier selected.

Based on the information he has to this point, what recommendation should Mr. Dalton make to the management committee?

b) Mr. Dalton fears that the management committee will criticize him for not pursuing the lowest possible price. He decides to contact the representatives of the two competing suppliers to ask them whether they have any last-minute changes to make to their tenders, without indicating whether they have been awarded the contract. The Alpha representative says he has no changes to make to his tender. The Delta representative is happy to inform him that his company has a new policy of offering three quantity discounts. The Delta tender must be adjusted to reflect the following changes:

Lot ordered	Unit price
0–499 wheels	$25
500–999 wheels	$24
1,000 or more wheels	$22

---

[*] Based on a case designed and written by Roger Handfield.

Does this last-minute change affect Mr. Dalton's recommendation? If so, explain how and justify your answer.

c) At the management committee meeting, Mr. Dalton makes his recommendation with confidence. As soon as he has finished, Mr. Dawson, the Production manager, says, "Once again, Purchasing has made a recommendation that ignores production requirements. Whenever an emery wheel has to be changed, we have 15 minutes of machine downtime, and there goes $8 of profit out the window."

Disconcerted, Mr. Dalton retorts that this has nothing to do with the question under discussion.

Is Mr. Dalton right? Why or why not?

9. Digitotal Inc. is a computer manufacturer. It expects demand for its computers to be 12,000 for each of the next three years.

It has always purchased screens from subcontractors. Now, wishing to minimize costs, the procurement manager uses the EOQ method, and has just received the following two tenders for screens:

Supplier A		Supplier B	
Quantity	Unit price	Quantity	Unit price
1–99	$60	1–499	$58
100–599	$58	500 or more	$56
600 or more	$56		

Supplier A delivers free of charge, whereas supplier B charges $100 for each delivery, regardless of the lot size. The procurement manager knows that the annual carrying cost for screens is $12 and that internal administrative costs are $50 for each order.

a) Which supplier should the procurement manager choose in order to minimize total costs? What quantity should be ordered each time? Justify your answers with the appropriate calculations.

b) Knowing that there is constant demand for screens in all 52 weeks of the year, the management of Digitotal Inc. wonders whether the company could not manufacture these screens itself for less. Studies show that the company could produce 300 screens a week, with a setup cost of $60 for each run.

What would be the maximum unit manufacturing cost of phased production allowing the company to match the suppliers' best offer, as determined in a)?

c) After some analysis, Digitotal's managers find that it is impossible for the company to manufacture these screens at a competitive price. They decide to go with the best offer received, in the appropriate quantity. The supplier guarantees delivery two weeks after receiving the order.

If Digitotal Inc. wants a service level of 99% for its customers, and demand is normally distributed with a standard deviation of five units per week, at what inventory level (Rop) should the company place an order?

10. Casino manufactures various models of gaming tables. Oak is the main raw material used in one of these models, the Montreal Deluxe. The demand for this model is expected to be stable for the coming year, at 30 tables a week (for a year of 50 weeks). The manufacture of each Montreal Deluxe table takes 120 linear feet of oak boards. The company has a production capacity for these tables of 50 units a week.

a) Two suppliers can meet the demand for oak. The first offers the following prices:

Quantity	Price
1–14,999 linear feet	$1.50 per linear foot
15,000 or more linear feet	$1.40 per linear foot

The second supplier offers no quantity discount. Its price is $1.35 per linear foot regardless of the quantity ordered.

The unit cost is $300 for orders placed with the first supplier. The second supplier is further away, and the cost would be $1,000 per order. In both cases, the annual unit carrying cost would be equal to 25% of the inventory value.

Which supplier can offer Casino the required quantities of oak at the lowest total cost? What size lot should be ordered to obtain the lowest total price? What is the difference between the lowest total price and the lowest price from the other supplier?

b) The unit manufacturing cost for the Montreal Deluxe table, excluding ordering, purchase and carrying costs for the oak boards, is $380. Unit setup costs are $2,000 per production run. The percentage to be used in calculating the carrying cost remains 25%.

Determine the optimal quantity to be manufactured and the unit cost price for each table manufactured with this optimal quantity, taking all the relevant costs into consideration.

11. Canplast produces a number of plastic household items using various manufacturing methods. The extrusion process used in much of its production requires metal dies that have to be replaced regularly. The company manufactures its own dies in a shop it has designed specially for this purpose. A metal manufacturing company, Saskalum, would like to obtain a contract from Canplast to manufacture these dies. The production manager at Canplast decides to take a serious look at Saskalum's offer. For purposes of comparison, he asks the company for a firm tender for die No. 2019, one of the most heavily used items at Canplast. Saskalum sends him the following price list:

Die No. 2019	
Quantity	Unit price
1–299 units	$42
300 or more	$40

The information available to the production manager shows that:

- Die No. 2019 is used in manufacturing 250,000 units per year of 250 working days.

- Manufacturing these dies internally entails the following costs:
  - setup cost: $540 per production run;
  - manufacturing cost: $50 per die;
  - annual unit carrying cost: 25% of the value of dies in inventory.
- The manufacturing process used by Canplast can produce 30 dies a day; each of these dies can be used to make 100 units of the company's product, on average.
- For the dies offered by Saskalum, ordering costs would be $200 per order, and the carrying cost would remain at 25% of the value of dies in inventory.
- The dies offered by Saskalum are of slightly poorer quality than those manufactured by Canplast, and each of them can be used to manufacture only 80 product units, on average.

a) Is it more economically sound for Canplast to purchase die No. 2019 or to manufacture it internally? How much can it save?

b) For one of the types of plastic it uses, Canplast relies on a perpetual inventory reorder method. The raw-materials inventory manager maintains that the job would be much easier if he could take periodic inventories of this product. The production manager is opposed to the change because the safety stock would rise by at least 25%. The average weekly demand for this type of plastic is normally distributed with a mean of 1,200 lbs and a standard deviation of 300 lbs. The delivery lead time is two weeks, and periodic inventories are taken every four weeks. The company wants to ensure a service level of 95% in restocking this kind of plastic. Who is right, the production manager or the raw-materials inventory manager?

12. Potato Inc. produces frozen french fries for a major fast-food chain. The customer's annual demand of 900,000 bags of french fries is considered constant and deterministic. Ordering costs are evaluated at $10, and annual carrying costs at $0.45 per unit. The customer's restaurants are open 365 days a year and Potato Inc. can produce 10,250 bags of fries daily.

a) What will be the most economic quantity to produce?

b) How many lots will the company have to produce per year?

c) How many days will it take to produce each lot?

d) Now assume that you are the inventory manager for the fast-food chain and that Potato Inc. offers you the following quantity discounts:

Quantity	Discount
7,000	5%
7,500	10%
12,000	13%
195,000	16%

If the price of a bag of french fries is $1.11, what quantity should you buy?

13. A production management analyst at Wellmanaged Inc. has been asked to develop an inventory-management system for the company. He has prepared the following tables, among others:

TABLE 1

Part No.	Units used	% of total	Cost price	Value	% of value
P110	150	1.6	$225.00	$33,750	25.2
111	175	1.9	$102.00	$17,850	13.3
114	42	0.4	$ 82.00	$ 3,444	2.6
115	3,200	34.3	$ 1.50	$ 4,800	3.5
116	700	7.5	$ 5.25	$ 3,675	2.7
117	110	1.2	$ 52.00	$ 5,720	4.3
119	250	2.7	$ 7.50	$ 1,875	1.4
121	1,100	11.7	$ 1.25	$ 1,375	1.0
122	400	4.3	$ 20.00	$ 8,000	6.0
123	650	6.9	$ 16.00	$10,400	7.8
131	110	1.2	$ 43.00	$ 4,730	3.5
132	225	2.4	$ 8.00	$ 1,800	1.3

TABLE 1 (*cont.*)

Part No.	Units used	% of total	Cost price	Value	% of value
135	190	2.0	$ 11.25	$ 2,138	1.6
136	200	2.1	$ 14.00	$ 2,800	2.1
138	150	1.6	$110.00	$16,500	12.2
140	1,500	16.0	$ 4.25	$ 6,375	4.8
141	150	1.6	$ 11.50	$ 1,725	1.3
142	60	0.6	$120.00	$ 7,200	5.4
Total	**9,362**	**100.0**		**$134,157**	**100.0**

TABLE 2

Part No.	Ordering cost	Carrying cost	Delivery lead time
P110	$25	30%	2 weeks
111	$25	30%	3 weeks
115	$25	30%	1 week
123	$25	30%	4 weeks

The demand for each part varies from week to week and is not perfectly constant over a given year, but these fluctuations are sufficiently minor that constant deterministic demand can be assumed if necessary. The work year is 50 weeks, and the target service level is 95%.

a) Using Table 1, complete an ABC-type analysis. What is the purpose of this kind of analysis?

b) What inventory-control system should be used for each inventory class identified in *a*)? Explain your answer.

c) Calculate the EOQs and the *Rops* for parts P110 and P115.

d) Does one particular inventory-control system seem more appropriate for the management of part P121? Explain your answer.

e) To calculate the safety stock required, the analyst proposes a service level of 90% for class A parts, 98% for class B and 99% for class C. Comment on these choices.

14. The president of Duratex wants to retain your services to help his company better manage its many raw materials and, more specifically, its stocks of $H_2S_4O_2NaO_2$, more commonly referred to as product ABC. After carrying out a detailed study of the company's various operations and an examination of the main budget and accounting records, you obtain the following information:

- The company estimates that it will need 1,000,000 lbs of ABC next year.
- The average market cost for a pound of ABC is $10.

Duratex will have to allocate funds to cover all expenses related to ABC for the coming year. Since it does not own the building, it must spend $1 per pound annually on warehouse rental. Expenses directly related to the product are:

- Average cost of order preparation: $1.50
- Average postage for placing an order: $0.50
- Handling charges: $1.00 per lb
- Insurance on inventory: $1.00 per lb per year
- Stocktaking: $1.00

Then there are additional specific expenses whenever Duratex places an order with its supplier:

- Average receiving costs per order: $11.00
- Average accounting costs per order: $5.00

Moreover, the company estimates that the average obsolescence cost is 20% and the estimated opportunity cost is 40% of the average inventory cost.

a)   What are the storage and ordering costs?

b)   What is the EOQ for the coming year, if all the amounts estimated turn out to be accurate?

c)   If the supplier offers the following quantity discounts, what quantity should be ordered?

Lot ordered	Price per lb
0–4,999 lbs	$10.00
5,000–9,999 lbs	$ 9.80
10,000 lbs or more	$ 9.50

15. Novatech managers are in a quandary. First, they can't decide whether they should aim for a service level of 95% for component X22. Second, they are wondering whether they should use a fixed-quantity or fixed-period inventory system to manage this component.

Novatech buys an average annual quantity of 1,000 X22s. The company's managers estimate the annual unit carrying cost at $15 and the unit ordering cost at $48. The delivery lead time is invariably five days.

The daily demand (the plant works 250 days a year) is normally distributed, with a standard deviation in daily demand of 1.2 units.

a)   What kind of inventory management system should Novatech use? Briefly justify your answer.

b)   In the situation described above and for each of the two inventory-management methods, how many units should be ordered, and when?

c)   If demand is deterministic and constant, when should X22s be ordered according to each of the inventory-management methods?

d)   In the above situation, should Novatech keep a safety stock? Justify your answer.

REFERENCES

1. BRITNEY, R.R., "Productivity and Inventory Turnover: How High Is High Enough?", *Business Quarterly*, Spring 1982, pp. 61-74.

2. JESSE, R.R. Jr., A. MITRA and J.F. COX, "EOQ Formula: Is It Valid under Inflationary Conditions?", *Decision Sciences*, July 1983, pp. 370-374.

3. LEENDERS, M.R., and H.E. FEARON, *Purchasing and Materials Management*, 10th ed. Homewood, Illinois: Richard D. Irwin, 1993.

4. MILLER, J.G., and P. GILMOUR, "Materials Managers: Who Needs Them?", *Harvard Business Review*, July-August 1979, pp. 143-153.

5. NADDOR, E., *Inventory Systems*. New York: John Wiley & Sons, 1966.

6. RHODES, P., "Inventory Carrying Cost May Be Less than You've Been Told," *Production & Inventory Management*, October 1981, pp. 35-36.

7. SCHMENNER, R.W., *Production/Operations Management, Concepts and Situations*, 4th ed. New York: Macmillan, 1990, p. 474.

8. TERSINE, R.J., and R.L. PRICE, "Temporary Price Discounts and E.O.Q.," *Journal of Purchasing and Materials Management*, Winter 1981, pp. 23-27.

9. VOLLMANN, T.E., W.L. BERRY and D.C. WHYBARK, *Manufacturing, Planning and Control Systems*, 3rd ed. Homewood, Illinois: Richard D. Irwin, 1992.

10. WIGHT, O.W., "Let's Obsolete Safety Stock," *Production & Inventory Management*, October 1982, pp. 62-63.

Demand Forecasting and Management

ROGER HANDFIELD, *main author*
JEAN NOLLET, *contributor*

OPERATIONS AND DEMAND MANAGEMENT

4.1   Demand Forecasting and Management and Their Importance to Operations Management

Operations planning and inventory management are two basic elements of the POM control system. Accurate knowledge of the demand to be met by the company's production system is a prerequisite, however, and one that is difficult for most firms. Without a full slate of guaranteed orders for several quarters ahead, data on demand over the necessary planning horizons must be based only on forecasts of varying degrees of reliability. Nevertheless, managers are obliged to use all the means at their disposal to obtain accurate measurements of future sales.

Forecasting meets this need. Using a rational approach, managers attempt to identify future events (in this case, demand) by first systematically grouping together data on variables that may influence these events, and then analysing these data and determining the effects of trends on the variables in question. This rational approach is what distinguishes forecasting from *prediction*, which often is an attempt to determine future events intuitively or with unscientific methods.

Forecasting is a prerequisite to operations planning. It helps managers to estimate what is likely to happen, such as the sales demand that operations will have to meet. The purpose of planning, on the other hand, is to determine company action; a series of plans sets out how the operational system will be used to effectively meet customer demand.

Companies that serve a highly seasonal market—manufacturers of snowmobiles, for instance—must do their best to spread their output throughout the year. A new management technique, *demand management*, has been developed for this purpose, mainly in the last 10 years. The most widely accepted definition of demand management is "accurately determining the total demand to be satisfied and providing the managers concerned with this information at the proper time and in the proper form." In addition, there are all the administrative activities necessary to co-ordinate the extent and pace of total demand on the one hand, and the company's production capacity on the other.[1, 4, 5]

Demand management thus becomes the essential link between the company's customers and the heads of the Marketing, Finance and POM functions. The group responsible for managing demand will have the following responsibilities:

- collecting data on the various types of demand that the company must meet, such as customer demand for finished products, demand from customers and from customer service for replacement units and spare parts, demand from the distribution network, demand from production units, and demand for special promotions, for charitable purposes and to replenish safety stocks and accumulate seasonal stock;

- assembling information on all this demand from various quarters and informing the departments concerned;

- if the company cannot meet total demand without experiencing major problems, designing and implementing ways to make demand more acceptable; this may include negotiating with customers to change delivery dates or

volumes ordered, taking steps to simplify such negotiations (price discounts, storage costs assumed by the supplier), promotional campaigns, or developing products with countercyclical demand in order to level out total demand;
— establishing realistic delivery deadlines and ensuring that they are met.

Demand managers may have a broad spectrum of responsibilities. They must possess the knowledge and communication skills to work closely with all the parties involved, within and outside the firm. These responsibilities are normally assigned to a group of managers from various departments: POM, Marketing, Finance, Economic analysis and others.

In a company with demand management activities as defined above, the task of the production planner and controller is relatively simplified. As we will see in the next chapter, it is much easier to design low-cost, easily implemented production plans when the demand to be satisfied is known as accurately and as far in advance as possible, and when demand remains as stable as possible all year long.

4.2   Operations Management Forecasting Needs

Operations managers rely on forecasts for most of the decisions they make, even if they do not always do so explicitly. Forecasts are useful in a wide variety of contexts—for instance, in decisions on whether to adopt new technology, change capacity or alter plant location and layout and in equipment and inventory management.

Such forecasts most often concern demand, but they may also have to do with price and cost trends, frequency of equipment breakdowns, availability and productivity of labour, time necessary to introduce new technology, or changes in the relative importance of factors in plant location. The demand forecasting methods described in this chapter can prove useful to managers seeking to assess future trends in the other decision-making variables listed above.

A few general rules apply to demand forecasting:
— The forecast must concern independent demand—that is, demand relating to finished products and spare parts, rather than dependent demand, which concerns components, raw materials and parts for which the quantities needed in future will be calculated as a consequence of operations scheduling decisions.
— Forecasts for families of products are preferable to those for individual products, since they are likely to be more accurate because of the compensatory demand for similar products.
— Short- or medium-term forecasts are best; the longer the range of a forecast, the less dependable it is.
— Forecasts are not guaranteed; by their very nature they are subject to error and must be used on the assumption that the true value of demand lies within an interval of the forecast values plus or minus a standard error.

A classic article by George W. Plossl[3] contains many recommendations on the proper use of forecasting methods by operations managers.

MAIN FORECASTING TECHNIQUES

4.3   Classification and Choice of Forecasting Techniques

Forecasting techniques or models can be divided into two main groups: *qualitative* and *quantitative*. Some of these techniques are illustrated in Table 4.1. The first group is based mainly on carefully analysed opinions, and involves no mathematical analysis of data or historical observations. The second group systematically analyses historical data, attempts to define the best model for explaining trends in the data, and then uses this model to produce forecasts.

Quantitative techniques may be further subdivided into causal methods and time-series methods. *Causal methods*, first of all, make it possible to discover the actual quantifiable factors that may have influenced past behaviour in a forecast variable, to evaluate the importance of each of these factors in explaining past variations, and to integrate the changes in these variables into an appropriate forecast model. For instance, the goal may be to forecast demand for personal computers on the basis of explanatory factors such as expected growth in population and personal income, falling computer prices, rapid growth in their processing capacity, new technologies making them more desirable or easier to use (integration of multimedia technologies, for example), changes in the percentage of the labour force working at home, etc. *Time-series methods*, on the other hand, ignore explanatory variables, or at least all but one: the passage of time. The goal of these methods is to devise a mathematical

TABLE 4.1 ►
Demand Forecasting Techniques

Qualitative techniques	Quantitative techniques
– Market research	**Causal methods**
– Opinions of sales staff	– Simple regression
– Delphi method (groups of experts)	– Multiple regression
– Historical analogies	– Econometric models
	– Input-output tables
	Time-series methods
	– Statistical mean
	– Moving average
	– Simple exponential smoothing
	– Double moving average
	– Double exponential smoothing
	– Simple regression
	– Multiple exponential smoothing
	– Classical decomposition
	– Multiple regression
	– Harmonics

model explaining the historical evolution of the forecast variable, a model belonging to one of the three very specific categories we will look at in sections 4.7 to 4.9, and to produce forecasts by extrapolating this model over time.

4.4   Qualitative Techniques

As we have seen, these forecasting techniques do not involve any extensive mathematical analysis of historical data; rather, they are intended to produce forecasts by combining the know-how and experience of many sources knowledgeable about expected trends in certain phenomena. Qualitative techniques, if poorly applied, can easily deteriorate into pure intuition. Needless to say, they must be used with strict controls, even though they are not based on mathematical models.

Qualitative techniques are used in situations in which there are no numerical data on historical events, such as when a new product is launched. In recent years, companies have not been able to satisfy the demand in the months following the introduction of new products, because of a lack of adequate forecasts (replacement blades for the Gillette Sensor razor, for instance, and Loblaw's energy-efficient fluorescent bulbs).

These techniques can also provide valuable results in the following cases:

- when historical data do exist but are not reliable enough for forecasting purposes;
- when it is deemed appropriate to compare forecast results with those obtained by quantitative models;
- for major scientific developments that will have significant repercussions for the cost of a product and, accordingly, for the demand for the product;
- when a major advertising campaign is planned or competitors' strategies have invalidated historical data;
- when major changes in values or behaviours can lead to far-reaching social changes (for example, the consequences of growing environmental awareness).

Depending on the circumstances, one of the models briefly described below may be suitable (see Table 4.1):

1. **Market research:** Testing specific products on potential customers in order to determine demand. There is no shortage of marketing references that may be consulted on this subject.

2. **Opinions of managers and sales representatives:** Forecasts are often based on the opinions of sales representatives. Managers and representatives know the market well and can quickly provide inexpensive forecasts, often implicitly taking account of various factors that can influence demand. The main drawback is their frequently optimistic bias–except in cases where sales representatives or managers are entitled to bonuses when they exceed sales projections!

3. **The Delphi method:** This approach involves obtaining a consensus of the opinions of a group of experts. The opinion of each expert is sought, then transcribed and distributed to the rest of the group for discussion purposes. The result of this

step is a second series of opinions, and often a third will be necessary to reach a consensus. The final opinion may well consist of a range of values rather than a single number, in which case the major advantage is the variety of factors considered, whereas the disadvantage is the tendency for extremes to be moderated.

4. **Historical analogies:** Sales trends for a new product may well correspond to those of products already on the market. Any plausible analogy or other link with an indicator can greatly simplify the job of forecasting. The product life-cycle curve, a classic marketing tool, can be used to fine-tune the forecast.

4.5   Quantitative Techniques

We have noted the specific nature of quantitative forecasting techniques and the basic differences between causal and time-series methods. Since we will be discussing time-series methods in greater detail in sections 4.6 to 4.9, we will limit ourselves to a brief discussion of certain causal methods here.

These methods offer a more in-depth analysis of the factors that affect trends in a forecasting variable such as historical demand. They thereby offer greater accuracy in long-term forecasts or those that involve major economic indicators (GNP, consumer price index, age groups). On the other hand, they also have several disadvantages. Identifying explanatory factors could prove very complex and costly. In addition, building the appropriate mathematical models frequently takes a great deal of time and effort, and these models may be cumbersome. Finally, an enormous number of factors must often be considered, and the results can be seriously distorted if a single one of these is overlooked. Hydro-Québec, for instance, relies on a causal model with 700 parameters in forecasting overall power demand trends. Accordingly, operations managers should reserve these methods primarily for strategic forecasting.

Some of the most common causal methods are:

1. **Simple regression:** In this model, a dependent variable relates to an independent variable, based on a mathematical model, often a linear one consisting of a straight-line regression. Depending on the degree of dependence, or *correlation*, between the two variables, the value of the dependent variable can be forecast with some accuracy from the value of the independent one. Note that the independent variable must represent a real factor, other than the passage of time, for this method to fall into the category of causal methods.

2. **Multiple regression and econometric models:** These methods are similar to simple regression, except that the dependent variable varies with the combined effects of several independent variables. Computers are normally used to solve such equations because of the many calculations involved. In some cases a number of regression equations must be solved simultaneously, in which case we speak of econometric models.

3. **Input-output tables:** Forecasters establish links between all the main economic indicators using a table to show quantitative relationships. It is then possible to forecast trends in one or more of these indicators based on variations in related components. This tool is used mainly by economists.

TIME-SERIES ANALYSIS TECHNIQUES

4.6   Steps in the Method

Those techniques grouped together here under the heading "time-series techniques" are particularly well suited to forecasting in operations management. Generally speaking, they are sufficiently accurate for a time horizon of one year or less (which meets most POM forecasting needs); they require relatively few data (simply a series of historical observations of the forecast variable); many of them involve only simple calculations, and software programs are readily available for handling more complex work; finally, they are generally based on an easily understandable analysis method and the user can measure the risk of error for the forecasts obtained.

Time-series methods require four steps, as shown in Figure 4.1.

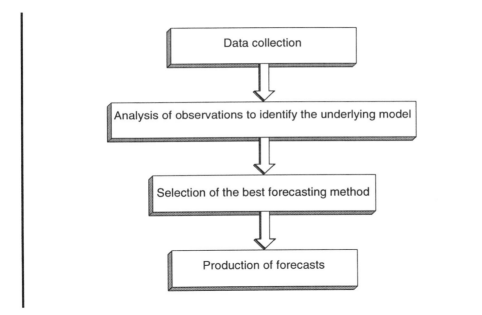

◄   **FIGURE 4.1**
**Steps
in a Time-Series
Analysis**

1. **Data collection:** In this first step, a series of observations is compiled on the values of the forecast variable (demand, in this case) over a given number of past periods. Generally speaking, the longer the series of observations (starting from the most recent period), the more accurate the forecasts will be. Observations are occasionally excluded, in particular when they concern atypical periods (during strikes at major customers, for example) or when significant phenomena produce major changes in the underlying forces that shape demand (the introduction of new technology or access to new markets following a free-trade agreement, for example). In the latter case, it is best to consider only those observations that deal with periods following the phenomenon in question. If a forecasting software program is used, this step ends with the input of observations in the form of numerical data.

2. **Data analysis:** The objective in this step is to define the underlying model that most faithfully represents historical demand trends. In time-series analyses there are three types of underlying models, which will be studied in detail later. For the moment, we will briefly describe two techniques used to establish the appropriate type of model. The first is visual observation. We will see that the three types of underlying models are quite different, and often simple visual examination of a graph showing historical trends in data is sufficient to identify the appropriate one. In other cases, however, this technique does not produce the desired degree of certainty, particularly when the data do not behave according to a "pure" basic model but have characteristics of a number of types. A second, more statistical, technique, called *data autocorrelation analysis*, may then be used. We will not describe this technique in detail, but simply point out that it can be used to measure the extent to which the observations are related to each other. Depending on the significance of this relationship or on the lag, if any, between periods, the proper underlying model can easily be determined, even in complex situations. We will return to this point in the discussion of methods appropriate to each kind of model.

3. **Selection of the best forecasting method:** For each type of underlying model, a number of forecasting methods can be used. The selection of the best method means that the methods belonging to the underlying model selected must be systematically tested and the results studied with one of the techniques described in sections 4.10 to 4.12.

4. **Production of forecasts:** This is the simplest step if the preceding steps have been carried out correctly. The variable representing the passage of time, in the equations for the method selected in step 3, is assigned the values corresponding to future periods to obtain a series of forecasts over as long a period as desired, through manual or computer-assisted calculations.

4.7   Stable Model

In this model, the observed data vary randomly around a stationary central value called the *stable level*. The forces affecting demand seem to act together to bring it back toward this central value whenever it moves away. Figure 4.2 shows a case of demand that fits well with this model. For cases where the fit is less clear, autocorrelation analysis can be used. If all the calculated autocorrelation values remain below the significance point, then this model is suitable.

FIGURE 4.2 ▶
Stable Model

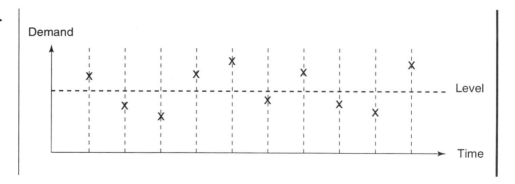

Now we will look at three forecasting models suited to demand that fits a stable model.

Statistical mean: With this method, the value of the level is calculated by taking the mean of all observations, according to the following formula:

$$\bar{X}_t = \frac{\sum\limits_{1}^{n} X_i}{n}$$

where X_t = the statistical mean at time t,

X_i = the value observed at time i,

n = the number of observations.

The forecast for any future period is equal to the mean:

$$F_{t+j} = X_t$$

where F_{t+j} = forecast for any future period.

The monthly demand for a type of fine paper varied as follows over the last 12 months (in tonnes):

Example
∎

January	33	February	36	March	29
April	37	May	34	June	28
July	26	August	38	September	34
October	35	November	28	December	30

A quick look at these data shows the production planner that demand for this product meets the criteria for a stable model. The production planner forecasts demand for the next month using the statistical mean and the following calculations:

$$F_{13} = \frac{\text{Sum of monthly demands}}{12} = \frac{388}{12} = 32.33$$

Note that, for the moment, this forecast also applies for all periods following period 13. When the real value of demand for period 13 is known, other observations will be added and the value of the mean calculated again, to obtain a forecast for month 14 that takes the value for month 13 into account.

Moving average: The statistical mean discussed above has one drawback. It assigns equal weight to all past observations, even those quite far in the past. The moving average overcomes this disadvantage in that it is calculated only on the basis of a limited number of the most recent observations.

We start by selecting a fixed number of data to be used in calculating the moving average, with the following equation:

$$F_{t+j} = \overline{X_{A_t}} = \frac{\sum\limits_{t-a+1}^{t} X_i}{a}$$

where $\overline{X_{A_t}}$ = weighted average calculated at time t,

a = number of periods used in calculating the moving average.

Example
■

Using the data from the previous example, the production planner may prefer to calculate a moving average rather than a statistical mean. Suppose the production planner wishes to use six observations. The forecast obtained at the end of December would be:

$$F_{13} = \overline{X_{A_{12}}} = \frac{X_7 + X_8 + \ldots + X_{12}}{6} = \frac{26 + 38 + \ldots + 30}{6} = \frac{191}{6} = 31.83$$

We will assume that we are at the end of January (month 13) and that actual demand for this new period is now known, and is 36 tonnes. The planner can now produce a new demand forecast for February (month 14), as follows:

$$F_{14} = \overline{X_{A_{13}}} = \frac{X_8 + X_9 + \ldots + X_{13}}{6} = \frac{38 + 34 + \ldots + 36}{6} = \frac{201}{6} = 33.5$$

The number of periods remains the same from one forecast to the next; however, the oldest period is replaced by the newest one. There are no hard and fast rules for selecting the best number of periods. In practice, moving averages ranging from three to 15 are used. Only experience can show the manager the number of periods that produces the most accurate results.

Simple exponential smoothing: Although the moving average can be used to take the latest observations into account in calculating the average, this technique still has the drawback of assigning a constant weight to all observations in the group selected. Many experts feel that the influence of forces that shape demand during a certain period gradually become less significant with time, and that the weighting of an observation should also decrease progressively. The technique of simple exponential smoothing can be used to calculate this kind of weighted average. For this purpose, a parameter called α is used, which varies from 0 to 1. The smaller this value, the more slowly the weight assigned to an observation decreases. If the planner has reason to believe that market forces are changing very quickly, on the other hand, a value of α closer to 1 can be used. In practice α usually takes a value of from 0 to 0.3.

With exponential smoothing, the weighted average is calculated using the following equation:

$$\overline{X_{W_t}} = \alpha X_t + \alpha (1 - \alpha) X_{t-1} + \alpha (1 - \alpha)^2 X_{t-2} + \dots + \alpha (1 - \alpha)^{n-1} X_{t-n+1}$$

where X_{W_t} = weighted average at time t,

X_t = observation at time t

n = number of observations,

α = weighting factor of from 0 to 1.

Once the weighted average has been calculated for a given period, it can easily be determined for the next period, with the new equation:

$$X_{W_{t+j}} = X_{W_1} + \alpha (X_t - X_{W_1})$$

Using the data from the previous example and a value of 0.3 for the α parameter, the forecast for January (month 13) can be obtained as follows:

Example ∎

$$F_{13} = \overline{X_{W_{12}}}$$

$$= 0.3 (30) + 0.3 [0.7 (28)] + 0.3 [0.7^2 (35)] + \dots + 0.3 [0.7^{11} (33)]$$

$$F_{13} = 30.89$$

Once the weighted average for month 12 has been determined, the averages for the following months can be calculated directly with the second equation:

$$F_{14} = \overline{X_{W_{13}}} = \overline{X_{W_{12}}} + 0.3 (X_{13} - \overline{X_{W_{12}}})$$

$$= 30.89 + 0.3 (36 - 30.89) = 32.42$$

4.8   Trend-line Model

Unlike the previous model, in the trend-line model demand does not oscillate around a stable level, but rather tends to continually increase or decrease. It begins at a certain level and rises or falls by much the same amount in each period. The magnitude of the mean variation observed from one period to the next is the measurement of the trend. Figure 4.3 shows data that meet the criteria for this model.

If simple visual examination is not sufficient to determine whether the demand fits this model, then an analysis of data autocorrelation—that is, measurement of the degree of correlation among the observations—may be helpful. In this case, the autocorrelation for a lag of one period is quite significant (nearly +1 for an upward trend, and –1 for a downward trend) and becomes less and less significant as the lag increases.

FIGURE 4.3 ▶
Trend-line Model

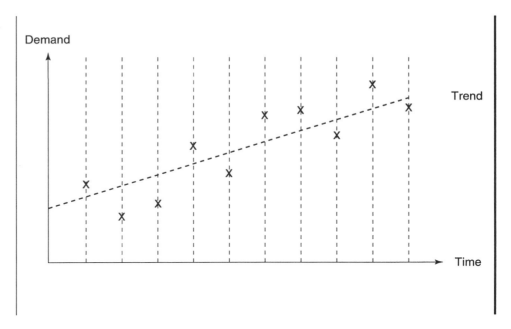

The forecasting methods suggested for the stable model are ill-suited to this model, since there will be a significant lag before the model accurately reflects the effects of the trend. Instead, special methods have been developed for the application of this model; these are described in the works listed in the references at the end of this chapter.

Double moving average: This method allows planners to evaluate the moving average using two equations, one to evaluate the starting level and the other the magnitude of the trend. The same number of observations is used in both equations.

Double exponential smoothing: With this technique the weighted average is calculated using two equations. Some researchers (Brown) recommend that a single parameter (α) be used, whereas others (Holt) suggest that two (α, β) are better.[2]

Simple regression: We have already looked at this technique as one of the causal methods. It can also be used in analysing time series, by making time the only explanatory variable.

4.9   Cyclical Model

In the cyclical model, seasonal or cyclical phenomena affect demand, which is particularly strong at some points during the year and weak at other times. This model applies to many products that people buy at specific times of year: seasonal clothing, sporting goods, ice cream, etc. These products are said to have a seasonal cycle. Similarly, major economic phenomena may have a cyclical effect on demand for certain items, and such cycles may well last for more than a year.

Such cycles cause demand to vary around a sine curve, as shown in Figure 4.4*a*. Note that a cycle may combine with a trend (Figure 4.4*b*).

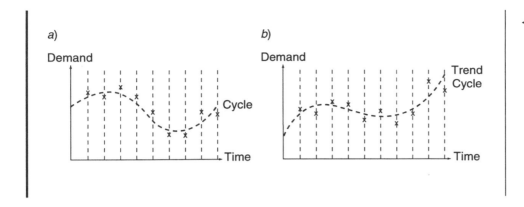

The presence of this kind of cycle may be detected through simple visual examination of data, or through autocorrelation analysis, in which case the most significant autocorrelation occurs when the lag corresponds to the length of the cycle.

Most forecasting methods have been developed for this kind of model. Since operations managers generally need forecasts with a time horizon of one year at most, they are interested primarily in seasonal cycles. We will briefly describe a few of the forecasting methods developed to meet this need.

Multiple exponential smoothing: Winters (in Makridakis and Wheelwright[2]) developed a model for evaluating the respective influence of the base level (stationarity), trend and seasonality on demand, using equations with three parameters (α, β and γ). Determining the optimal values for these parameters can be a very complex task, but there is software available that will do so automatically.

Classical decomposition: With this method the planner uses successive calculations to isolate the base level, trend and cyclical factors from the observed data. The cycle is first evaluated and its value subtracted from the observations. Then the trend is measured and removed, leaving the value of the base level. The *Census II*[2] method used by the U.S. Federal Bureau of Statistics is one such decomposition method.

Multiple regression: This method is similar to the one presented in our discussion of causal methods, but time, expressed in various ways, is the only explanatory variable.

Harmonics: Since Fourier's time, mathematicians have been aware that any curve can be represented by a sum of sinusoidal curves, with frequencies of multiple whole numbers and variable amplitudes. Harrison (in Makridakis and Wheelwright[2]) developed a forecasting method based on this approach.

SELECTING THE BEST FORECASTING TECHNIQUE

Now that we have examined a number of forecasting methods suited to the appropriate underlying model, the following are some criteria for choosing the most appropriate technique, one that gives optimal results for the criteria discussed below.

4.10 Main Error Measurements

Forecasting methods must give the most accurate forecasts possible. Since it is impossible to measure the error (or deviation) of a model's forecasts in comparison with actual demand for the future period in question, we must measure the error that would have occurred if this method had been used to forecast data for past periods. We will discuss the three most common error measurements used in forecasting.

Root mean square deviation: This measurement is frequently used in combination with regression techniques. In simple, or linear, regression, statistical theory tells us that the best straight line to represent the trends in data is one that minimizes the root mean square of the deviation between data and the corresponding points on the line (these deviations are also called *residuals*). This measurement of deviation (or error) is favoured by many forecasting specialists. It is calculated as follows:

$$RMS_t = \frac{\sum_{1}^{n}(F_i - X_i)^2}{n}$$

where RMS = root mean square deviation.

Mean absolute deviation: This measurement is normally expressed as a percentage, and considers the magnitude of deviations, but not their sign. Accordingly, positive and negative deviations do not cancel each other out. A low mean absolute deviation value means that the method produces forecasts that are close to actual demand values. It is calculated as follows:

$$MAD_t = \frac{100\sum_{1}^{n}\frac{|F_i - X_i|}{X_i}}{n}$$

where MAD = means absolute deviation.

Bias: This measurement differs from MAD simply in that it considers deviations in terms not only of their magnitude but also of their sign. Consequently, negative deviations are perfectly offset, more or less, by positive ones. For a sufficiently large number of observations, the bias value should be close to 0%. A positive value means that the method in question tends to produce forecasts that exceed real values, while a negative value indicates the opposite. The equation for calculating bias is:

$$BIAS_t = \frac{100\sum_{1}^{n}\frac{F_i - X_i}{X_i}}{n}$$

Measurements of deviation are used mainly for comparison purposes. A forecasting method that has lower values for each of these three measurements than other methods is very likely to produce more accurate forecasts. In many cases, however, no method is applicable for all measurements of deviation, in which case other criteria must be used in choosing the best model.

4.11   Autocorrelation of Residuals and Graphic Analysis

The ideal forecasting method would permit explanation of all the variations in observations as fully as possible. In other words, the values calculated should depart from observations only by an inexplicable residual due solely to chance. A valuable indicator of random distribution of deviations is that they are not interrelated in any significant way. Most forecasting software can be used to calculate the degree of interrelation (or autocorrelation) of residuals. A forecasting method is considered statistically valid if there is no significant autocorrelation between residuals, regardless of the lag observed.

The indicators described above give us information on the ability of a forecasting method to properly depict the past, on average. Of course, what managers seek when they attempt to produce forecasts is information on the future. Often, a method that offers good results in terms of deviation scores is less successful in evaluating demand during periods that are particularly important for operations managers—that is, when demand is highest or lowest. For this reason it is a good idea to graph the forecasts from each of the methods tested, and then compare them with historical observations to determine which ones are most successful in extrapolating past trends.

REVIEW QUESTIONS

1. What is the difference between a forecast and a prediction?

2. How does demand management differ from simple forecasting?

3. What are the main forecasting needs of operations managers?

4. What is the difference between qualitative and quantitative forecasting techniques?

5. What are the main steps in using time-series techniques?

6. Briefly describe the three types of underlying models used in time-series analyses.

7. What major criteria are used in selecting the best forecasting technique?

8. What are the main types of costs related to forecasting?

DISCUSSION QUESTIONS

1. "A forecast should give a better picture of the future than does a prediction." Comment.

2. Discuss the potential contribution of demand management to a company's operations. What organizational problems can occur when a group is set up to oversee demand management?

3. Can qualitative forecasting techniques be as rigorous as quantitative techniques? Under what circumstances should each be used, respectively?

4. Under what circumstances should data autocorrelation analysis be used when identifying the underlying model?

5. Discuss the importance of the number of periods used in calculating the moving average, and the value of the α parameter in exponential smoothing.

6. How is it possible to choose the best forecast for a given period, when a number of forecasting methods have been tested?

7. Why is graphic analysis useful in selecting the best forecasting technique, when there are more scientific tools available such as measurements of deviation and autocorrelation of residuals?

8. Discuss the contribution of computers in producing forecasts.

9. What variables, in addition to demand, should be forecast for purposes of decision-making in POM?

10. The Dean of the Faculty of Law has a report stating that enrolment may fall by 5% from 1995 to 1998 inclusive. This potential decline is expected to affect a number of faculties, including the Faculty of Law, and would apply to both the number of applications received and the number accepted.

   What forecasting method should the Dean use for the period 1995 to 1998?

PROBLEMS AND CASE STUDIES

1. Mr. Brisson is head of the operations planning department in a medium-sized firm. He is examining the forecasting method now used by the firm, a moving average with six periods. In the past, some forecasting errors affecting the company's most important product have resulted in major planning and production control problems. Mr. Brisson wonders whether this forecasting technique is still the most appropriate one. Demand for the product over the last year has been as follows:

Month	Demand (units)
January	4,500
February	6,000
March	6,500
April	5,200
May	5,300
June	4,100
July	3,200
August	3,800
September	5,500
October	6,300
November	5,800
December	5,400

a) What underlying model seems appropriate for these data?

b) Calculate the forecasts obtained for the last six months with the moving average technique used by the company.

c) For the same months, calculate the forecasts that would have been obtained had the company used:
   - a statistical mean;
   - a moving average with three periods;
   - exponential smoothing with $\alpha = 0.1$;
   - exponential smoothing with $\alpha = 0.3$;
   - exponential smoothing with $\alpha = 0.7$.

d) Calculate the three standard measurements of deviation (root mean square deviation, mean absolute deviation and bias) for each of these forecasting techniques.

e) What forecasting technique should Mr. Brisson adopt?

2. YearRound Sports manufactures hockey and baseball equipment. Demand for the company's products is seasonal, but its planners continue to use simple forecasting methods such as moving averages or exponential smoothing. Last year, overall demand for all models of hockey gloves was as follows:

Month	Demand (pairs)
January	5,200
February	4,100
March	6,500
April	3,100
May	900
June	600
July	400
August	1,200
September	4,400
October	6,700
November	3,200
December	8,300

a) Using a moving average for three periods and exponential smoothing with α = 0.2, show the forecasts that would have been obtained for the last nine months of the previous year. Calculate the values of the three error measurements.

b) For each of the methods in a), calculate the forecast for January of this year.

c) Should the company continue to use these forecasting methods?

3. The Faculty of Law of a university received the following applications for enrolment over the last five years:

Year	Applications
1989	3,440
1990	3,610
1991	3,500
1992	3,650
1993	3,800

How many applications can be expected in 1994 if the following methods are used:

a) statistical mean?

b) moving averages based on three, four and five years, respectively?

c) simple exponential smoothing with a parameters of 0.1, 0.5 and 0.9?

4. The management of an airline expects that the seat occupancy rate will be high during the summer season. However, it wishes to forecast demand for flights to Europe so that it can more efficiently allocate its resources. The company calls on a Business Administration graduate to explain the moving average method, and supplies the following data from the previous summer.

Week	Number of passengers	Week	Number of passengers
1	8,400	8	11,400
2	8,900	9	10,700
3	9,500	10	10,100
4	11,000	11	9,400
5	10,800	12	8,700
6	11,100	13	8,600
7	11,000		

Management would like to estimate demand for weeks 11, 12 and 13 of this year, with forecasts based on data from the previous summer. Calculate the results obtained if the graduate applies the statistical mean, moving average with five periods, and simple exponential smoothing with α = 0.3 to these data (e.g., determine the forecast for the 11th week of this year from the first 10 weeks of last year); calculate the measurements of error, and comment on the results.

5. The number of U.S. tourists visiting Canada has increased sharply in the last 15 years or so. This growth is attributable to greater disposable income, but also to the exchange rate. An economist has determined that the following equation applies for forecasting the number of U.S. tourists who will visit Canada:

$$Y = 310,800 + 121.8X_1 + 101,400X_2$$

where Y = number of U.S. tourists visiting Canada in a given year,

X_1 = average disposable income of U.S. residents,

X_2 = U.S. dollar premium over the Canadian dollar (in %).

Determine the expected number of tourists according to these two cases:

Scenario	Disposable income	Premium
1	$17,400	30
2	$18,100	40

6. Carbo Inc., a carburetor manufacturer, has sold the following quantities over the last eight months. The sales manager at Carbo Inc. feels that all demand for this period has been met.

Month	Number of carburetors
November	14,200
December	13,600
January	18,400
February	16,800
March	17,400
April	19,700
May	21,100
June	20,800

The sales manager wishes to use the best possible forecasting method to estimate demand for July. You are asked to test the following forecasting methods, based on the data from the last eight months:

a) statistical mean;

b) moving average with three periods;

c) exponential smoothing with $\alpha = 0.7$. In addition, evaluate the results obtained for the period from January to June, using the following error measurement techniques:

– root mean square deviation;

– mean absolute deviation;

– bias.

REFERENCES

1. FOGARTY, D.W., J.H. BLACKSTONE and T.R. HOFFMANN, *Production & Inventory Management*, 2nd ed. Cincinnati: South-Western Publishing, 1991, p. 18.

2. MAKRIDAKIS, S., and S.C. WHEELWRIGHT, *Interactive Forecasting*, 2nd ed. San Francisco: Holden-Day, 1978.

3. PLOSSL, G.W., "Getting the Most from Forecasts," *Production and Inventory Management*, 1st quarter, 1973, pp. 1-15.

4. SMITH, S.B., *Computer Based Production and Inventory Control*. Englewood Cliffs, New Jersey: Prentice-Hall, 1989, p. 21.

5. VOLLMANN, T.E., W.L. BERRY and D.C. WHYBARK, *Manufacturing Planning and Control Systems*, 2nd ed. Homewood, Illinois: Dow-Jones Irwin, 1988, pp. 405-447.

CHAPTER 5

Operations and Production Planning

ROGER HANDFIELD, *main author*

MATTIO O. DIORIO, *contributor*

OPERATIONS PLANNING

5.1   Objectives of Operations Planning

Operations planning allocates the company's resources to meet its strategic objectives, in light of existing constraints and forecast demand. Managers have long recognized the importance of long-, medium- and short-term planning and the need for operations plans to optimize the use of available resources. It comes as no surprise, therefore, that operations planning is an essential part of production and operations management. POM managers endeavour to meet customers' expectations as determined by the Marketing function, in terms of quality, volume, location, time and costs. They take into account the financial, human, technological and other constraints that limit the company's manoeuvrability and make constant and effective interdepartmental co-ordination essential for the entire firm.

The need to plan operations according to different time frames calls for a variety of management approaches, involving managers at various levels in the company. For long-term planning, they attempt to define the company's overall objectives with respect to growth, development and profitability over a period of up to 10 or even 20 years, depending on economic sector. It is the responsibility of senior management to formulate an overall strategy for the long term, taking everyone's needs and resources into account. In this they will be supported by managers from each of the main management functions. Each function will then have to define its own long-term objectives, in keeping with those of the company, and make appropriate long-term plans. In POM, such long-term planning is increasingly facilitated by such methods as manufacturing resources planning *(MRP II)*.

In the control system, operations planning focuses mainly on the medium and short terms. Whereas in long-term planning it is possible and often necessary to consider far-reaching changes to production capacity (by building new production units or adopting new technologies, for example), operations planning assumes that the firm's production capacity will not change significantly over the planning period. Managers adjust production volumes by varying the use of existing production resources (overtime, for instance), changing the quantities of resources used—normally within strict limits, if it can be done quickly enough (temporary hiring or laying off or short-term leasing of equipment), or turning to outside suppliers (occasional subcontracting).

The *objectives* of operations planning in the control system, then, are to determine the quantities to be produced in the short or medium term (*priority planning*) and specify the quantities of resources to be used (*capacity planning*), in order to meet operational objectives (as measured by quality, volume, location, time and costs).

5.2   Steps in Operations Planning

The authors of the principal works on operations planning[1, 2, 3] and the organizations in the field (such as the Canadian Association for Production and Inventory Control [CAPIC], which is associated with the American Production and Inventory Control

Society [APICS]) recommend a four-step approach. These steps make it possible to design plans with decreasing time horizons but increasingly detailed planning elements.

These four steps are illustrated in Figure 5.1, along with their interrelationships (the output of each step serves as the input for the next step) and the considerations at each step—namely, the objective, inputs, type of products, horizon, time unit and output. The process for transforming an input (essentially different kinds of information) into an output (a plan) will be explained in detail in sections 5.9 to 5.11 and in chapters 6 and 7. We will first look at considerations other than those involved in the transformation process for each of the four steps.

Step 1: Production planning (also known as aggregate planning)

Objective: To determine, using a common unit of measurement, the *overall quantities of finished products to be produced* during each of the time units (periods or intervals) constituting the planning horizon, and calculate the quantities of the main resources to be used, in order to satisfy all the forecast demand for the period.

Inputs: Information on the demand to be satisfied (usually in the form of forecasts), the relevant technical considerations (quantities of resources available, standard production time and costs, overall inventory of finished products) and company policies that must be considered by the planner (policies concerning fluctuations in manpower, overtime, subcontracting, inventories and stockouts, for example).

Production units: A common unit of measurement that applies to all the company's products. This *equivalent unit* serves as a common denominator for comparing all the products manufactured, production inputs and resources, as applicable. The method used in determining the most appropriate equivalent unit is explained in section 5.5.

Horizon: The longest planning horizon used for the control system. Although a *one-year* horizon seems to be the most common, production plans are sometimes also drawn up for periods of six months to two years. A horizon of more than two years leaves time for major changes to the operations system, and so has more to do with the design and improvement of production systems than with the control system.

Unit of time: A *month* is generally used as the unit time period or interval.

Output: The result of the information (input) transformation process for this first step is the *production plan*. This is the term recommended by CAPIC, and we use this standardized terminology as much as possible in the chapters on production and inventory planning and control. Some companies still use the term *aggregate plan*.

Step 2: Detailed planning

Objective: First, to determine the quantities of each *type of finished product to be produced* in each period. These quantities must satisfy customer demand while respecting the constraints set out in the production plan. At this point, customer demand is determined on the basis of forecasts (for each specific type of finished product), confirmed orders, or a combination of the two. Confirmed orders ordinarily have specified delivery times. Respecting these time limits becomes the key objective at this second step, in the way that determining the quantities to be produced was the main objective at the first step.

▼ **FIGURE 5.1**
Planning Priorities

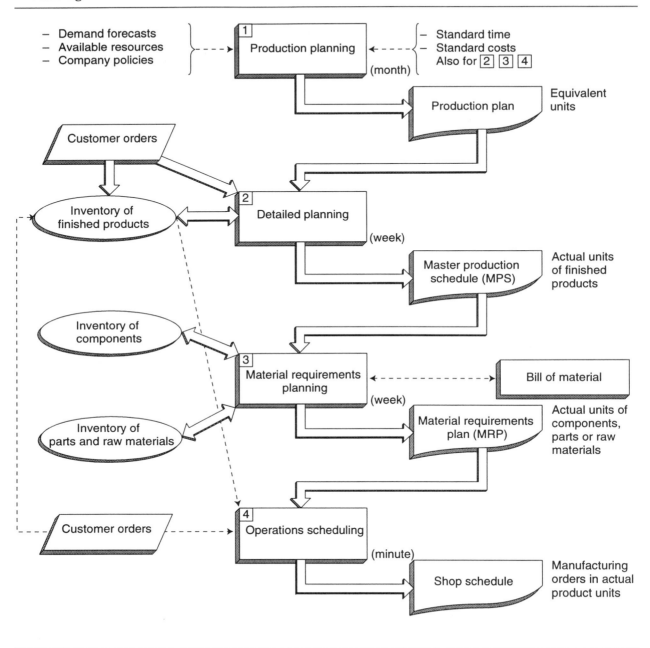

Input: The main inputs at this step are constraints plan (overall quantities to be produced and available resources), confirmed orders, or, lacking these, demand forecasts, technical aspects mentioned in step 1 (but in greater detail at this point) and the inventories of finished products, if any.

Product units: The various finished products must be counted in *actual units* applicable to each product (units of each model of furniture, litres of each type of paint, metres of each kind of metal wire, and so on).

Horizon: At this step, the planning horizon should be shorter than that used for the production plan. With a few exceptions (products with a very long production time, such as ships), the horizon used in this detailed planning step should not exceed six months and is most often a *quarter*.

Unit of time: A *week* is generally used. Sometimes variable units are preferred, shorter at the beginning of the planning horizon (one day, for instance) and longer toward the end (one week).

Output: The document that results from this step is called the *master production schedule*, or *MPS*.

Step 3: Material requirements planning

Objective: To determine *when* and *how much of each raw material, part or component to order* (from external suppliers or the internal production system, as applicable) in order to carry out the master production schedule drawn up in the previous step. This third step is necessary only for companies with production systems comprising several stages (modules), in which products are manufactured according to some variation of the following general process: manufacture of parts, assembly of components, final assembly. However, a number of firms with more direct production systems (proceeding from raw material to final product in a single step, for example) nevertheless use material requirements planning to determine when and in what quantities to order raw materials from suppliers.

Inputs: The master production schedule, the bill of material (indicating the necessary quantities of components, parts or raw materials for each unit or lot of finished products), the inventory of components, parts and raw materials and the table of lead times for ordering or producing components, parts and raw materials.

Product unit: In this case, *actual units* of each component, part or raw material are used.

Horizon: Generally speaking, material requirements planning uses the same planning horizon that detailed planning does, *one quarter*.

Time unit: The same unit is used as for detailed planning, generally *one week*.

Output: The document resulting from this step is called the *material requirements plan*, or *MRP*.

Step 4: Operations scheduling

Objective: To identify *the product to which each component of the operations production system should be assigned* (workstation, worker, machine) so that the various plans and programs drawn up at the previous steps can be carried out; in other words, when each operation necessary to produce a product should be performed. Operations scheduling often has other objectives in addition to this main goal, such as maximizing the use of production resources, minimizing average order processing time or reducing the number of backorders.

Inputs: Mainly the master production schedule and the material requirements plan. A *route sheet* is also often used at this step, specifying the sequence of operations to be carried out for each product and the quantities of production resources necessary. Finally, standard manufacturing times and costs are also used.

Product unit: Real product units (finished products, components or parts) are combined, for the purposes of this final step, into *orders* or *manufacturing orders*. It is these orders that must be allocated at this step to each resource unit, in a specific sequence.

Horizon: The planning horizon varies in length but is generally shorter than for the previous steps, usually from one week to one month.

Time unit: As short as necessary, depending on the operating characteristics of the production resources: *day*, *hour*, *minute* or *fraction of a minute*.

Output: The document resulting from this final step is used as a first-line guide for operations. It is known as the *production schedule* or *manufacturing or shop calendar* or *schedule*.

Companies wishing to plan their operations rationally should proceed through all four steps. Nonetheless, some firms, because of a lack of resources, time or the small number of orders to be processed, elect to short-circuit the process recommended above and proceed directly to the scheduling step. They draw up a production schedule solely on the basis of customer orders. Figure 5.1 also illustrates this situation.

On the other hand, other companies with extremely complex production systems add intermediate steps to those we have discussed here. For instance, firms whose final assembly operations are complex and have long lead times (often carried out in separate production units) separate the detailed planning step into two substeps: planning of final assembly (which takes account of assembly operations for the finished product) and detailed planning of main components, which then replace the finished products in the master production schedule. A new document is then added and used as an output at the first substep: the *final assembly schedule*.

Before closing this section, we should note that operations planning requires that the steps described be carried out in chronological order. If, however, because of constraints imposed by a plan at an earlier step it proves impossible to arrive at a plan that will achieve the company's objectives, the planners will have to return to the previous steps to alter the data (usually the master production schedule) used in the preceding plans. Thus, sequential theoretical process described above is often an iterative one in practice.

5.3   Priority and Capacity Planning

As noted at the end of section 5.1, operations planning objectives relate to both the estimated resources necessary for production and the quantities to be produced. Planners attempt to reach both these goals at once. It may be that for steps 2 (detailed planning) and 3 (material requirements planning) drawing up the plans involves manipulating such a huge amount of data that it is preferable to approach the two separately, yet simultaneously.

As shown in Figure 5.2, steps 1 and 4 in the planning process remain separate. Planners examine priorities (quantities to be produced) and capacities at the same time. Steps 2 and 3 overlap. The terms *detailed planning* and *material requirements planning* are reserved for priority planning, and the *rough-cut capacity planning* and *capacity requirements planning* steps are introduced at the appropriate levels.

The objectives and methods specific to these two capacity planning steps are discussed in Chapter 6. For the moment, we will simply emphasize the need for those in charge of priority planning and those responsible for capacity planning to constantly share information, to ensure that their final plans are compatible.

5.4 Importance of Computers in Operations Planning

Operations planning involves the collection, storage and processing of enormous quantities of numerical data, of the following types:

- *technical*, including all specifications for the products to be manufactured and the available production resources (labour, equipment, power sources, technologies);

- *quantities*, including all information relating to the number of units required, products or resources, either individually (bills of material or capacity) or overall (customer orders, purchase orders or manufacturing orders);

- *time*, combining all the relevant temporal data (fixed dates, lead time, standard or actual time);

- *cost*, including all the relevant monetary data (price, unit or total, standard or actual costs, cost prices).

In addition, in endeavouring to produce the best possible plans, operations planners can use quantitative optimization models or simulations. Operations research has long employed such models and methods. Few POM managers used these methods or models until recently, however, because of the complex calculations involved and the amount of time it took to obtain the desired results using manual calculations. But with the advent of computers and the availability of user-friendly software for solving the complicated mathematical problems involved in operations planning, planners have been changing their approach.

Today, planners have PC-based software packages that can solve most of the constrained optimization problems that crop up at the various planning stages. We will show how they are used in production planning in section 5.10. Electronic spreadsheets (Lotus 1-2-3, Excel and others) make it possible to run simulations to test a number of possible solutions (section 5.9). Finally, commercial software packages for operations management (there are dozens on the market, of varying complexity—Myte Myke, Inmass, Copics and Mac Pac, to name only a few) contain all the modules necessary to compile, store and process the data needed for decision-making at each step in operations planning.

FIGURE 5.2 ▶
Priority and
Capacity Planning

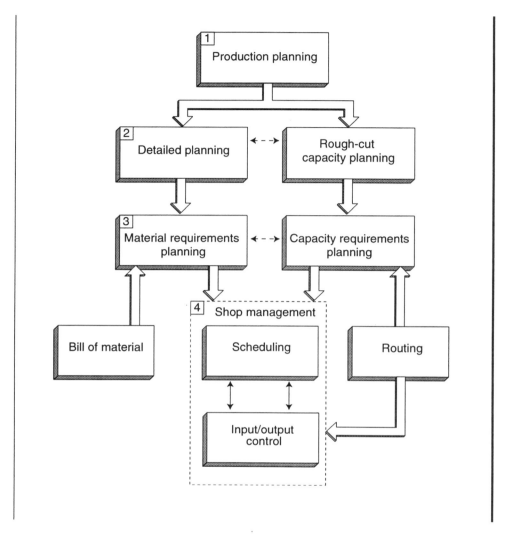

PRODUCTION PLANNING

5.5   Production Planning: Conditions and Constraints

The production planning (or aggregate planning) process gives operations managers an opportunity to answer many vital questions, such as: can the workforce be varied, in order to cope with fluctuations in demand? Is it best to carry an inventory of finished products, to call on subcontractors, or to combine these two methods with others, to meet demand? What are the costs and consequences of the different options?

Production planning also serves to determine how best to combine internal resources (inventory, labour and equipment) and external resources (subcontractors) to meet customer demand, in keeping with the company's competitive strategy. Managers use different means to handle seasonal and cyclical variations in demand, some of which have repercussions for the production plan.

Before planners begin drawing up the production plan, the company's policies and strategic objectives must be established and made known. At this point in the planning process, the company's physical facilities are considered fixed, by convention, but managers may vary their rate of use to meet production requirements.

Few authors deal with the matter of the *planning horizon* at the production planning step, yet this is an essential decision for the company's operations. The planning horizon can have a significant effect if it is long enough to allow managers to identify variations and trends in aggregate demand, and to devise and implement means of handling these variations. The horizon may be different from one company to the next, depending on how the firm manages demand and its production technology, which is why horizon periods range from six months to two years. Finally, the period chosen must allow a flexible transition from one production plan to another, in case the control of operations or some unforeseeable event makes changes necessary.

The choice of *equivalent unit* used in planning calculations is another essential facet of the production plan. The unit chosen must be applicable to all the company's products. The obvious choice is a typical *finished product* as a common denominator, so that all the other products can be measured in terms of this unit. For example, a company that specializes in manufacturing armchairs may select a typical model of armchair (the most popular one, perhaps) and make this chair its standard. Each unit of this model reordered or produced will represent an equivalent unit. One unit of a more complex or more costly model will represent more than one equivalent unit, while a simpler model will represent less than one unit. Before this technique can be used, the planner must draw up a conversion table that specifies each product in equivalent units.

This simple method is not appropriate for every company, however. The most important characteristic to be considered in the selection of an equivalent unit is ease of use. A company with a broad and varied product line (e.g., armchairs, tables, beds and wardrobes) may find it impossible to identify a typical product against which all other products can easily be measured.

In this case operations planners have two choices. If the inputs used in production are similar or if one of these inputs is a major part of all the products the company makes, a unit of this *key input* may be selected as the equivalent unit. For instance, refineries often transform a single raw material (crude oil or unrefined sugar) into a relatively wide range of finished products. They may find it easier to measure their finished products in terms of units of this raw material. Where neither the company's inputs nor its finished products are homogeneous enough for this purpose, one option remains. The planner may select a resource with a major effect on production capacity, and use a unit of this *key resource* as the equivalent unit. In a production system where production capacity is dependent on the availability of direct labour, the appropriate equivalent unit could be a person-hour, with each product unit being measured in terms of the number of hours of labour required to make it. Note that in general the same equivalent unit must be used for production planning as for determining the capacity of the operational system.

Another constraint on production planning is imposed by the company's policies with regard to *variations in the rates of use* of production resources. It is not always possible for operations managers to hire or lay off workers in order to meet the number required by the initial production plan, or to vary the workforce as often as might be desirable to minimize total costs. Similarly, companies often have very specific policies regulating overtime, and these may be included in collective agreements. Finally, production planners' options may be limited by company policies concerning inventory, stockouts and subcontracting. Planners must be skilled in combining the various means of varying production rates, and this task can represent a substantial challenge.

One last constraint is the need to satisfy *total demand* over the planning horizon, including the difference between total quantities in inventory at the beginning and end of the period. Even if company policy allows for some lag between demand and production over the period, with the attendant risk of overstocking or stockouts, total production over the entire planning horizon must be equal to total demand, plus or minus inventory adjustments.

5.6   Strategic Elements and Their Costs

Because demand tends to fluctuate from month to month and season to season, operations planners must use specific strategies and techniques. In making their selections, they usually consider the costs associated with each strategy and technique. Table 5.1 lists the possible strategies in production planning and the associated costs. The costs shown in the table are over and above those for the production of an equivalent unit in standard time.

A few explanations are necessary concerning some of the strategic considerations listed in Table 5.1 and their costs.

- Not all the strategic elements listed are necessarily available to all companies at all times; the company's policies may restrict or prohibit the use of some of them.

- The table shows only the most easily measured additional cost; most of the strategic elements shown entail other indirect costs (for instance, reduced efficiency because of many variations in the workforce or excessive overtime, reduced product quality because of machines being run too rapidly).

- The additional costs associated with subcontracting result from the fact that this method is used only when demand is very high. We are not referring to structural subcontracting, whereby a company regularly contracts out part or all of its production to benefit from lower costs, among other advantages.

5.7   Preparing an Optimal Production Plan

The preparation of an optimal production plan requires careful attention to the following steps.

Step 1: Collecting the necessary information

Whether the information is provided by different company departments or collected by operations planners themselves, the planners absolutely must obtain it before embarking on the other production planning steps:

Strategies	Associated costs
Workforce	
– Varying the workforce	– Hiring (recruitment, training), layoff (separation allowances)
– Overtime	– Overtime premium
– Extra shift	– Organizational costs, premium, greater overhead
Equipment	
– Changing the operating speed	– Lower reliability, increased maintenance costs
– Temporary leasing	– Leasing costs, lower efficiency
Lag between production and demand	
– Excess inventory	– Opportunity costs, storage costs, holding costs
– Stockouts	– Loss of business, compensation for backorders, foregone profits
External resources	
– Subcontracting	– Additional costs

◄   **TABLE 5.1**
**Strategic Elements
in Production
Planning**

- forecasts of aggregate demand for each time unit in the planning horizon;
- aggregate finished products inventory at the beginning of the planning horizon, and the quantities desired for final inventory;
- current or potential availability of each key production resource (labour, equipment);
- standard production time for an equivalent unit for each key resource; the planner may simply calculate the time or may determine the number of equivalent units that can be produced by a unit of each resource;
- standard costs for the use of resources;
- quantified values (where possible) of the consequences of the applicable company policies.

Step 2: Analysis of unit costs of strategic elements

In the previous section we listed the main strategic elements that production planners may consider when drawing up an optimal production plan. Now we will reduce these costs to an equivalent unit basis and compare these strategic elements to determine a crossover point. This will allow us to answer questions such as: Is it better to produce goods ahead of time and hold them in inventory, or to produce them at the last minute, at the risk of having to resort to overtime? Is it less costly to adjust the workforce temporarily though overtime or through hiring and laying off? If additional equipment capacity is required temporarily, is it better to lease additional equipment or to increase the operating speed of existing equipment? How does temporary subcontracting compare in terms of costs with other strategic elements?

This analysis will guide us in the subsequent steps. Specific examples of calculations are given in section 5.9.

Step 3: Preparing plans corresponding to various strategies and evaluating their economic viability

Based on an examination of trends in aggregate demand (as represented by forecasts of demand on the planning horizon) and the results of step 2, planners now turn to designing different production plans corresponding to a number of possible strategies (section 5.8), and determining their total cost in order to measure the economic advantages of each. Sections 5.9 and 5.10 give examples.

In this step, planners make use of quantitative optimization or simulation methods, and computers may prove useful to quickly determine either the least costly plans (optimization) or the exact difference in total cost among a wide range of plans (simulation). Depending on the approach chosen, this step may involve a fairly direct approach (optimization) or an iterative process (simulation).

Step 4: Integration of variables and non-quantified constraints

The economic benefits of a production plan are an essential consideration in selecting an optimal plan. Nevertheless, a number of key variables (often those affected by company policies) and some constraints cannot be included in mathematical models, either because they are not suited to the type of model used (a linear model, for example) or because some constraints are excluded from the model to keep it from becoming unwieldy. The planner must have a thorough knowledge of the organization and culture of the company in order to carry out this step correctly, relying on experience and, in some cases, intuition.

Step 5: Selecting the optimal plan

The most desirable plan of those tested will be the one with the optimal combination of benefits and drawbacks (minor it is hoped). This plan will become the input for the subsequent steps in operations planning.

5.8   Types of Strategies in Production Planning

For planning purposes, strategies have been divided into two broad groups: on the one hand, those that deal with the frequency and size of variations in production volume over the planning horizon; on the other hand, those that concern the number of strategic elements used.

In the first category are *extreme* and *moderate* strategies. Extreme strategies may be broken down, in turn, into *level* and *chase* strategies.

A *level strategy* involves the establishment of a steady average production rate for the entire planning horizon, even if forecasts indicate fluctuations in demand from one period to another. The rate used corresponds to the average demand per period, corrected to take account of any difference between the initial inventory and the desired final inventory. Irregularities in demand are smoothed out by accumulating inventory during slow periods and depleting it (with the possibility of stockouts) during high-demand periods. Obviously, this strategy facilitates planning, but it runs the risk of being more costly than a moderate strategy because of its lack of flexibility in response to demand. It may be the best method, however, when demand is stable.

A *chase strategy*, on the other hand, involves producing exactly to demand. Thus the production rate always corresponds to demand for a given period. Although this extreme strategy virtually eliminates inventory, it generally results in wide variations in the workforce, overtime and, often, subcontracting requirements. It can prove very costly and difficult to put into practice.

Moderate strategies fall somewhere between these two "extreme" strategies. There are variations in the production rate, but they occur less often and are less severe than fluctuations in demand. Often the optimal and least costly strategy, all things considered, will be of this type.

In the second category, strategies are grouped into *pure* and *mixed* types, depending on the number of strategic elements used. Pure strategies rely on only one element to absorb fluctuations in demand, whereas mixed strategies call for a combination of the elements available. A pure strategy may be aimed at achieving the necessary changes in production rates simply by varying the workforce. On the other hand, when a combination of changes in the workforce and overtime is used for the same purpose, we speak of a mixed strategy. A pure strategy may prove the best choice if one of the strategic elements available is much less costly than all the others. Most often, however, the optimal strategy is to be found in the mixed group.

USING A PRACTICAL TOOL

5.9   The Heuristic or Graphical Method

This iterative method uses easily developed production plans to prepare a series of increasingly less expensive solutions that respond more and more to the requirements of company policy and other production constraints. It is often called the *graphical method*, since unit or cumulative graphs are used (Figures 5.3 and 5.4) to guide planners in preparing the different plans. It has a number of *advantages*, in that it is easy to understand, imposes no cost constraints, can include as many strategic elements as necessary and makes it possible to compare the economics of a number of plans. Within certain limits, calculations can be made manually, although electronic spreadsheets can greatly reduce the effort required. The main *disadvantages* of this method are the frequently high number of trials necessary to obtain acceptable plans and the fact that it does not show the difference between the total costs of the plans tested and the minimum possible costs.

Before using this method, planners must carry out the steps described in section 5.7, bearing in mind the following points with respect to step 3 (preparation of plans corresponding to various strategies and economic evaluation of these plans) and step 4 (integration of non-quantified variables).

1. The first plans prepared must correspond to *pure* strategies. Ordinarily, two plans are prepared: the first will be a level strategy, the second a chase strategy.

2. Each of these two plans is examined to determine whether one of them may already be satisfactory in economic terms. If so, planners move on to step 4. Otherwise, they continue step 3 with the following addition.

3. Based on existing plans, the study of trends in forecast demand and an analysis of unit costs of strategic elements (step 2), planners devise new plans that correspond in general to a moderate mixed or pure strategy. Then they evaluate the comparative benefits and drawbacks of these plans with regard to total costs and other quantifiable variables, before moving on to step 4.

The following example shows how the heuristic method is used, and the calculations necessary to establish and compare different production plans.

Example
∎

NKD, a manufacturer of household appliances, has forecast demand as follows (expressed in equivalent units):

January	16,000	May	15,000	September	30,000
February	14,000	June	22,000	October	30,000
March	12,000	July	25,000	November	25,000
April	10,000	August	25,000	December	22,000

The relevant unit costs are as follows:

– labour cost at regular wage rate: $2,000 per employee per month;

– labour cost at overtime wage rate: 1.5 times the regular wage rate;

– hiring cost: $2,400 per employee;

– layoff cost: $3,200 per employee;

– inventory carrying cost: $4 per unit per month;

– stockout cost: $12 per unit per month.

The following considerations result from company policy or other production constraints:

Example
(*cont.*)

– the inventory of finished goods at the beginning of the year is 2,000 units, and the company wishes to increase it to 4,400 by the end of the year;

– there are currently 180 workers;

– variations in the workforce are allowed, but should never affect more than 30% of the workforce at a time or occur more than four times a year;

– overtime hours may not exceed 50% of regular hours per month;

– at the regular wage rate, the production rate is 100 equivalent units per employee, per month;

– maximum inventory capacity is 30,000 units;

– the company prefers not to have any stockouts but is ready to tolerate them provided they do not exceed 2,000 units and do not occur two months in a row;

– company policy is not to subcontract work or set up a second shift;

– production capacity depends solely on the workforce variable and is not affected by equipment capacity;

– all costs and all capacities are linear and vary directly with the quantity of resources used.

Solution with the heuristic method

Step 1: Collecting the necessary information

The above data provide all the necessary information.

Step 2: Analysis of unit costs of strategic elements

The problem data suggest that production planners have four strategic elements on which they can base different plans: overtime, variations in the workforce, inventory and stockouts. They must begin by calculating the unit cost (in equivalent units) of each of these elements.

Overtime

Planners must calculate the value of the overtime premium in equivalent units. It is known that each employee costs $2,000 per month at the regular wage rate and can produce 100 equivalent units. The unit cost at the regular wage rate, then, will be $2,000 ÷ 100 equivalent units = $20. Since the overtime premium is 1.5 times the regular rate, this gives $20 × 0.5 = $10.

(N.B.: for the rest of this example we will use "EU" to mean equivalent unit.)

Variations in the workforce

The calculations for this purpose are somewhat more complex, since the workforce can vary in three ways:

Example
(*cont.*)

— a person may be hired during the period and remain with the company to the end of the period;

— a person working for the company at the beginning of the period may be laid off during the period;

— a person may be hired and laid off during the period or laid off and replaced by a new employee.

For each of these possibilities there will be a different unit cost. In addition, the unit cost must take account of the length of employment during the period, since this cost declines with the length of employment. Table 5.2 shows how this unit cost is calculated, given the costs of hiring and laying off ($2,400 and $3,200, respectively) and the length of employment. The calculations apply for periods of up to six months, but can be extended if necessary.

TABLE 5.2
Unit Costs of Variations in the Workforce

Length of employment	Unit costs of various possibilities		
	Hiring only	**Layoff only**	**Combined hiring and layoff**
1 month	$2,400 ÷ 100 EU = $24	$3,200 ÷ 100 EU = $32	$24 + $32 = $56
2 months	$2,400 ÷ 200 EU = $12	$3,200 ÷ 200 EU = $16	$12 + $16 = $28
3 months	$2,400 ÷ 300 EU = $8	$3,200 ÷ 300 EU = $10.67	$8 + $10.67 = $18.67
4 months	$2,400 ÷ 400 EU = $6	$3,200 ÷ 400 EU = $8	$6 + $8 = $14
5 months	$2,400 ÷ 500 EU = $4.80	$3,200 ÷ 500 EU = $6.40	$4.80 + $6.40 = $11.20
6 months	$2,400 ÷ 600 EU = $4	$3,200 ÷ 600 EU = $5.33	$4 + $5.33 = $9.33

Inventory and stockouts

These two unit costs are part of the problem data, and are $4 and $12 per EU per month, respectively.

Before completing this step, the planners must determine the crossover points of the various strategic elements and make the necessary trade-offs. Five comparisons are possible.

Overtime and variations in the workforce

Based on the unit costs calculated above:

- having employees work overtime is better than hiring additional employees if the hiring period is two months or less;

- it is less costly to use overtime than to hire and lay off a person within a period of less than six months.

Overtime and inventory

Since it costs $10 more to produce a unit using workers on overtime and since the monthly unit inventory holding cost is $4, the crossover point between these two strategic elements is 2.5 months ($10 ÷ $4 = 2.5). This means:

- it is better to wait and use workers on overtime to produce units that could be produced ahead of time by workers at the regular rate, but which would have to be carried in inventory for three months or more before being used;

- if the inventory carrying period is two months or less, the opposite applies.

Overtime and stockouts

In this case the crossover point is 0.8 months ($10 ÷ $12). Thus it is better to have employees work overtime (within the stipulated limits) than to accept a stockout.

Inventory and variations in the workforce

Here the comparison becomes more complex, since the two strategic elements in question have unit costs that vary with their length of use. There will be a different crossover point depending on how long each element is used. To determine these points, we will simply consider the option of hiring followed by layoffs to effect variations in the workforce.

Length of variation in the workforce	Unit cost	Crossover point for inventory
1 month	$56.00	$56.00 ÷ $4 = 14 months
2 months	$28.00	$28.00 ÷ $4 = 7 months
3 months	$18.67	$18.67 ÷ $4 = 4.7 months
4 months	$14.00	$14.00 ÷ $4 = 3.5 months
5 months	$11.20	$11.20 ÷ $4 = 2.8 months
6 months	$ 9.33	$ 9.33 ÷ $4 = 2.3 months

Example
(*cont.*)

Accordingly:

– it is better to produce goods ahead of time and carry them in inventory for less than 14 months than to be obliged to hire employees at the last minute for only one month;

– the option of varying the workforce is preferable if it makes it possible to avoid carrying goods in inventory for longer than 14 months.

The reasoning would be similar, with different values, for hiring periods exceeding one month.

Variations in the workforce and stockouts

The same reasoning is used:

Length of variation in the workforce	Unit cost	Crossover point for stockouts
1 month	$56.00	$56.00 ÷ $12 = 4.7 months
2 months	$28.00	$28.00 ÷ $12 = 2.3 months
3 months	$18.67	$18.67 ÷ $12 = 1.6 months
4 months	$14.00	$14.00 ÷ $12 = 1.2 months
5 months	$11.20	$11.20 ÷ $12 = 0.9 months
6 months	$ 9.33	$ 9.33 ÷ $12 = 0.8 months

Accordingly:

– it is better to vary the workforce, even for a single month, if it helps to avoid a stockout of five months or longer;

– a stockout of four months or less is preferable to varying the workforce for one month.

Step 3: Drawing up plans corresponding to various strategies and evaluating their economic benefits

As we saw at the beginning of this section, the heuristic method calls for two plans, one corresponding to a level strategy and the other to a chase strategy. Now we will quickly look at the principles to be applied in preparing these plans.

Level strategy

Example
(*cont.*)

The *quantity to be produced* each month is equivalent to the mathematical mean of monthly demand forecasts, adjusted to take account of the difference between the initial and final inventories. This gives:

$$P_t = \frac{\sum\limits_{1}^{12} D_t - S_I + S_F}{12}$$

where P_t = quantity to be produced in month t,

D_t = forecast demand for month t,

S_I = initial inventory

S_F = final inventory desired.

In this example, the calculations give:

$$P_t = \frac{16{,}000 + 14{,}000 + \ldots + 25{,}000 + 22{,}000 - 2{,}000 + 4{,}400}{12} = 20{,}700$$

NKD must produce 20,700 EU every month.

Since production remains constant throughout the period, it seems reasonable to keep a stable workforce as well. The *size of the workforce* is calculated as follows:

$$E_t = \frac{P_t}{C_t}$$

where E_t = employees required for month t,

C_t = monthly production capacity per person, regular wage rate.

Consequently, NKD will need a workforce of 207 employees (20,700 ÷ 100). The other data for the plan must still be calculated (inventory or stockout, hiring or layoff, overtime) and the costs evaluated using the normal economic principles.

Inventory or stockout (if $S_t < 0$):

$$S_t = S_t - 1 + P_t - D_t$$

Hiring ($V_t = E_t - E_{t-1}$)

Overtime (O_t) (if $P_t > E_t \times C_t$):

$$O_t = \frac{P_t - (E_t \times C_t)}{C_t}$$

where O_t = number of employees at the regular wage rate needed to work the overtime hours in month t.

Example
(*cont.*)

Annual inventory holding cost:

$$\sum_{1}^{12} S_t \times CS_t$$

for any $S_t > 0$ and where CS_t = unit inventory holding cost for month t.

Annual stockout cost:

$$\sum_{1}^{12} (-S_t) \times CP_t$$

for any $S_t < 0$ and where CP_t = unit stockout cost for month t.

Annual hiring cost:

$$\sum_{1}^{12} V_t \times CH_t$$

for any $V_t > 0$ and where CH_t = cost of hiring a person in month t.

Annual layoff cost:

$$\sum_{1}^{12} (-V_t) \times CL_t$$

for any $V_t < 0$ and where CL_t = cost of laying off an employee in month t.

Annual labour cost at the regular wage rate:

$$\sum_{1}^{12} E_t \times CR_t$$

where CR_t = monthly cost of an employee working at the regular wage rate.

Annual overtime cost:

$$\sum_{1}^{12} O_t \times CO_t$$

where CO_t = cost of an employee working a number of equivalent overtime hours at the regular wage rate, for month t.

▼ **TABLE 5.3**   **Example**
  NKD's Production Plan—Level Strategy   (*cont.*)

NKD
Production plan 1
Level strategy
Stable workforce

	Initial conditions	January	February	March	April	May	June	July	August	September	October	November	December
Demand and shipments		16,000	14,000	12,000	10,000	15,000	22,000	25,000	25,000	30,000	30,000	25,000	22,000
Production plan		20,700	20,700	20,700	20,700	20,700	20,700	20,700	20,700	20,700	20,700	20,700	20,700
Inventory (− = stockout)	2,000	6,700	13,400	22,100	32,800	38,500	37,200	32,900	28,600	19,300	10,000	5,700	4,400
Number of workers	180	207	207	207	207	207	207	207	207	207	207	207	207
Hiring		27	0	0	0	0	0	0	0	0	0	0	0
Layoffs		0	0	0	0	0	0	0	0	0	0	0	0
Overtime (months/worker)		0	0	0	0	0	0	0	0	0	0	0	0

Cost of plan 1:		
	Carrying cost	$1,006,400
	Stockout cost	0
	Hiring cost	64,800
	Layoff cost	0
	Labour cost	
	Regular rate	4,968,000
	Overtime rate	0
	Total cost	**$6,039,200**

Given the repetitive nature of these calculations, the use of an electronic spreadsheet or other appropriate software is strongly recommended. Table 5.3 shows the plan arrived at by NKD.

Example
(*cont.*)

Chase strategy

In a plan corresponding to a chase strategy, the *quantity to be produced* each month will be equal to the forecast demand for the month—except for the first month, when the initial inventory must be subtracted from forecast demand, barring instructions to the contrary, and for the last month, when the final inventory must be added to forecast demand.

▼ TABLE 5.4
NKD's Production Plan—Chase Strategy

NKD
Production plan 2
Chase strategy
Variable workforce

	Initial conditions	January	February	March	April	May	June	July	August	September	October	November	December
Demand and shipments		16,000	14,000	12,000	10,000	15,000	22,000	25,000	25,000	30,000	30,000	25,000	22,000
Production plan		14,000	14,000	12,000	10,000	15,000	22,000	25,000	25,000	30,000	30,000	25,000	26,400
Inventory (− = stockout)	2,000	0	0	0	0	0	0	0	0	0	0	0	4,400
Number of workers	180	140	140	120	100	150	220	250	250	300	300	250	264
Hiring		0	0	0	0	50	70	30	0	50	0	0	14
Layoffs		40	0	20	20	0	0	0	0	0	0	50	0
Overtime (months/worker)		0	0	0	0	0	0	0	0	0	0	0	0

Cost of plan 2:

Carrying cost	$17,600
Stockout cost	0
Hiring cost	513,600
Layoff cost	416,000
Labour cost	
Regular rate	4,968,000
Overtime rate	0
Total cost	**$5,915,200**

The *size of the workforce* is calculated as for the level strategy, except that it can vary from one month to the next. In the chase strategy, fluctuations in demand are absorbed by varying the workforce. Table 5.4 shows the plan obtained using this strategy.

Example (*cont.*)

An examination of these two plans leads to the following observations:

− the costs of the level plan exceed those of the chase plan by $124,000;

− the level plan exceeds the maximum inventory capacity (30,000 EU) for the period April to July;

− the chase plan does not respect the constraints concerning variations in the workforce, since the workforce varies nine times (rather than the maximum of four times); in addition, two of these variations, in May and June, exceed the maximum allowable level of 30%;

− all other constraints are respected.

The obvious conclusion is that at least one other mixed-strategy plan must be tested. This is where the method gets its alternative name of the *graphical method*, as graphs prove very useful at this point. As we mentioned at the beginning of this section, two types of graphs are used: unit and cumulative. Figure 5.3 shows a graph illustrating unit demand and production, while Figure 5.4 shows a cumulative graph.

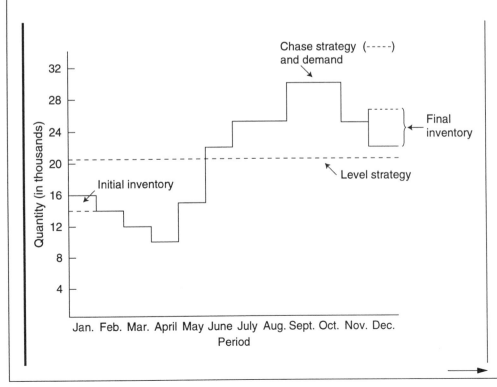

◄ **FIGURE 5.3 NKD's Monthly Demand and Production**

Example
(*cont.*)

Mixed strategy

If we examine Figure 5.3, in particular, and some results of the analysis of unit costs in step 2, we can draw up a plan corresponding to a mixed strategy:

–   the demand curve in Figure 5.3 shows that the year appears to be divided into two seasons: low demand for the first five months of the year and high demand for the last seven months; this leads us to believe that a good mixed strategy could have two different production rates during the year: one in months with low demand and the other in the high-demand season;

–   to absorb the rise in production volume that this new strategy implies when the production rate varies, managers could either vary the workforce or have employees work overtime—or they could choose a combination of the two; since the production rate must be increased for at least six months, the analysis of unit costs in step 2 indicates that it is preferable to hire new employees.

FIGURE 5.4 ▶
NKD's Cumulative Demand and Production

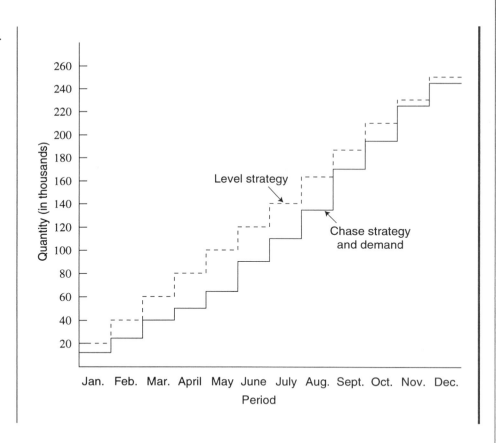

Now we need to determine the appropriate production rates and the extent of the variation in the workforce required. To limit the number of variations, we could keep the workforce of 180 employees at the beginning of the year and have them work at the regular wage rate, translating into a monthly production rate of 18,000 EU. An examination of demand in the first five months of the year indicates that this production exceeds forecast demand and that inventory will tend to increase. This accumulated surplus (Figure 5.4) will allow the company to maintain production at the same rate in June, even though forecast demand increases, and to defer the increase in the workforce until early July.

Example
(*cont.*)

▼ TABLE 5.5
NKD's Production Plan—Mixed Strategy with Variations in the Workforce

NKD
Production plan 3
Mixed strategy
Variable workforce

	Initial conditions	January	February	March	April	May	June	July	August	September	October	November	December
Demand and shipments		16,000	14,000	12,000	10,000	15,000	22,000	25,000	25,000	30,000	30,000	25,000	22,000
Production plan		18,000	18,000	18,000	18,000	18,000	18,000	23,400	23,400	23,400	23,400	23,400	23,400
Inventory (− = stockout)	2,000	4,000	8,000	14,000	22,000	25,000	21,000	19,400	17,800	11,200	4,600	3,000	1,400
Number of workers	180	180	180	180	180	180	180	234	234	234	234	234	234
Hiring		0	0	0	0	0	0	54	0	0	0	0	0
Layoffs		0	0	0	0	0	0	0	0	0	0	0	0
Overtime (months/worker)		0	0	0	0	0	0	0	0	0	0	0	0

Cost of plan 3:	Carrying cost	$617,600
	Stockout cost	0
	Hiring cost	129,600
	Layoff cost	0
	Labour cost	
	Regular rate	4,968,000
	Overtime rate	0
	Total cost	**$5,715,200**

Example
(cont.)

If the company operates in this way for the first half of the year, it will accumulate inventory of 21,000 EU by late June, and will have to produce at an average monthly rate of 23,400 EU for the last six months of the year to meet forecast demand and wind up with the desired final inventory of 4,400 EU. With employees working at the regular wage rate, this production rate calls for a workforce of 234, meaning that the company will have to hire 54 new employees (equal to the maximum allowable variation of 30%) at the beginning of July. Table 5.5 illustrates this third plan. Total costs are $200,000 lower than in the previous plan, and all the quantified constraints are respected.

Other plans corresponding to mixed-moderate strategies, which would be less expensive and would meet all the quantified constraints, could doubtless be devised. It might be helpful to study the graphs and the analysis of unit costs in greater detail. But we might well come up against the two major weaknesses of this method:

– it is impossible to know whether the plan prepared, although it may meet the quantified constraints, represents the lowest possible cost;

– since this method relies on successive approximations, there is no simple way of evaluating ahead of time the impact on total cost and respect for constraints of any changes made that affect several strategic elements at once.

Consequently, we will remain with the third plan for the time being.

Step 4: Integrating variables and non-quantified constraints

Now planners must take account of various elements that are not included in the economic model (considerations relating to company policies or to other management concerns, for example), such as the difficulties involved in implementing and carrying out the plans in question. Since it calls for only one variation in the workforce and the production rate over the year, the production plan corresponding to a moderate strategy does not seem to raise any particular problems in this respect; the level plan would cause even fewer problems, while the chase plan is much more problematical.

Step 5: Selecting the optimal plan

In view of the economic advantages of the plans developed, their respect for quantified constraints and the other elements to be considered, the plan corresponding to a moderate strategy (Table 5.5) would seem to be the best in this case.

REVIEW QUESTIONS

1. What are the main objectives of production planning?

2. How does production planning in the control system differ from other planning efforts in POM?

3. For each of the operations planning steps, state the objectives, product units, inputs, planning horizon, time units and output. Briefly describe each one.

4. At which steps in operations planning do priority planning and capacity planning coincide? At which steps are they done in parallel?

5. What are the main conditions and constraints applying to production planning?

6. Why are equivalent units used in production planning?

7. What are the main strategic elements available and the main associated costs in production planning?

8. What is meant by an *extreme* strategy? A *moderate* strategy? A *pure* strategy? A *mixed* strategy?

9. Why is the heuristic method also called the *graphical method*?

DISCUSSION QUESTIONS

1. "Determining the capacity of the operations system and operations planning are closely linked." Comment.

2. Is it worthwhile to proceed by steps in operations planning? Discuss.

3. Why are priority planning and capacity planning carried out simultaneously at certain steps in operations planning?

4. "Production planning makes it possible to maximize the use of resources." Comment.

5. Discuss the specific importance of each of the steps described in preparing an optimal production plan.

6. How could the planning techniques described in this chapter apply to a company in the service sector? What specific points would merit particular attention?

7. A systematic approach to POM highlights the importance of the links between decisions on designing and improving the operations system on the one hand, and decisions affecting the control system on the other hand. Illustrate this point by showing the links between determining capacity and planning operations.

PROBLEMS AND CASE STUDIES

1. At company XYZ, demand for the next six months corresponds to the following forecast:

Month	Forecast in equivalent units
January	300
February	500
March	400
April	100
May	400
June	300

The following information is also available:

- initial inventory: 60 equivalent units;
- carrying cost: $5 per EU per month;
- stockout cost: $20 per EU per month;
- number of hours of work per month, at the regular wage rate: 160 hours per person;
- time required to produce one EU: 5 hours;
- hiring cost: $100 per person;
- layoff cost: $50 per person;

- average wage: $8 per hour at the regular rate, 25% premium for overtime;
- subcontracting: $250 per EU;
- other production costs: $140.

To meet this forecast demand, the company is considering three production plans:

- Vary the number of employees in such a way as to satisfy total demand without risking stockouts and without resorting to overtime.
- Maintain a constant number of employees—corresponding to the number of workers required to produce the six-month forecast, divided by the average capacity of an employee during the period—and satisfy total demand without risking stockouts or resorting to overtime or subcontracting. If the production capacity at the regular rate exceeds demand in a month, stop production at the demand rate and pay employees for idle time.
- Complete production for the period with a constant workforce working all anticipated hours at the regular wage rate, even if it means risking stockouts or excess inventory.

a) Evaluate the total cost of each plan.

b) Draw a graph of cumulative demand and the proposed plans. What conclusion can be drawn from the graph?

c) Try to establish a production plan with a total cost less than that of the proposed plans.

d) Given all the strategic elements to be taken into consideration by the firm, which plan should be recommended? Briefly justify your answer.

2. Altalight specializes in table and bedside lamps. The company is preparing its production plan for the coming year. The operations planner has the following information on which to base her decision.

Unit costs (per person or per equivalent unit)

- cost of labour at the regular wage rate: $2,650 per month;
- cost of labour at the overtime rate: 1.5 times the regular rate;

- hiring cost: $2,000;
- layoff cost: $2,750;
- carrying cost: $11 per month;
- stockout cost: $24 per month.

Other information

- The company seeks to increase its inventory of finished products from an initial level of 2,000 EU to 14,000 EU by the end of the period.
- At the beginning of the year, the workforce is 240 employees.
- The production rate at the regular rate is 75 EU per person per month.
- The maximum inventory capacity is 3,000 EU.
- The production capacity varies with the number of workers, and may fluctuate by up to 25% per month.
- It is company policy to meet total demand for the year; however, the company can tolerate a stockout during the period, provided that it lasts no longer than one month at a time.
- Overtime must not exceed 20% of regular time on a monthly basis.
- The workforce must not exceed 320 employees.

Forecast demand (in equivalent units)			
January	9,800	July	8,400
February	6,800	August	16,900
March	10,400	September	15,300
April	8,200	October	10,600
May	17,100	November	22,200
June	23,300	December	32,000

a) Analyse the unit costs of the different strategic elements to be considered.

b) Draw up the plans necessary for the heuristic method, namely:
- a level plan,
- a chase plan,
- a plan corresponding to a moderate strategy.

c) Analyse the strengths and weaknesses of each plan.

d) Identify the plan that minimizes total costs and briefly analyse it.

e) Draw up an optimal production plan.

3. Gopathec is a company in a manufacturing sector where demand is subject to considerable seasonal variations. Thus it is very important that the company, if it is to be profitable, draw up an optimal production plan. The production planner has to use the following information to prepare various production plans for the upcoming year.

Forecast demand (in equivalent units)

January	64,000	July	10,000
February	55,000	August	12,000
March	31,500	September	32,000
April	28,000	October	48,000
May	28,000	November	73,000
June	15,000	December	85,000

Unit costs

– monthly labour cost at the regular wage rate: $2,200;

– hiring cost: $3,000 per person;

– layoff cost: $5,000 per person;

– overtime premium: 50% of the regular wage rate;

– monthly carrying cost: $6;

– monthly stockout cost: $12.

Other information

– The workforce at the beginning of the year is 200 employees.

– Each person can produce 180 EU per month working at the regular wage rate.

– It is possible to have employees work overtime, but overtime must not exceed 20% of regular hours on a monthly basis.

– The workforce may vary if necessary, but by no more than 40 employees from one month to the next.

– The initial inventory of finished products is 10,000 EU, and the company wishes to double it by the end of the year.

– The physical inventory capacity for finished products is 60,000 EU.

– Stockouts are acceptable, but must never exceed 10,000 EU at the end of the month; in addition, the company will not tolerate more than three months of stockouts during the year.

a) Using numerical analysis, show how the crossover point between overtime and variations in the workforce could be determined.

b) Prepare a level plan and a chase plan and analyse them.

c) Prepare a plan to minimize total production costs.

d) Prepare an optimal production plan and justify your choice.

4. Ms. Young is Director of Production Planning at Anisco, a vacuum-cleaner manufacturer. She is in charge of drawing up the company's production plan for next year. The demand forecasts, in equivalent units, are as follows:

Forecasts by period

January	8,900	July	7,700
February	7,500	August	7,600
March	9,500	September	13,900
April	9,100	October	11,700
May	15,600	November	20,200
June	21,200	December	29,100

Ms. Young has the following information concerning the relevant costs:

– labour cost, regular wage rate: $2,400 per month per person;

– labour cost, overtime rate: 1.5 times the regular rate;

– hiring cost: $1,800 per person;

– layoff cost: $2,500 per person;

- inventory carrying cost: $10 per equivalent unit per month;
- stockout cost: $25 per equivalent unit per month.

The following information might also be of use in drawing up a production plan:

- The inventory of finished products, 3,000 equivalent units, is to be reduced to 2,400 EU by the end of the year.
- At the beginning of the year, the workforce is 225 employees.
- The production rate at the regular wage rate is 60 EU per person per month.
- The maximum inventory capacity is 20,00 EU.
- The production capacity varies directly with the number of employees.
- Company policy is to meet demand for the year; it can tolerate stockouts during the year, but prefers to avoid them.
- Overtime must never exceed 20% of regular hours in a month.
- The workforce must not exceed 300 employees.

With the help of an appropriate software package, Ms. Young has prepared the following three production plans.

a) What kind of strategy is represented by each of these plans?

b) List two major strengths and two major weaknesses of each plan.

c) Ms. Young is very tempted to adopt plan C because of its low total cost. However, she finds the high overtime costs worrisome. How could this plan be changed so as to respect all the constraints, without significantly increasing the total cost? Justify your answer with the appropriate calculations.

PLAN A

Production plan

Period	Final inventory	Sales forecast	Production
0	3,000		
1	3,000	8,900	8,900
2	3,000	7,500	7,500
3	3,000	9,500	9,500
4	3,000	9,100	9,100
5	3,000	15,600	15,600
6	3,000	21,200	21,200
7	3,000	7,700	7,700
8	3,000	7,600	7,600
9	3,000	13,900	13,900
10	3,000	11,700	11,700
11	3,000	20,200	20,200
12	2,400	29,100	28,500

Workforce

Period	Workforce	Hiring	Layoffs
0	225		
1	148	0	77
2	125	0	23
3	158	33	0
4	152	0	6
5	260	108	0
6	353	93	0
7	128	0	225
8	127	0	1
9	232	105	0
10	195	0	37
11	337	142	0
12	475	138	0

Costs of the plan

Hiring cost	$1,114,200	12.59%
Layoff cost	922,500	10.42%
Labour cost (regular rate)	6,456,000	72.94%
Overtime cost	4,800	0.05%
Carrying cost	354,000	4.00%
Stockout cost	0	0%
Total	**$8,851,500**	**100%**

PLAN **B**
Production plan

Period	Final inventory	Sales forecast	Production
0	3,000		
1	7,550	8,900	13,450
2	13,500	7,500	13,450
3	17,450	9,500	13,450
4	21,800	9,100	13,450
5	19,650	15,600	13,450
6	11,900	21,200	13,450
7	17,650	7,700	13,450
8	23,500	7,600	13,450
9	23,050	13,900	13,450
10	24,800	11,700	13,450
11	18,050	20,200	13,450
12	2,400	29,100	13,450

PLAN **C**
Production plan

Period	Final inventory	Sales forecast	Production
0	3,000.00		
1	5,028.57	8,900	10,928.57
2	8,457.14	7,500	10,928.57
3	9,885.71	9,500	10,928.57
4	11,714.28	9,100	10,928.57
5	7,042.86	15,600	10,928.57
6	-3,228.57	21,200	10,928.57
7	0	7,700	10,928.57
8	3,328.57	7,600	10,928.57
9	357.15	13,900	10,928.57
10	4,428.57	11,700	15,771.43
11	0	20,200	15,771.43
12	2,400.00	29,100	31,500.00

Workforce

Period	Workforce	Hiring	Layoffs
0	225		
1	225	0	0
2	225	0	0
3	225	0	0
4	225	0	0
5	225	0	0
6	225	0	0
7	225	0	0
8	225	0	0
9	225	0	0
10	225	0	0
11	225	0	0
12	225	0	0

Workforce

Period	Workforce	Hiring	Layoffs
0	225.00		
1	182.14	0	42.86
2	182.14	0	0
3	182.14	0	0
4	182.14	0	0
5	182.14	0	0
6	182.14	0	0
7	182.14	0	0
8	182.14	0	0
9	182.14	0	0
10	262.86	80.71	0
11	262.86	0	0
12	262.86	0	0

Costs of the plan		
Hiring cost	$0	0%
Layoff cost	0	0%
Labour cost (regular rate)	6,480,000	76.30%
Overtime cost	0	0%
Carrying cost	2,013,000	23.70%
Stockout cost	0	0%
Total	**$8,493,000**	**100%**

Costs of the plan		
Hiring cost	$145,285.64	1.9%
Layoff cost	107,142.90	1.40%
Labour cost (regular rate)	5,826,856.00	76.37%
Overtime cost	943,716.06	12.37%
Carrying cost	526,428.50	6.90%
Stockout cost	80,714.31	1.06%
Total	**$7,630,143.50**	**100%**

5. The following is an aggregate production plan produced with a software package, followed by some relevant data. Answer the following questions, referring to this plan, and explain your answers as appropriate.

a) What is the production level in period 4?

b) What is the inventory level at the end of period 12?

c) How many units can an employee produce per month, working overtime only in periods 6, 7, and 8?

d) Calculate, in three different ways, the total labour cost for units produced by employees working overtime in periods 6, 7, and 8.

e) What is the cost of laying off an employee?

f) For practical reasons, the production manager decides to prepare a level plan rather than an aggregate plan. What will be the total labour costs at the regular wage rate for this level plan, based on the data provided in the previous answers?

g) Evaluate the production plan from the employees' standpoint. Will they be satisfied with it?

h) Prepare a trade-off analysis for unit costs of overtime hours as compared with inventory carrying costs.

Production plan

Period	Final inventory	Sales forecast	Production
0	500		
1	2,000	1,000	2,500
2	2,500	2,000	2,500
3	2,000	3,000	2,500
4	2,000	4,000	
5	1,000	5,000	4,000
6	0	6,000	5,000
7	0	6,000	6,000
8	0	5,000	5,000
9	0	4,000	4,000
10	0	3,000	3,000
11	0	2,000	2,000
12		1,000	

Workforce

Period	Workforce	Hiring	Layoffs
0	20		
1	20	0	0
2	20	0	0
3	20	0	0
4	32	12	0
5	32	0	0
6	32	0	0
7	32	0	0
8	32	0	0
9	32	0	0
10	24	0	8
11	16	0	8
12	16	0	0

Costs of the plan

Hiring cost	$18,000	1.61%
Layoff cost	24,000	2.15%
Labour cost (regular rate)	924,000	82.68%
Overtime cost		10.74%
Carrying cost	31,500	2.82%
Stockout cost	0	0%
Total	**$1,117,500**	**100%**

REFERENCES

1. FOGARTY, D.W., J.H. BLACKSTONE and T.R. HOFFMANN, *Production & Inventory Management*, 2nd ed. Cincinnati: South-Western Publishing, 1991.

2. SMITH, S.B., *Computer Based Production and Inventory Control*. Englewood Cliffs, New Jersey: Prentice-Hall, 1989.

3. VOLLMANN, T.E., W.L. BERRY and D.C. WHYBARK, *Manufacturing, Planning and Control Systems*, 2nd ed. Homewood, Illinois: Dow-Jones Irwin, 1988.

CHAPTER 6

Detailed Production Planning and Material Requirements Planning

CLAUDE R. DUGUAY, *main author*
MATTIO O. DIORIO, *contributor*

THE MASTER PRODUCTION SCHEDULE (MPS)

6.1   Dependent and Independent Demand

In the first part of this chapter we will discuss production planning for goods subject to independent demand, and describe the master production schedule, or MPS, and its role in the company. In the second part we will present some technical aspects of preparing and using the MPS. In the third part we will look at material requirements planning (MRP), which focuses on planning for dependent demand goods, from the same angle. Before we delve any deeper into this subject, however, we must make a distinction between *dependent demand* and *independent demand*. This difference is clearly explained by Joseph Orlicky,[6] one of the pioneers of MRP, a forerunner of the MRP II approach developed by Oliver Wight.[10]

Independent demand goods are those products or components (spare parts, options, accessories, etc.) that are delivered to the company's customers or intermediaries (wholesalers, distributors, agents, warehouses and so on). Independent demand is *estimated* on the basis of forecasts and confirmed orders (Figure 6.1).

Dependent demand goods are the subassemblies and components used to manufacture independent demand goods. Dependent demand is *calculated* on the basis of the planned production of finished products as set out in the MPS. For instance, the planned production of 1,000 bicycles, with independent demand, will lead to dependent demand for 2,000 wheels, 1,000 pedal assemblies, etc.

Individual items may fall into both categories—for example, a part that is used in manufacturing a product but is also sold to customers as a spare part. In such a case.

FIGURE 6.1 ▶
Independent and Dependent Demand

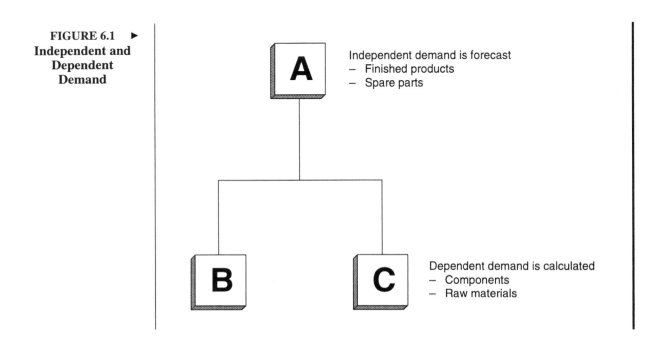

it is assumed to be subject to independent demand, but is placed at the appropriate level in the MRP process so as to meet all manufacturing needs.

6.2 Nature and Purpose of the MPS

Once the production plan is completed, the next step is detailed production planning. The purpose of the production plan is to determine the use of production capacity for all coming periods combined. For our purposes, we will use a month as the aggregate planning interval or period, and a week for detailed planning purposes. Although these are the periods most often used by companies, they may vary. A company must select planning periods that meet its specific needs. Detailed planning is used to determine what the company's production capacity will be used for—i.e., to what goods will production capacity be allocated for each of the coming weeks. The output of this detailed planning process is the MPS, which establishes the quantities of the firm's main products that will be manufactured in each period.

If a company manufactures a limited range of products and then carries them in inventory ("made to stock"), the MPS establishes what quantities of each finished product will be manufactured every week. In many cases there is such a variety of finished products—upholstered furniture, for instance—that final assembly will not take place until a confirmed order is received. In such cases, the company relies on a final assembly schedule to plan production. The MPS then serves as a basis for the manufacture of components and the acquisition of raw materials, and is drawn up according to types of finished products or the equivalent.

Generally speaking, the MPS is used to:
- establish and meet delivery dates;
- make efficient use of capacity;
- reach the objectives of the production plan;
- determine trade-offs between production and marketing.

The MPS has an essential role to play in the operation of an integrated production and inventory planning and control (PIPC) system. For each period, it offers the opportunity to establish a balance between the company's resources for that period and the demand to be met. Any unsolved problems that lead to backorders will prevent the company from following the MPS. By the same token, failure to implement the MPS will result in backorders. The MPS, then, is involved whenever there is any kind of disruption in production, such as delays, or in the sales environment, such as fluctuations in demand.

The MPS planning horizon includes at least the cumulative lead times for the manufacture and purchase of all components and raw materials required to produce the goods in question. Any changes in these lead times may mean that the company cannot order and receive the components within the necessary time limits.

The first objective of the person in charge of the MPS, or the Master Scheduler, is to provide good service—i.e., to deliver orders on time within a competitive lead time. The second objective is to make optimal use of resources, by carrying minimal inventory on the one hand, and ensuring that operating conditions guarantee efficient operations and purchasing on the other.

6.3   Role of the MPS in an Integrated Production and Inventory Planning and Control (PIPC) System

In an integrated production resources planning system, the production plan (PP) and the MPS are often included in the same closed-loop subsystem. In such cases, the activities in this loop begin with the preparation of the PP, which determines the aggregate rate of use of production capacity for each of the periods in question. The MPS allocates this capacity to various products or types of products[4] for more detailed periods (months, weeks), and must respect the aggregate capacity and aggregate inventory level stipulated in the production plan (Figure 6.2).

The information needed for preparing the MPS is obtained mainly from Marketing (demand forecasts, order entry), so that demand for each product or product type can be determined, and from the Inventory Management and Production Planning functions, so that supply, by which is meant the resources available to meet this demand (inventory, manufacturing) can be determined. Figure 6.3 gives an overview of these relationships upstream of the MPS.

FIGURE 6.2 ▶
The PP-MPS Loop

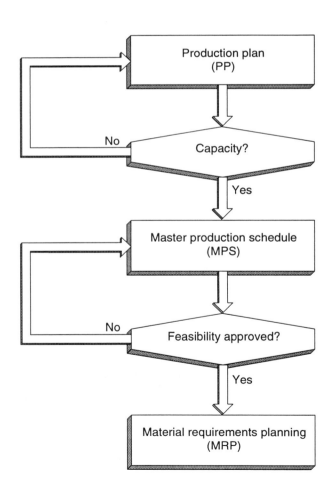

▼ **FIGURE 6.3**
Relationships between the MPS and Other Activities

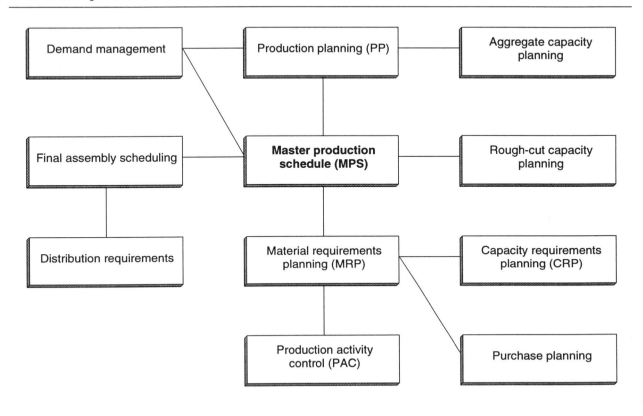

Source: Adapted from a figure by Fogarty.[5]

Based on this information and on company policy, the firm's planners draw up a preliminary version of the MPS for the coming periods. Then the feasibility of this version must be tested. Obviously, it must respect the aggregate capacity guidelines set out in the production plan. Experience has shown that it is also wise to ensure that the MPS is realistic for each of the key steps in the manufacturing process. This is the purpose of "rough-cut capacity planning."

Once it has been successfully tested, the MPS is used as an input for MRP, to calculate the components and raw materials required. The MPS is either a manufacturing schedule for finished products that have already been ordered or that can be considered sold, or an anticipated manufacturing schedule for finished parts and subassemblies, in cases where the company plans a to-order final assembly phase. As an input to the MRP process, the MPS allows planners to ensure that the necessary components and raw materials will be available when the time comes for final assembly.

Demand management will use the MPS on an item-by-item basis to determine when an order can realistically be accepted, or to evaluate whether the MPS should be revised in view of orders received from customers.

6.4   Strategic Choices and the MPS Environment

Delivery lead time is a key aspect of a company's position in the market. From this point of view there are three major types of production systems. When the delivery lead time is very short, the company must manufacture its finished products to be carried in inventory *make to stock*. When it can demand a delivery lead time longer than its own cumulative production lead time, it can manufacture goods to order *make to order*. When its delivery lead time falls between these two cases, the company manufactures some of its components for inventory and completes the finished products when it receives orders *assemble to order*. Figure 6.4 illustrates these three systems,[7] along with a fourth case, *engineer to order*.

FIGURE 6.4 ▶
Delivery and Production Lead Times and Positioning

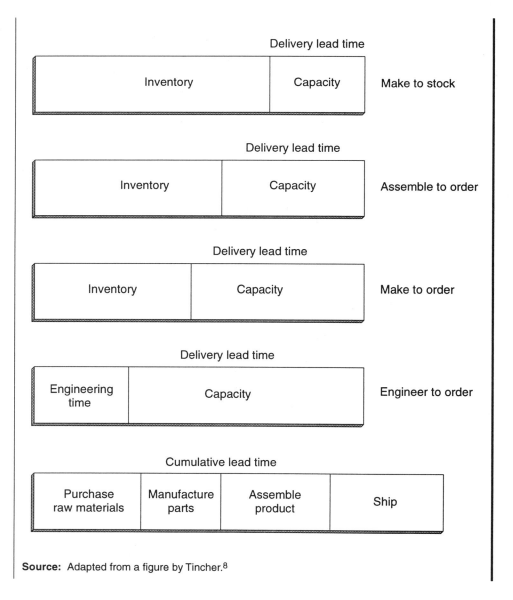

Source: Adapted from a figure by Tincher.[8]

The company's positioning depends a great deal on the nature of demand and competition. Although few companies will fall into just one of these groups for all their products, one group will tend to predominate.

The *first category* includes companies that make to stock, where managers have drawn up demand forecasts for all products. These companies then produce to meet these forecasts, and carry the finished products in inventory in the hope of selling the forecast quantities. It is the finished products that are to be carried in inventory that are considered in the MPS. Sales are tracked closely to ensure that forecasts are consistent with demand, the MPS and sales. Pharmaceutical companies and household appliance manufacturers fall into this category, as do McDonald's restaurants. Burger King restaurants, on the other hand, fall into the second category, since they assemble their sandwiches to order.

The *second category* takes in companies that assemble to order and have a short delivery lead time. Such companies hold subassemblies in inventory and use them to assemble finished products to match the customer's specifications. This approach calls for two plans: an MPS based on demand forecasts, used as a guide in manufacturing components; and a master assembly schedule based on actual orders and limited by the availability of the components in inventory. Manufacturers of automobiles, industrial machinery, heavy appliances and prefabricated houses all have these characteristics, along with upscale restaurants.

The *third category* consists of companies that make to order and have a long delivery lead time. Orders are most often unique, so neither components nor even raw materials, in some cases, are stockpiled. The final product design may not be completed until shortly before it is to be manufactured. In this case, the approach taken in managing the MPS is similar to that used in the critical path method. Given the importance of project planning and control, Chapter 8 is devoted to this method.

TECHNIQUES USED IN THE MPS

6.5 Preparing the MPS

Just as in production planning, a whole range of techniques is available for preparing the MPS, from simple planning grids to simulation models. We will describe a few of the most common basic tools and practices below, to illustrate the nature and scope of the MPS. We will then offer an example in the simplest category, making to stock, and discuss the key administrative considerations.

To produce an MPS, planners begin with the data available on demand, the aggregate available capacity as defined in the production plan, and indications for the aggregate level of inventory at the end of the period (Figure 6.3).

The MPS record shown in Figure 6.5 is the basic format for an MPS, and similar records are prepared for each product in question. These records allow planners to efficiently organize the information available for each product, and to project the expected trends in available inventory over the coming periods in the MPS horizon. In addition, they are similar in many respects to the planning grid shown in Chapter 3. We will first describe the various parts and then employ a simple example to show how these records are used. In the format recommended by the American Production.

FIGURE 6.5 ▶
Master Production
Schedule Record

	Period									
	1	2	3	4	5	6	7	8	9	10
Forecast demand										
Confirmed orders										
Projected inventory										
Inventory available to promise										
Planned production (MPS)										

FIGURE 6.5 ▶ Master Production Schedule Record

and Inventory Control Society (APICS), an individual record consists of five rows and a number of columns corresponding to the number of periods in the planning horizon. The horizon must be at least equal to the cumulative production lead time. A horizon of 13 weeks, corresponding to a quarter (three months), is frequently used in theoretical exercises, while in actual practice companies use a wide variety of records that often have one section for the near future, in weeks, and another part for the middle to long term, with longer intervals.

The first two lines give information on product demand: one shows demand forecasts for each of the periods in the horizon, and the other shows confirmed orders for these periods. The third line indicates the projected inventory at the end of each period, given the forecast demand and planned production; planned production is shown on the fifth line. The planned production results from prior decisions by the Master Scheduler, based on forecasts, available capacity, scheduling policy and production lead time for the product in question and all other products.

S_i is calculated using the following formula:

$$S_i = S_{i-1} + P_i - \max [F_i, C_i]$$

where S_i = inventory available at the end of period i,

   P_i = planned production for period i (available at the beginning),

   F_i = forecast demand for period i,

   C_i = confirmed orders to be delivered during period i.

When $F_i > C_i$, choosing $F_i = \max [F_i, C_i]$ assumes that forecast demand for period i will be met before reaching the period, even if confirmed orders are less than forecast demand at this time. When $F_i < C_i$, choosing $C_i = \max [F_i, C_i]$ means that for period i actual demand C_i exceeds forecast demand, for purposes of calculating the remaining inventory. The line for projected inventory on hand provides information for dealing with potential problems of adjusting to forecast demand and planned production.

When there is a negative quantity in period i on this third line, it indicates that if everything goes as planned from now until the period when the negative quantity appears, the company will suffer a stockout. To avoid this, it will either have to plan to produce more by period i or turn down orders for certain periods, which will cut sales to below forecast levels and so avoid exceeding the available quantities. In short, any negative quantity on this line indicates that production of this item will have to be increased or some orders will have to be refused in future.

The fourth line of the MPS record shows the quantities of the product that are still available to promise. This line is used mainly for managing demand once the MPS has been approved, and its importance and calculation will be explained in section 6.7.

Lines 3 and 4 on the record are calculated using the data provided in lines 1 and 2 and the decisions shown on line 5. A spreadsheet consisting of all the planning records can be very useful for quickly showing the impact of changes in demand or production or the consequences of the planners' decisions.

The MPS is prepared with two major goals in mind: avoiding stockouts and using all available capacity without exceeding it.

Where supply is concerned, planners can rely on various methods such as forward scheduling or backward scheduling to determine the use of capacity over time. In slack periods they can move some production up. In periods of excess demand planners must either find additional capacity or delay certain orders.

To determine the amounts to be produced, planners rely on scheduling techniques, but they must also be able to adapt their decisions to take account of available capacity and lead times.

The Hearright company, which makes three kinds of hearing aids, has asked you to come up with an MPS for the next 12 weeks, in keeping with the company's production plan.

The company provides you with some information to help you in your assignment.

— Forecast demand for the next 12 weeks is distributed as follows for the firm's three products:

	1	2	3	4	5	6	7	8	9	10	11	12
D	140	160	158	137	270	138	160	160	145	152	142	125
E	140	130	177	188	100	175	160	139	160	135	157	147
F	140	170	195	175	125	157	160	161	160	143	126	128
Total	420	460	530	500	495	470	480	460	465	430	425	400

Example*
■

*   Prepared by Carole Belazzi, research assistant, 1984.   ⟶

Example
(*cont.*)

- The orders received are as follows:

  Product D: 90, 100 and 50 for periods 1, 2 and 3;

  Product E: 120, 100 and 80 for periods 1, 2 and 3;

  Product F: 130, 120, 170 and 100 for periods 1, 2, 3 and 4.

  - The cost of each product is:

  Product D: $240

  Product E: $168

  Product F: $168

  - Annual inventory carrying cost is 20% of the value of the product.

In addition, the following information is available from the quarterly production plan.

- The normal work week for the next quarter is 40 hours, corresponding to 480 units per week.
- Quantities in inventory at the beginning of the quarter are:

  Product D: 200 units

  Product E: 280 units

  Product F: 320 units

Total: 800 units

- The production plan calls for an inventory of 1,000 units at the end of the quarter.
- Company policy prohibits overtime and subcontracting.
- Stockouts are not allowed.
- The setup cost is $4,000 and equipment is set up outside of normal working hours.
- The company can manufacture only one type of product at a time.

Solution

The first step is to draw up a preliminary MPS, without regard to constraints on capacity, using production lots of 480 units whenever the projected inventory on hand falls below zero. The MPS for product D is calculated as follows:

First, let us determine the projected inventory on hand, using the equation:

$$S_i = S_{i-1} + P_i - [F_i, C_i]$$

Period 1: $S_1 = 200 + 0 - 140 = 60$ where $P_i = 0$

Period 2: $S_2 = 60 - 160 = -100$; since S_2 is negative, the company must produce $P_2 = 480$; so $S_2 = 60 + 480 - 160 = 380$

Period 3: $S_3 = 380 - 0 - 158 = 222$

Period 4: $S_4 = 222 - 0 - 137 = 85$

Example
(cont.)

		1	2	3	4	5	6	7	8	9	10	11	12
		\multicolumn{12}{c}{**Period**}											
Forecast demand	F_i	140	160	158	137	270	138	160	160	145	152	142	125
Confirmed orders	C_i	90	100	50									
Projected inventory on hand (200)	S_i	60	380	222	85	295	157	477	317	172	20	358	233
Inventory available to promise	ATP_i	110	330			480		480				480	
Planned production	P_i		480			480		480				480	

Period 5: Since the forecast of 270 exceeds the projected inventory on hand of 85, the company must produce a lot of 480; so $S_5 = 85 + 480 - 270 = 295$, and so on for the other periods.

The next step is to calculate the inventory available to promise ATP_i – that is, the number of units that can be promised for delivery on a given date. ATP_i is calculated for the first period, whether or not there is planned production, and then only for periods when there *is* planned production (section 6.7).

For the first period, $ATP_i = S_0 + P_1 - C_1$

So $ATP_1 = 200 + 0 - 90 = 110$.

For the other periods, ATP_i is obtained by subtracting the C_i for the following periods from P_i up to the C_i of the next period when there is production, but not including that period.

$$ATP_2 = 480 - (100 + 50 + 0) = 330$$

$$ATP_5 = 480 - (0 + 0) = 480$$

$$ATP_7 = 480 - (0 + 0 + 0 + 0) = 480$$

$$ATP_{11} = 480 - (0 + 0) = 480$$

Proceeding in the same way for the other three products, we obtain the preliminary MPS shown in Figure 6.6.

Note that on the last line of Figure 6.6 there are periods that call for two setups, which conflicts with the last two constraints given in the problem data. Accordingly, the line for Planned production must be changed so that there is only one setup per period, still respecting the other constraints. Figure 6.7 shows the results. Since there have been changes in the production periods, there must also be

Example
(*cont.*)

changes in the projected inventory on hand and inventory available to promise. This solution is aimed above all at avoiding stockouts, and then at setting up equipment on the weekend. Although it is not optimal, it is acceptable, since it respects the constraints of the production plan.

▼ **FIGURE 6.6**
Preliminary MPS for Hearright

		Period											
		1	**2**	**3**	**4**	**5**	**6**	**7**	**8**	**9**	**10**	**11**	**12**
D	Forecast demand	140	160	158	137	270	138	160	160	145	152	142	125
	Confirmed orders	90	100	50									
	Projected inventory on hand (200)	60	380	222	85	295	157	477	317	172	20	358	233
	Inventory available to promise	110	330			480		480				480	
	Planned production		480			480		480				480	
E	Forecast demand	140	130	177	188	100	175	160	139	160	135	157	147
	Confirmed orders	120	100	80									
	Projected inventory on hand (280)	140	10	313	125	25	330	170	31	351	216	59	392
	Inventory available to promise	60		400			480			480			480
	Planned production		480	480			480			480			480
F	Forecast demand	140	170	195	175	125	157	160	161	160	143	126	128
	Confirmed orders	130	120	170	100								
	Projected inventory on hand (320)	180	10	295	120	475	318	158	477	317	174	48	400
	Inventory available to promise	70		210		480				480			480
	Planned production			480		480				480			480
	Setups	0	1	2	0	2	1	1	1	1	0	1	2

▼ **FIGURE 6.7**
Hearright MPS Grid

		Period											
		1	2	3	4	5	6	7	8	9	10	11	12
D	Forecast demand	140	160	158	137	270	138	160	160	145	152	142	125
	Confirmed orders	90	100	50									
	Projected inventory on hand (200)	540	380	222	565	295	157	477	317	172	20	358	233
	Inventory available to promise	440			480			480				480	
	Planned production	480			480			480				480	
E	Forecast demand	140	130	177	188	100	175	160	139	160	135	157	147
	Confirmed orders	120	100	80									
	Projected inventory on hand (280)	140	10	313	125	25	330	170	31	351	696	539	392
	Inventory available to promise	60		400			480			480	480		
	Planned production			480			480			480	480		
F	Forecast demand	140	170	195	175	125	157	160	161	160	143	126	128
	Confirmed orders	130	120	170	100								
	Projected inventory on hand (320)	180	490	295	120	475	318	158	477	317	174	48	400
	Inventory available to promise	190	90			480			480				480
	Planned production		480			480			480				480
	Setups	1	1	1	1	1	1	1	1	1	–	1	2
	Stockouts	–	–	–	–	–	–	–	–	–	–	–	–
	Total production	480	480	480	480	480	480	480	480	480	480	480	480
	Forecast production	480	480	480	480	480	480	480	480	480	480	480	480
	Discrepancy	0	0	0	0	0	0	0	0	0	0	0	0

The available capacity is fully used and it is expected that total inventory at the end of the horizon will be 1,025, or 25 more than was desired. There are no stockouts, although the projected inventory on hand for certain periods is fairly low—for instance, for product E in periods 2 and 8. There are 11 setups, since only one setup is necessary for product E in periods 9 and 10.

Proceeding by trial and error, it may be possible to find a better solution. Once the Master Scheduler feels that the plan is a good one, it will be submitted for approval to the heads of the Operations and Marketing functions.

6.6   MPS Approval

As with the production plan, the company's various departments, when preparing the MPS, must agree to work together as closely as possible (Tincher[8]). Once again, the objectives of each function do not always coincide (Figure 6.8).

Production and Purchasing favour an MPS that makes fairly even use of all available capacity and that requires few revisions, if any. They also prefer to have orders that fully respect the cumulative production lead time. Marketing for its part, would like an extremely flexible MPS, with 100% reliability for agreed delivery dates, to ensure full customer satisfaction. Experienced sales representatives know that the lead times used in planning are often approximations, and that it is possible to shorten them; this is not as true for companies for which reducing lead times is a strategic objective. And the Comptroller-Treasurer would like to reduce the investment in inventory.

▼ **FIGURE 6.8**
The MPS Loop

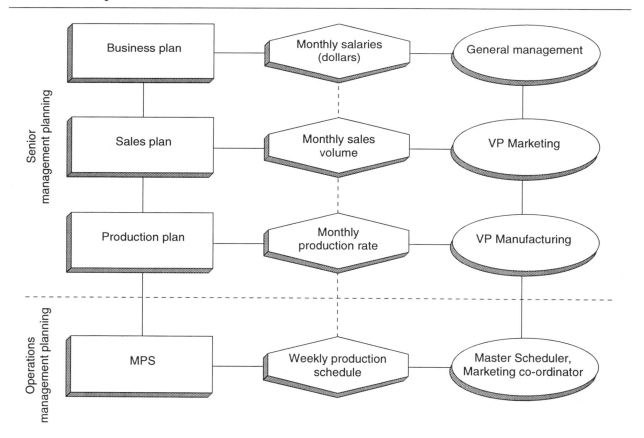

Source: Adapted from a figure by Tincher.[8]

No MPS can satisfy all the parties involved. The CEO and the management team, rather than the Master Scheduler, are responsible for deciding on the trade-offs that are often necessary. The Master Scheduler collects data, sketches out possible solutions and analyses the consequences of any trade-offs.

It is up to management to establish policies concerning the MPS, while the Master Scheduler develops the schedule in light of these policies, and the various functions involved must reach a consensus every week on the MPS for coming periods. This plan must then be updated and carefully adjusted to take account of any disruptive changes. An organization that cannot share responsibilities in this way and apply the necessary discipline cannot benefit from integrated operations management.

6.7   Putting the MPS into Practice: Administrative Aspects

Once the MPS has been approved, it serves as the basis for MRP—that is, planning the acquisition or production of components to be used in manufacturing the firm's finished products. If a company makes goods to stock, the MPS indicates when products will be available. If, on the other hand, it assembles to order, the MPS will indicate what subassemblies of components must be manufactured in order to assemble the final products that will be ordered, according to the firm's forecasts. Forecasts will be borne out little by little as orders are accepted for a certain date. The MPS, given the information it contains on inventory available to promise, is a valuable tool when deciding whether orders can be accepted, setting specific deadlines in routine cases and deciding on trade-offs in more complex cases.

The inventory available to promise is generally indicated section by section, with each section consisting of the period when the production of an item is planned and all the following periods until the next production run. Thus one section occupies one or more columns (periods) on an MPS record. If no production is planned for the first period, the first section consists of all the periods until the period when the first production run is planned. Only one number is shown in each section, and it is in the first period for the section. This number indicates the quantity from this section that is still available for future sales. For sections other than the first, the quantity available to promise is calculated as the difference between production for the period and the sum of the orders received during the periods in this section. This information is calculated using the following formula:

$$ATP_i = P_i - C_i - C_{i+1} - \ldots - C_{i+k-1}$$

where ATP_i = inventory available to promise at period i,

$\quad$ P_i $\quad$ = planned production for period i,

$\quad$ C_i $\quad$ = total quantity required for confirmed orders for period i,

$\quad$ $i + k$ = period of the next planned production run.

To simplify the appearance of the table, boxes in the "Inventory available to promise" line are usually left empty for periods in which there is no production.

The first section is a special case. The inventory available to promise, ATP_1, is calculated as follows:

$$ATP_1 = S_0 + P_1 - C_1 - C_2 - \ldots - C_{j-1} - \ldots - C_{k-1}$$

where S_0 = inventory at beginning of period 1,

P_1 = production planned for period 1,

C_j = total quantity required for confirmed orders for period j,

k = period of the next planned production run.

The use of an MPS record to manage orders is illustrated in the following example.

Example
■

Product MSL has a cumulative production lead time of four weeks, consisting of:

- one week for final assembly;
- one week for manufacturing the components;
- two weeks for acquiring raw materials and other components from outside suppliers.

After the MPS for the next seven periods is approved, the MPS record for product MSL is as follows.

MPS record Code: *MSL*							
	Period						
	1	**2**	**3**	**4**	**5**	**6**	**7**
Forecast demand	30	45	40	80	20	70	15
Confirmed orders	25	60	15	55	25	35	
Projected inventory on hand	10	50	10	30	5	35	20
Inventory available to promise	15	25		20		65	
Planned production		100		100		100	
Initial inventory: $S_0 = 40$							

Ms. Martin, the Master Scheduler, must use this information to answer the following questions:

1. Can she accept order No. 10, for 20 units of MSL for period 2?

2. Can she accept order No. 20, for 30 units for period 3, if she accepts order No. 10 in period 1?

3. Can she accept order No. 30, for 300 units for period 7?

Example (*cont.*)

1. Yes, because the inventory available to promise in period 2 is 25 units.

2. No, because after accepting order No. 10, there are only 20 units available to promise, 5 in period 2 and 15 in period 1.

3. Yes, if there is enough capacity, because she has the time to plan production based on the acquisition of raw materials.

Solution

Whenever a period ends, each record must be updated to reflect the passage of time, along with events that may have occurred and decisions that may have been taken.

Computers have now made it much easier to keep production schedules up to date. The problem no longer lies with processing the changes, but rather with their impact on the efficiency of production operations.

Most software programs update the schedule by regeneration *(regeneration MRP)*—that is, by calculating all the items at the end of each period. When computers were less powerful, the *net change MRP* was more common; only the elements affected by a transaction were recalculated, as the transactions occurred. This kept records constantly up to date, which is an advantage when there are few regenerations.

6.8 Changes in the MPS

Before integrated PIPC systems were introduced, making it possible to keep production plans and schedules on target, there was often a good deal of scepticism among the people in charge of putting them into practice. Continual changes within manufacturing companies made such schedules irrelevant shortly after they were approved. Despite this drawback, everyone had to work to carry out the agreed schedules. This led to the *order launching-expediting* approach.

Table 6.1 gives an idea of the multitude of changes that a manufacturing plant may be faced with. As can be seen, every occurrence may disrupt production plans.

But when, and to what extent, should production schedules be changed to reflect these events? There are three opinions: freeze the MPS for a certain number of periods, take a time-fence approach and adopt a system of confirmed planned orders.

A confirmed planned order cannot be changed automatically by the software; it must be changed by the planner. On redoing the calculations to take account of any

TABLE 6.1 ▶
**Ten Factors that
May Disrupt
Production Plans**

1. Delay by a parts supplier	6. Work stoppage
2. Urgent order from a major customer	7. Retooling
3. Defective tools	8. Absenteeism
4. New product	9. Waste
5. Engineering change order	10. Breakdown

Source: Factors derived from Buffa and Miller.[2]

changes that have occurred, the planner considers confirmed planned orders as data to be taken into account in decisions regarding other planned orders.

The time-fence approach, introduced in the 1970s,[8] was a major breakthrough in PIPC systems. These fences define time periods within which it is increasingly difficult to make changes.

The basic idea of time fences is that the later a change in the MPS occurs, the more difficult (or costly) it will be to implement. A time-fence policy is not intended to systematically prevent changes to the MPS required by Marketing in response to changing market trends, but rather to manage the changes made, by introducing discipline based on the costs and consequences of these changes, and to encourage Marketing and Production to agree on the policies and steps to be applied.

The elements in the cumulative production lead time for a given item make it possible to specify the time-fence policy for the item. Generally speaking, production lead time is broken down into three periods:

- assembly lead time;
- lead time for manufacturing components;
- lead time for acquiring raw materials or components from outside suppliers (Figure 6.9*a*).

Three time fences correspond to these three periods, reflecting the degree of difficulty involved in implementing these changes (Figure 6.9*b*).

- **Firm time fence:** Within this time fence, only emergency changes are allowed, and they require the approval of senior management; either one customer must be given precedence over another, or additional costs must be incurred to overcome the constraints imposed by normal lead times.

- **Mix time fence:** Within this time fence, changes may be made if the necessary materials and capacity are available. They remain fairly difficult, nonetheless, and require the consent of the Director of Materials.

- **Rate time fence:** Past this time fence, the Master Scheduler can redesign the schedule within the capacity parameters of the production plan. Within this time fence, options are limited by any purchased materials with long delivery lead times. Changes are relatively simple past this time fence, provided that they respect aggregate capacity constraints (Figure 6.9*b*).

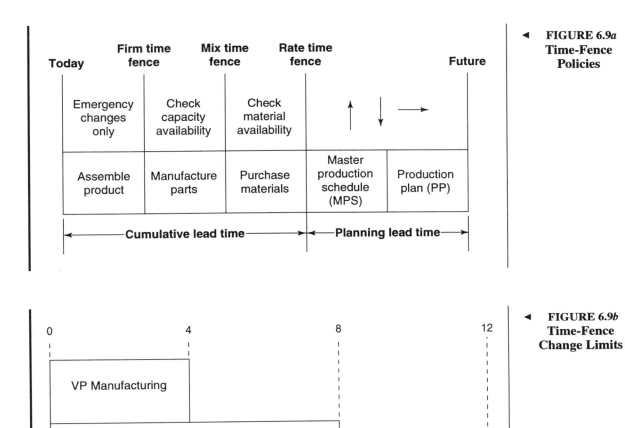

Source: Adapted from a figure by Tincher.[8]

6.9   Final Assembly and Planning Bills of Materials

The selection of units to be recorded is an important decision in managing the MPS. According to Vollmann,[9] this is one of the major interfaces between Marketing and Production. The choice depends mainly on two related factors, the variety of finished products and the delivery lead time. In section 6.4 we discussed the link between cumulative production lead time, delivery lead time and whether the company makes to stock, assembles to order or makes to order. In the latter case, the production of finished products is determined only shortly ahead of time, based on confirmed orders. The MPS is then drawn up by product type to calculate requirements in terms of parts.

For large lines of finished products, it my be necessary to include the entire group of products in the MPS, because of difficulties in forecasting demand for individual items. When a company offers a wide range of finished products, the demand for each product may well be relatively low and difficult, if not impossible, to forecast. Orlicky[6] gives the example of a farm tractor with 6,912 different possibilities, since 25 options are available for 11 different features: the arrangement of wheels, type of fuel, etc. It is easy to imagine how difficult it would be for Marketing to provide reliable forecasts for such a diversity of products! In general, it is easier to forecast sales of a product type than for each individual product, since variations in demand for individual products tend to even each other out.

When production must be determined on the basis of sales forecasts, because of the delivery lead time, and these forecasts are difficult to determine due to the extensive line of finished products, then products are grouped into subsets that can more easily be forecast; the units to be entered in the MPS are determined by means of planning bills of materials (BOMs). For MRP, product BOMs are replaced by planning BOMs. In the MPS, aggregate units (or superproducts) are used. This implies two planning operations, for:

- manufacture of components and subassemblies, mainly from *forecasts*, using planning BOMs;
- final assembly, mainly based on received orders, from the *BOM*s, reduced to components and subassemblies. This is carried out by means of a single-level BOM.

A more detailed treatment of these considerations would be beyond the scope of this book, but it is worthwhile noting their potential for linking the strategic and operational aspects of planning, thanks to advances in information technology combined with a thorough understanding of the production process.

6.10 Role of the Master Scheduler

The Master Scheduler plays a crucial role in carrying out the companys's plans. According to Wight,[10] he or she is the pivotal point between the Marketing and Production departments. Vollmann[9] gives a description of the Master Scheduler's duties in an integrated production planning and control system.

1. Oversees the maintenance of the information system, by adding records ou updating files with information to be included in the MPS (product bills of materials, inventory status, etc.).

2. Breaks down the production plan into a master production schedule (in actual units) so that decisions made on the basis of the MPS conform to the PP and other plans.

3. Analyses problems and submits those that do not fall under his or her responsibility to senior management.

4. Monitors sales and completed production and compares these data with plans, to make any necessary corrections and determine what steps should be taken to cope with delays.

5. Contributes to diagnoses of problems in the company by explaining the effects on the MPS.

6. Co-operates with the Order Entry and Sales Forecasting department.

7. Co-operates with the Production Control department to evaluate the feasibility of changes in capacity.

8. Keeps plans constantly updated to maintain efficiency up to the end of the period, taking capacity constraints into account.

9. Co-operates closely with the Marketing manager, the Production manager and the Planner, who contribute the data and different viewpoints necessary for drawing up the MPS.

MATERIAL REQUIREMENTS PLANNING (MRP)

6.11 Role of Material Requirements Planning

Material requirements planning (MRP) serves as the interface between detailed operations planning and short-term scheduling (Figure 6.10). Its role is to determine the amounts to be produced, along with manufacturing, assembly and order dates for items subject to dependent demand—that is, raw materials and components—so as to produce the quantities stipulated in the MPS the proper time. MRP is used to co-ordinate the fabrication and procurement of the goods the company has agreed to deliver and the production operations that must be carried out to complete these orders on schedule. In many firms that turn out complex products such as automobiles, televisions, computers or washing machines, this is an essential step in overall co-ordination.

Although MRP is a simple concept, it could not be applied efficiently to operations until the advent of computers. Joseph Orlicky is considered to have refined the knowledge that led to the popularity of MRP,[6] and consultants Oliver Wight and George Plossl, with the support of the American Production and Inventory Control Society (APICS), are credited with promoting the training that led to its widespread use. The introduction of computers into factories has led to a whole new approach to production methods, and the considerable training required to achieve the desired success.

Computers were initially used only to calculate net requirements for components and raw materials, on the basis of the planned quantities of finished products in the MPS and inventory on hand.

It quickly became clear that the system could be used for much more than simply accounting for materials. It could also be used to plan the release of orders for components and to make the adjustments to releases necessitated by various disruptions over a given period. If a component was not available when it came time to assemble the finished product, the rapidity of the system made it possible to shift priorities and to reschedule production.

The basic idea of rescheduling to keep production on track was made reality by the development of the *closed loop MRP* system, which was enhanced by combining priorities planning with MRP and the company's aggregate business plan. Thus the system has extended to the planning of production resources and has become commonly known as *manufacturing resources planning*, or *MRP II*.[1]

FIGURE 6.10 ▶
MRP: Between
Operations
Planning and
Short-Term
Scheduling

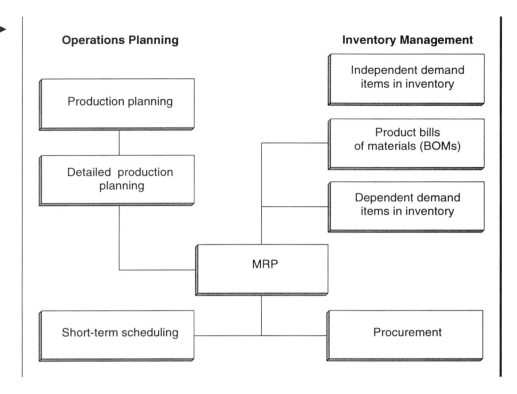

MRP is now used as much for planning as for control—i.e., for following up on various steps and details. In this context, control is also intended to remedy any serious departure from the schedule (usually a delay), in particular if it may mean changes to the MPS. MRP is also used to direct the use of resources; once the manufacturing quantities and dates and the order dates are known, short-term scheduling can proceed.

In short, MRP is designed to answer three questions:

1. What components or raw materials will the company need in order to carry out the MPS?

2. How many units of each item must be purchased and manufactured, given the inventory on hand?

3. When should purchase orders be placed, and when should manufacturing begin?

These questions are answered by "exploding" each product in the MPS and by establishing production and procurement schedules, taking care to properly offset the lead times for the delivery, manufacturing and assembly of these items. The quantities calculated by MRP are taken directly from the MPS forecasts. As a result, the accuracy of the MPS affects the validity of the planned production quantities specified by MRP. The close links between MRP and the MPS highlight the dependent demand for components and raw materials. These calculations are reviewed periodically in the light of events.

The speed of computers makes such reviews possible. Another important technological advance for MRP is the improvement in data capture and transmission—remote terminals, bar codes, etc., which speed up operations and reduce errors. The information provided by the system is thus more up-to-date and accurate.

6.12 Lumpy Demand

Dependent demand may be relatively stable. If weekly demand for a specific item identified in the MPS is stable, it is assumed that demand for components and raw materials will be as well. But management efforts to synchronize different demands may lead to instability. For instance, the company may plan to produce a given type of item only once every four weeks, in which case derived demand is no longer stable. This is termed *lumpy demand*, or demand characterized by sudden variations. Figure 6.11 shows the difference between stable weekly demand and lumpy demand. Three weeks with no demand is followed by one week with demand. Note that if the figure represented time in four-week periods rather than one week at a time, even the lumpy demand would actually appear fairly stable.

Lumpy demand may be *dependent* or *independent*; *stable* or *unstable*; *regular* over time or *random*. It is considered stable when there is little variation from one period to another, and regular when the time interval between orders is fixed, or almost fixed. All these types of demand have different consequences for the manager. Lumpy demand that is dependent, stable and regular makes it easier to plan the use of productive resources. However, independent demand must be forecast, and this becomes more complex if it is largely unstable. Planning for large orders received on a random basis is more difficult. This type of order, particularly in the manufacturing sector, corresponds to dependent lumpy demand that results directly from independent lumpy demand (orders).

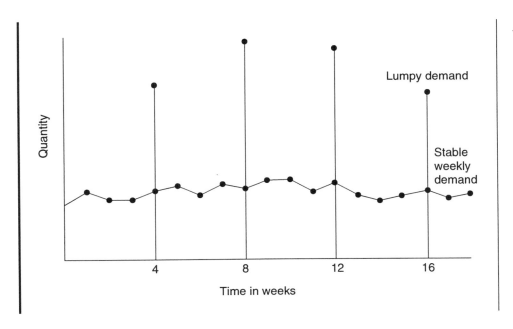

◄ **FIGURE 6.11
Stable versus
Lumpy Demand**

OPERATION OF THE MRP SYSTEM

6.13 System Inputs

An MRP system requires three main inputs to make the development of an MRP possible: the MPS, the BOM, and inventory levels. Manufacturing and assembly lead times and delivery lead times for raw materials are also essential information, and are recorded for each item in the master inventory file. Figure 6.12 provides the information necessary into drawing up an MRP. It is impossible to prepare an acceptable plan if any of the three inputs is missing or out of date. We will now take a brief look at each of these inputs.

The first input, the *master production schedule* (MPS), specifies the quantities of finished products that must be manufactured or assembled to meet forecast demand. Management must first verify that production capacity is available to meet MPS requirements. The desired quantity of finished products influences gross requirements for components, which are calculated with product BOMs.

FIGURE 6.12 ▶
Main Inputs to the MRP System

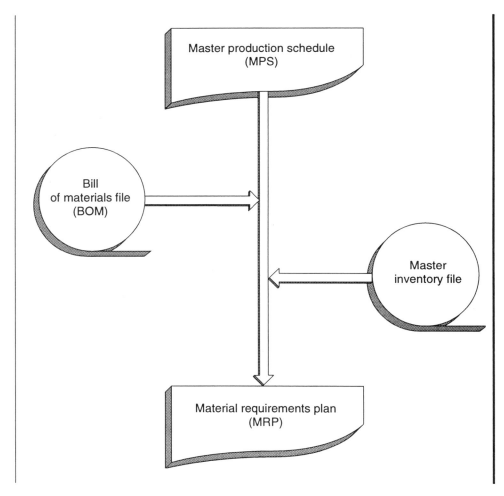

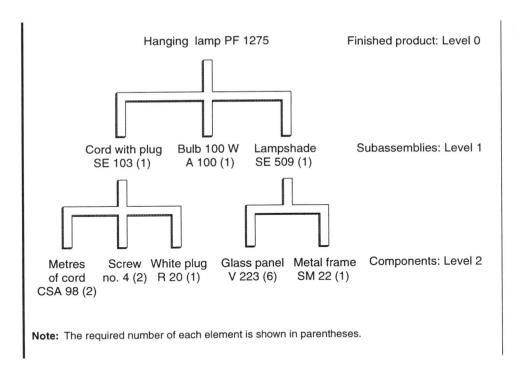

Hanging lamp PF 1275   Finished product: Level 0

Cord with plug   Bulb 100 W   Lampshade   Subassemblies: Level 1
SE 103 (1)   A 100 (1)   SE 509 (1)

Metres   Screw   White plug   Glass panel   Metal frame   Components: Level 2
of cord   no. 4 (2) R 20 (1)   V 223 (6)   SM 22 (1)
CSA 98 (2)

Note: The required number of each element is shown in parentheses.

◄ **FIGURE 6.13**
Bill of Materials in Tree Form for a Hanging Lamp

The second input is the bill of materials (BOM) file, which lists and describes all the materials and components that go into the products to be manufactured or assembled by a company. Item A, assembled from one or more components, is called the *parent item*. It may be an assembled finished product, such as a table, or a subassembly that is itself part of another product, such as an aircraft engine. The BOM shows the product structure in the form of a tree or a list. It details the links between the raw materials, components and subassemblies that make up a finished product.

Figure 6.13 shows the BOM, in tree form, for a hanging lamp, while Figure 6.14 gives the BOM for the same product in list form. Six components are required to assemble the finished product.

The types and code numbers of these components must be clearly identified. There is also an intermediate level that corresponds to the assembly of both the lampshade and the electric cord with plug. For example, the lampshade is assembled from six glass panels (V 223) and one metal frame (SM 22). Items used directly in making the finished product are at level 1. Items used directly in making level 1 items are at level 2, and so on. An item used in the assembly of both a finished product and a component is listed at the lower of the two possible levels.

There is a detailed BOM for each finished product, and it must be updated in order to avoid the ordering or manufacture of components that are either obsolete or unnecessary. The purpose of regular updating is not to group together the components required for manufacturing or assembling various products. Such grouping is carried out only when the MRP is drawn up; the BOM is just one input of this plan. A detailed example will be provided later to illustrate this point.

FIGURE 6.14 ▶
**Bill of Materials
(BOM) in List
Form for a
Hanging lamp**

Hanging lamp	PF 1275	← Level 0
Description	Number	Total quantity in the product
Cord with plug	SE 103	1
Cord (in metres)	CSA 98	2
Screw	4	2
Plug	R 20	1
100 W Bulb	A 100	1
Lampshade	SE 509	1
Glass panel	V 223	6
Metal frame	SM 22	1

Level 1   Level 2

Computers are indispensable for updating BOMs and for MPS computations when there is considerable variety or complexity in the structure of the finished product. To facilitate computations, each component and subassembly must have its own unique identification number and code.

The third input, the master inventory file, provides information about the quantities of each of the items, components and subassemblies on hand, quantities of components on order but not yet delivered, acquisition lead times, lot sizes, safety stock, etc. It is essential that the information in the inventory file be complete and accurate, so that the net requirements for each item can be determined. The *net requirements* are calculated by subtracting the number of items in inventory from the gross requirements. If the quantity on hand is over- or underestimated, the repercussions of any error are absorbed by the net requirements amount, thereby undermining the advantages of MRP. At this step, since the objective is to determine the order and production or assembly release dates, and to determine the input quantities required to draw up MPS, the different lead times must be known. In fact, it is to compensate for these lead times that net requirements are offset.

Even though the number of hours, days or weeks of lead time must be known before the MRP can be draw up, it is sometimes difficult to determine all of them accurately. The more stable the actual lead times, the easier it is to determine them. However, if lead times vary substantially, which one should be used? A lead time that is set higher than that forecast will result in a longer and more costly carrying period, and a lead time set too low can result in stockouts and delays in manufacturing, assembly and product delivery. In both cases the objective of the MRP—to co-ordinate production and procurement efforts—will not be met. Accordingly, the reliability of external and internal supplier deliveries is particularly important.

Overall, the quality of the system's performance depends heavily on the quality of the information used in the MRP system. No effort must be spared to ensure the completeness and accuracy of all inputs, as they are essential to the effective operation of the system. Figure 6.15 gives an overview of MRP.

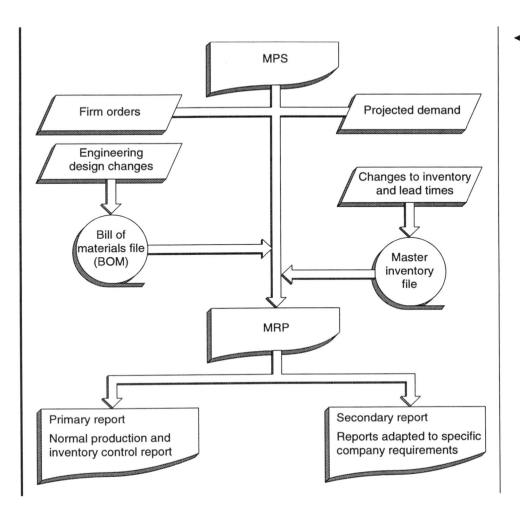

6.14 Preparing an MRP

Obtaining approval of the MPS and updating the input files for the MRP are the first essential steps in material requirements planning. The plan is prepared in successive levels, beginning with level 1 items—that is, the components that go directly into a finished product. As Figure 6.13 shows, level 0 is assigned to the finished product.

For each of the items at a given level, the chart shown in Figure 6.16 is used, representing the MRP record. There are as many records as there are items subject to dependent demand. Sometimes, to simplify the presentation of the MRP, a record is also completed for level 0 items, which simplifies analysis if it becomes necessary to reschedule orders because of unforeseen circumstances. However, releases at level 0 are not calculated with this system, but rather are determined by the MPS.

The first line in a record for an item shows the *gross requirements* for each of the periods in the time horizon, stemming from production decisions affecting all parent items at higher levels. These gross requirements are calculated using the product BOM for each of the parent items and the planned order releases for these items.

FIGURE 6.16 ▶
Record for MRP

	Period							
	1	2	3	4	5	6	7	8
Gross requirements								
Scheduled receipts								
Projected available balance								
Net requirements								
Planned order receipts								
Planned order releases								

The second line, *scheduled receipts*, indicates the quantities of this item stipulated in orders that have been already released, but that will not be completed until the period in which the quantity is shown. The other four lines are used for calculations and decision-making.

The *projected available balance* shows the inventory available at the end of each period, to meet gross requirements for later periods. Two different formulas are used to calculate this quantity, depending on whether the net requirements (NR) are positive or nil. The net requirements are calculated as follows:

$$NR_i = \max[(GR_i - RU_i - D_{i-1}), 0]$$

where NR_i = net requirements calculated for period i,

D_i = inventory available at the end of period i,

RU_i = orders scheduled for receipt at the beginning of period i,

GR_i = gross requirements calculated for period i,

PR_i = planned order receipts for the beginning of period i.

First case: $NR_i = 0, D_i = D_{i-1} + RU_i - GR_i$

Second case: $NR_i > 0$, that is, when $D_{i-1} + RU_i < GR_i$, the gross requirements for a period exceed the amount of inventory from the previous period and the quantity scheduled for receipt in period i; thus there are *net requirements* for this period, indicating a potential stockout. If there are no plans to produce the goods needed for the period, a stockout will indeed occur. Normally, a company will plan to cover these net requirements by producing sufficient goods during or before this period, depending on the offset corresponding to the lead time. The last two lines indicate *planned order releases* and the corresponding *planned order receipts*. Thus we have:

$$D_i = PR_i - NR_i$$
$$= PR_i - GR_i + RU_i + D_{i-1} + PR_{i-1}$$

Each of the records at the level in question must be completed before the next level can be approached. To move on to the following level we start from the quantities on the *planned order releases* line to calculate the gross requirements for the following level by exploding the BOMs. The example below illustrates these calculations.

Properly speaking, the MRP consists only of the *planned order releases* lines from each record. This line indicates when the purchase or manufacturing orders for each item are to be released, and in what quantities. However, it is often useful to have a wider view of the situation, as can be obtained from the complete record. The following detailed example is limited to two items sold by a lighting company and just a few periods in the planning horizon.

Example
■

The MPS for a small company called Lighting Inc. specifies that 30 lamps each of type PF 1275 and PF 1380 are to be delivered in week 6, along with 20 PF 1275 lamps in week 4, and 15 PF 1380 lamps in week 5. The production manager, who must draw up an MRP, decides to prepare the plan manually since there are only two products: hanging lamps PF 1275 and PF 1380.

The company manufactures the metal frames for the lamps and assembles all the lamps, because many customers prefer to assemble the lamps themselves. The on-hand inventory and delivery and the manufacturing lead times are shown in Figure 6.17 and the BOM is given in Figure 6.18. The company has decided that it will produce lampshades and their components on a lot-for-lot basis (Section 6.16), because they are needed for only these two finished products. Finally, a delivery of 100 units of V 323 is expected in period 3.

	On-hand inventory	Delivery and manufacturing lead time (weeks)
Finished products		
Lamp PF 1275	10	1
Lamp PF 1380	–	1
Subassemblies		
Cord with plug SE 103	30	2
Cord with plug SE 104	3	2
Lampshade SE 509	52	1
Lampshade SE 540	3	1
Light bulb 100 watts A 100	200	–

◄ **FIGURE 6.17 Inventory Record and Delivery and Manufacturing Lead Times**

⟶

Example
(*cont.*)

	On-hand inventory	Delivery and manufacturing lead time (weeks)
Components		
Metres of cord CSA 98	1,000	–
Screw no. 4	1,000	1
White plug R 20	60	1
White plug R 24	20	1
Glass panel V 223	23	3
Glass panel V 323	12	3
Metal frame SM 22	7	2
Metal frame SM 29	3	1

▼ **FIGURE 6.18**
Product Structure of Lamps

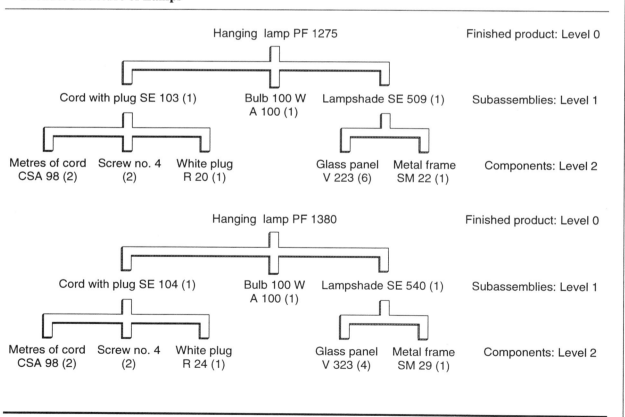

Level 0 consists of two items, lamps PF 1275 and PF 1380. For this level, only the *planned order releases* line counts, and it is given by the MPS.

At level 1 are five items—cords with plug SE 103 and SE 104, lampshades SE 509 and SE 540, and light bulb A 100. The records for these items can be completed with the above information. For cord with plug SE 104, the *gross requirements* are shown in periods 4 and 5. They correspond to the planned order releases at the higher level for lamp PF 1380 for these two periods. The gross requirements for SE 104 in period 4 are 15, since the product BOM shows that each PF 1380 lamp requires a single cord with plug SE 104. The gross requirements for SE 104 in period 5 are 30 for the same reasons. We can see that the BOM for the product is used to make the link between the planned releases of a parent item at one level and the resulting gross requirements for components at the next level. Try placing the records one under another to visualize the links between the levels established by these BOMs (Figure 6.19).

Example (*cont.*)

◀ **FIGURE 6.19 MRP Sheet**

Item no.	Lot size	Lead time	On-hand	Safety stock	Reserved	Level
PF 1275 Lamp	L/L	1	10	–	–	0*

Date:	Period						
	1	2	3	4	5	6	7
Gross requirements				20		30	
Scheduled receipts							
Projected available balance	10	10	10	0	0	0	
Net requirements				10		30	
Planned order receipts				10		30	
Planned order releases			10		30		

Item no.	Lot size	Lead time	On-hand	Safety stock	Reserved	Level
PF 1380 Lamp	L/L	1	0	–	–	0*

Date:	Period						
	1	2	3	4	5	6	7
Gross requirements					15	30	
Scheduled receipts							
Projected available balance	0	0	0	0	0	0	
Net requirements					15	30	
Planned order receipts					15	30	
Planned order releases				15	30		

* Level 0 is the level of items subject to independent demand for which planning is done in the MPS. These charts are for information purposes only.

Example
(*cont.*)

Item no.	Lot size	Lead time	On-hand	Safety stock	Reserved	Level
SE 103 Cord with plug	L/L	2	30	–	–	1

Date:	Period						
	1	2	3	4	5	6	7
Gross requirements			10		30		
Scheduled receipts							
Projected available balance	30	30	20	20	0		
Net requirements					10		
Planned order receipts					10		
Planned order releases			10				

Item no.	Lot size	Lead time	On-hand	Safety stock	Reserved	Level
SE 104 Cord with plug	L/L	2	3	–	–	1

Date:	Period						
	1	2	3	4	5	6	7
Gross requirements				15	30		
Scheduled receipts							
Projected available balance	3	3	3	0	0		
Net requirements				12	30		
Planned order receipts				12	30		
Planned order releases		12	30				

Item no.	Lot size	Lead time	On-hand	Safety stock	Reserved	Level
SE 509 Lampshade	L/L	1	52	–	–	1

Date:	Period						
	1	2	3	4	5	6	7
Gross requirements			10		30		
Scheduled receipts							
Projected available balance	52	52	42	42	12		
Net requirements							
Planned order receipts							
Planned order releases							

Example
(*cont.*)

Item no.	Lot size	Lead time	On-hand	Safety stock	Reserved	Level
SE 540 Lampshade	L/L	1	3	–	–	1

Date:	Period						
	1	2	3	4	5	6	7
Gross requirements				15	30		
Scheduled receipts							
Projected available balance	3	3	3	0	0		
Net requirements				12	30		
Planned order receipts				12	30		
Planned order releases			12	30			

Item no.	Lot size	Lead time	On-hand	Safety stock	Reserved	Level
A 100 Light bulb 100 W	L/L	–	200	–	–	1

Date:	Period						
	1	2	3	4	5	6	7
Gross requirements			10	15	60		
Scheduled receipts							
Projected available balance	200	200	190	175	115		
Net requirements							
Planned order receipts							
Planned order releases							

Item no.	Lot size	Lead time	On-hand	Safety stock	Reserved	Level
CSA 98 Metres of wire	L/L	–	1,000	–	–	2

Date:	Period						
	1	2	3	4	5	6	7
Gross requirements		24	80				
Scheduled receipts							
Projected available balance	1,000	976	896				
Net requirements							
Planned order receipts							
Planned order releases							

Example
(cont.)

Item no.	Lot size	Lead time	On-hand	Safety stock	Reserved	Level
Screw no. 4	L/L	1	1,000	–	–	2

Date:	Period						
	1	2	3	4	5	6	7
Gross requirements		24	80				
Scheduled receipts							
Projected available balance	1,000	976	896	816			
Net requirements							
Planned order receipts							
Planned order releases							

Item no.	Lot size	Lead time	On-hand	Safety stock	Reserved	Level
R 20 White plug	L/L	1	60	–	–	2

Date:	Period						
	1	2	3	4	5	6	7
Gross requirements			10				
Scheduled receipts							
Projected available balance	60	60	50				
Net requirements							
Planned order receipts							
Planned order releases							

Item no.	Lot size	Lead time	On-hand	Safety stock	Reserved	Level
R 24 White plug	L/L	1	20	–	–	2

Date:	Period						
	1	2	3	4	5	6	7
Gross requirements		12	30				
Scheduled receipts							
Projected available balance	20	8	0				
Net requirements			22				
Planned order receipts			22				
Planned order releases		22					

Example
(*cont.*)

Item no.	Lot size	Lead time	On-hand	Safety stock	Reserved	Level
V 223 Glass panel	L/L	3	23	–	–	2

Date:	Period						
	1	2	3	4	5	6	7
Gross requirements*							
Scheduled receipts							
Projected available balance							
Net requirements							
Planned order receipts							
Planned order releases							

* No gross requirements, since there are still SE 509 lampshades on hand.

Item no.	Lot size	Lead time	On-hand	Safety stock	Reserved	Level
V 323 Glass panel	L/L	3	12	–	–	2

Date:	Period						
	1	2	3	4	5	6	7
Gross requirements			48	120			
Scheduled receipts			100*				
Projected available balance	12	12	64	0			
Net requirements				56			
Planned order receipts				56			
Planned order releases	56						

* An order for 100 has been released, and is scheduled for receipt in period 3.

Example
(cont.)

Item no.	Lot size	Lead time	On-hand	Safety stock	Reserved	Level
SM 22 Metal frame	L/L	2	7	–	–	2

Date:	Period						
	1	2	3	4	5	6	7
Gross requirements*							
Scheduled receipts							
Projected available balance							
Net requirements							
Planned order receipts							
Planned order releases							

* No gross requirements, since there are still SE 509 lampshades on hand.

Item no.	Lot size	Lead time	On-hand	Safety stock	Reserved	Level
SM 29 Metal frame	L/L	1	3	–	–	2

Date:	Period						
	1	2	3	4	5	6	7
Gross requirements			12	30			
Scheduled receipts							
Projected available balance	3	3	0	0			
Net requirements			9	30			
Planned order receipts			9	30			
Planned order releases		9	30				

Example
(*cont.*)

Once the gross requirements have been identified for SE 104, the other parts of the record may be calculated using the data on inventory and orders in progress and the planning factors given in the example. The inventory of SE 104 in periods 1, 2 and 3 remains at three units. In period 4, the gross requirements of 15 absorb the inventory of three units and create net requirements of 12 units. To avoid a stockout, the company must cover these requirements with the planned receipt of at least 12 units. To have this delivery planned in period 4, the company must release a manufacturing order two weeks beforehand, since the manufacturing lead time for SE 104 is two weeks. Since the company has adopted a lot-for-lot policy for this item, the planned quantity for this release is exactly 12. With this release planned in period 2, the projected available balance at the end of period 4 will be 0. Thus the company will have a projected inventory of 0 to meet the gross requirements of 30 in period 5, meaning that there will be net requirements of 30 for this period. These net requirements must be covered by the planned receipt of 30 units in period 5. For this delivery to take place, a release of at least 30 units in period 3 must be planned. And with the lot-for-lot policy, the release will be exactly 30 units. Since there are no other gross requirements for SE 104 after period 5, planning is completed for this item.

We proceed in the same way for each of the level 1 items, and then move on to level 2, and so on, until we reach the lowest level. MRP is based on a series of simple and systematic calculations that are well suited to computer processing. Given the multitude of items and the frequency of events that make updating necessary, a computer system is in fact essential in performing the necessary calculations quickly and making the appropriate adjustments to operations.

The example of the lamps illustrates the basic concepts underlying the operation of MRP. On the one hand, the net requirements at one level become the gross requirements at the following level, once the appropriate adjustments are made to take account of the quantities in the product BOM; on the other hand, operations at one level begin when operations at the previous level are completed.

It is interesting to note the effect of higher-level stock on the amounts to be ordered, assembled or manufactured at lower levels—stock can serve to reduce planning needs considerably. For instance, the requirements for 50 PF 1275 lamps could have led to an order for 300 V 224 glass panels. However, none was required, since there are no net requirements for lampshade SE 509, which is part of PF 1275.

6.15 System Outputs

The outputs of an MRP system result from calculations of dates and quantities, and are presented in the form of MRPs and various reports. The efficiency of the MRP will depend on how the planner uses these reports.

The plan is the main MRP output. It consists of all the MRP records prepared for individual items. It serves as the main input in capacity requirements planning (CRP), to determine its feasibility. In addition, the plan is used to draw up action reports for manufacturing or purchase orders. Any planned order releases must be transformed into orders when they reach period 1 in the planning chart.

The immense memory and great speed of computers make it possible for the system to readjust priorities by issuing exception and pegging reports. *Exception reports* are intended to focus attention on items that call for immediate attention so that the planner can recommend the appropriate corrective steps.

Pegging reports make it possible to retrace gross requirements back to their source at any time. As Orlicky says,[6] the ability to track gross requirements is extremely valuable in making planning decisions such as which deliveries of finished products should be delayed in the event of a stockout or in rescheduling the arrival of components whose assembly has been delayed. They are also used to determine the production lot of an item, for purposes of quality control or completion control, particularly in the military, pharmaceutical, nuclear and aerospace industries.

The planning and replanning possibilities, to take account of internal or external disruptions, offered by MRP are why it has been extended beyond simply accounting for materials, as was originally intended.[6] MRP is a key module in a dynamic system that makes it possible to combine a vast amount of data and number of decisions into a coherent, up-to-date whole. Decisions on updating the system are some of those important ones, and we will look at this topic in the next section.

TECHNICAL ASPECTS OF MRP

6.16 Frequency of Updating and Lot Sizing

Updating is an essential feature of MRP, to ensure validity of system outputs. When should the plan be updated? Whenever new information becomes available, when conditions change, or at regular intervals?

Two approaches are used by managers in making this decision: *partial planning* (net-change MRP) and *total planning* (regeneration MRP). In the net-change method, only those aspects affected by a change in information are updated, and such modifications are made as soon as a change is known. With the regeneration method, all modifications are made at a predetermined time, often weekly. Thus there is a trade-off to be made between the cost and the benefits of updating.

Net-change MRP provides up-to-date but costly information. However, lower data-processing costs have made this approach significantly less expensive.

Nevertheless, Vollmann *et al.*[9] have found that the most common practice is still weekly regeneration, no doubt because the cost of excess information is underestimated in theory and also sometimes in practice. This cost, as well as those of updating and of less-effective decisions based on outdated information, must be evaluated by each company, taking its particular situation into account. Lower data-processing costs are an important benefit of regeneration.

The lot size to be manufactured is as important to determine as frequency of updating. Orlicky[6] described various methods, all of which are still in use today. Since that time, research on the subject has often concentrated on trying to prove that one method is more appropriate than another by attempting to generalize from specific cases.

	Period									
	1	**2**	**3**	**4**	**5**	**6**	**7**	**8**	**9**	**Total**
Net requirements	50	30	–	10	20	5	–	35	30	180
Planned orders										
1. Lot-for-lot	50	30	–	10	20	5	–	35	30	180
2. Economic order quantity (EOQ)	80	–	–	80	–	–	–	–	80	240
3. Period order quantity (POQ)	90	–	–	–	60	–	–	–	30	180

◀ **TABLE 6.2**
Some Lot-Sizing Techniques

The MRP identifies when items should be available to satisfy demand at the next level. Should an order be placed to fill quantity requirements for each period or for a group of periods? Carrying costs, ordering costs, variability of demand and the planning horizon must all be considered.

The simplest lot-sizing method is *lot-for-lot*, which consists of buying or manufacturing lots that meet the exact net requirements for the period. Table 6.2 illustrates this method as well as the other two that will be described in this section. The lot-for-lot method reduces carrying costs, but fails to consider ordering costs, which could be higher because one order is placed in each period in which net requirements occur. It is often used in mass or continuous production, and is particularly appropriate when demand is very discontinuous. In situations where a high purchase price leads the company to order small lots, this method is also justified. If need be, orders can be placed more than once during a given period if ordering or setup costs have been reduced significantly, as is often the case with just-in-time systems.

The *economic order quantity (EOQ)* method balances ordering and carrying costs to come up with the optimal order quantity—i.e., the quantity that minimizes these two costs. For the EOQ method (which is described in Chapter 3) to be applied successfully, a number of conditions must apply, including the assumption that demand is uniform and constant. This technique can yield excellent results when actual conditions match the assumptions closely enough. The following example shows how this method works. However, the notion of net requirements does not seem to be applicable to the model. Note that the demand distributed over the nine periods corresponds to approximately 9/52 of the annual demand of 960 units: Is demand discontinuous to the point of rendering the model inapplicable?

Where annual demand is 960 units, ordering costs $40 and carrying costs $1 per month per unit, the EOQ is as follows:

$$\sqrt{\frac{2 \times 960 \times 40}{12}} = 80 \text{ units}$$

With this method, the quantity to be ordered is greater than that arrived at using the lot-for-lot method. Total ordering costs are lower, but carrying costs rise because there are units on hand at the end of most periods.

Period order quantity (POQ) is the last technique we will examine here. It is most often used when demand is both unstable and distributed throughout the year. The POQ is based on a time interval between orders, which is computed using the EOQ model. It corresponds to the number of periods that inventory equal to the EOQ could cover, on average, and is calculated as follows:

$$POQ = EOQ = \text{Annual demand} \times \text{Number of periods in the year}$$

Accordingly, in the above example, this gives:

$$\frac{80}{960} \times 52 \text{ weeks} = 4.33 \text{ weeks, or about 4 weeks.}$$

This does not mean that an order should be placed every four weeks, but rather that an order should be calculated to satisfy the net requirements for four weeks. The POQ method usually results in lower costs than the EOQ, because of the balance between net requirements and the timing of orders placed at a fixed monthly frequency. The quantities ordered cover only what will be consumed during the time periods, or "time buckets," before the next order is placed.

Table 6.3 uses an example to detail the costs related to each of the above methods. Only nine time buckets are included in the calculation of costs. A longer planning horizon and different data could modify not only total costs but also the ranking of the three methods.

The example does not take into account the offsetting of demand. The order dates should be modified to take delivery lead times into consideration. Fixed lead times affect only order dates, and not costs.

TABLE 6.3 ▶
Ordering and Carrying Costs Related to Lot-Sizing Methods

	Ordering costs	Carrying costs	Total costs
Lot-for-lot 7 @ $40 0 @ $0.25	$280	–	$280
Economic order quantity (EOQ) 3 @ $40 310* @ $0.25	$120	$77.50	$197.50
Period order quantity (POQ) 3 @ $40 170* @ $0.25	$120	$42.50	$162.50

Assumptions: 1) The inventory carrying costs are $1 per month or about $0.25 per period.

2) Only the units on hand at the end of the period incur carrying costs.

	Period									
	1	2	3	4	5	6	7	8	9	Total
Quantity on hand according to EOQ	30	–	–	70	50	45	45	10	60	= 310
Quantity on hand according to POQ	40	10	10	–	40	35	35	–	–	= 170

At least six other lot-sizing techniques have been developed. The three best known are *least unit cost*, *least total cost* and the *Wagner-Within algorithm*. These techniques make it possible to simultaneously vary lot sizes and planning periods. Buffa and Miller[2] and Orlicky[6] provide more detail on this subject. Orlicky holds that, where costs are concerned, one method is almost as good as another when the uncertainty of future demand (even when dependent, it is not known in advance) and the characteristics of each company are considered. From an administrative point of view, however, fixed-quantity methods are more advantageous in that only the date, and not the quantity, need be altered if an order is changed. This makes for a less "nervous" system.

After carefully examining their own requirement, managers will find that only two or three methods are applicable and worthy of more thorough examination. It is doubtful that any one method will be clearly superior for an extended period; managers must be attentive to the changing conditions under which these techniques are applied.

6.17 Importance of Safety Stock

Safety stock helps reduce the uncertainties of independent demand. In theory, safety stock is unnecessary where demand is dependent, for once independent demand has been estimated, dependent demand is known. In practice, however, safety stock is often used, even in an MRP context. There are a number of reasons for this.

Components that are difficult to procure or that have long delivery lead times are sometimes ordered in larger quantities than specified by the lot-sizing method used. In fact, despite efforts to plan level 0 products, some users are sceptical of the validity of forecasts and the logic of the system. However, there are no grounds for this scepticism.

Indeed, safety stock is justified in only two instances of dependent demand: when a certain percentage of components is rejected as substandard, or when there are variations in delivery lead times. In both cases, it is essential that components be ordered in sufficient quantities to satisfy demand at higher levels. The problem becomes even more complicated when there is a given rate of substandard items or losses at many phases in the production cycle. Simulation then becomes a valuable technique for computing the stockout probability of different items. Choosing the appropriate stockout level depends on the costs involved. Because stockout costs may be high, most managers prefer to have a higher, rather than lower, level of safety stock.

The closer a stockout is to level 0 in a product structure, the more expensive it is. The value of work in process includes not only the costs of raw materials and components, but also labour and some overhead. For this reason, it is normally expected that the quantity of safety stock will be greater at higher levels in a product structure.

The use of safety stock and the production of sufficient lots to satisfy demand for many days ahead naturally run counter to the just-in-time approach explained in Chapter 9, the objective of which is to eliminate inventory.

However, the MRP approach only goes as far as reducing unnecessary quantities of dependent demand items. It seems difficult to reconcile such an objective with the existence of excessive inventory levels. MRP can improve the rate of inventory turnover, especially when no additional quantities are incorporated into inventory unless they are justified by MRP calculations.

OTHER MRP APPLICATIONS

6.18 MRP and the Service Sector

It has long been thought that MRP applications were limited to the manufacturing sector, with its tangible and stockable products. However, recent studies show that extending MRP to the service sector is not only possible but beneficial.

Planning resource requirements for a university academic year, for instance, is a complicated undertaking. Cox and Jesse[3] applied MRP to higher education. They believed that planning the number of courses more accurately and assigning students to courses more effectively could optimize the short-term use of teaching staff. In the longer term, it would be possible to plan and control resources by using course enrolment forecasts. Figure 6.20 shows the planning and control activities at the various steps.

First, the independent demand—the number of graduates per term—must be estimated. Next, various approaches are developed to create a feasible aggregate plan. By considering the major options chosen in each program for each term, it is possible to create an master curricula schedule (equivalent to an MPS). The next step is the preparation of a preliminary course priority requirements plan (equivalent to an MRP), using as inputs the bill of courses file (equivalent to a BOM file) and student record file. The resulting plan is then compared with available faculty and classroom capacity, and this iteration is repeated until satisfactory results are obtained.

MRP has also been used in the health-care environment. Steinberg *et al*[7] studied MRP in the context of surgical requirements in a hospital. Table 6.4 summarizes the analogy between a hospital and the manufacturing context, with specific reference to the three main inputs to the MRP system.

The *first input* is the weekly surgery schedule. The names of the surgeons responsible for specific operations (products) are listed on the schedule. Since two surgeons performing an identical operation may require different sets of surgical instruments, MRP identifies these operations as two different "products." The *second input* is a file listing the surgical materials and supplies requested by a surgeon for each operation. The *third input* is the inventory file, which can be broken down into disposable items, reusable instruments and sophisticated high-technology instruments. The surgical operations and their characteristics determine the nature of the inventory file.

TABLE 6.4 ▶
Comparing MRP Inputs in a Hospital and in Manufacturing

Hospital system	Manufacturing system
Weekly schedule of surgical operations	MPS organized by period
Surgical material and supply requirements file	BOM file, including components
Inventory file, including instruments	Inventory file

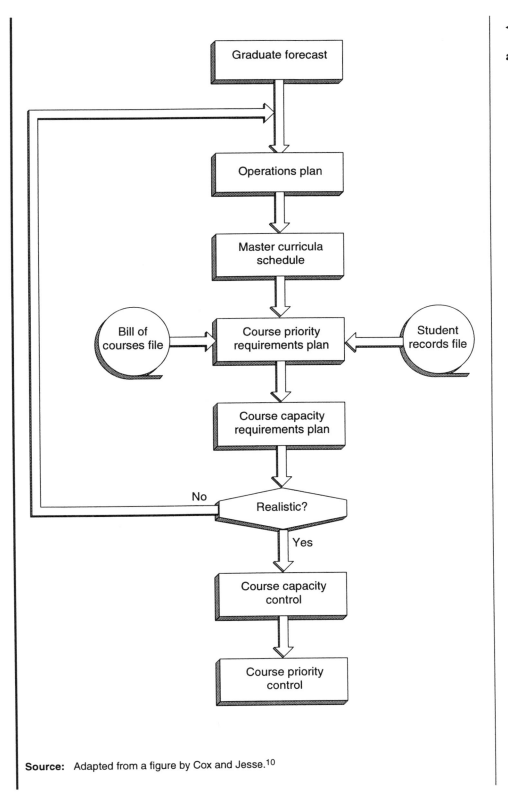

◄   **FIGURE 6.20**
Applying MRP in
a University Setting

Source: Adapted from a figure by Cox and Jesse.[10]

Applications of MRP in the service sector are promising and will most likely contribute to improved customer service and reduced costs. MRP can contribute greatly to improved co-ordination of planning and control in the service sector. Once again, it can be seen that an open-minded attitude can lead to valuable applications.

6.19 Feasibility of MRP and Capacity Requirements Planning

To be useful, it is essential that an MRP be feasible. It must be possible to carry out planned production in the planned periods. When an MRP is being prepared, the system determines planned order releases by considering only net requirements for components, internal or external delivery lead times and lot sizes. It does not take account of available capacity at the plant or at suppliers' facilities. The plan is drawn up on the assumption of unlimited capacity.

Capacity requirements planning (CRP) prepares a profile of the workload at each work centre, making it possible to identify workstations where the workload exceeds the available capacity. Capacity requirements are calculated by exploding releases in the MRP using routing for items, similar to the explosion of releases in the MPS using product BOMs. Taking the operating rules at the plant into account, the various operations necessary are distributed to each work centre.

Once the load profile has been drawn up on the assumption of unlimited capacity, capacity planning is completed by looking for solutions to any problems identified, such as too much or too little work. Some orders can be shifted to even out the work flow; other measures such as overtime, assigning a larger number of workers, etc., are also possible. If these corrective steps cannot overcome the problems identified, it will be necessary to review the MPS or to allocate more production resources than stipulated in the production plan. These extraordinary steps are sometimes necessary to keep the plan feasible. However, the details of capacity planning and control lie outside the limits of this textbook.

Once the MRP is sufficiently realistic, the planner can begin carrying it out, by releasing the purchase or manufacturing orders indicated in period 1 and triggered by the system. The next phases are capacity control and priority control, which lead us to short-term scheduling.

Planners must also ensure that the system runs smoothly and improve it where possible by identifying, analysing and eliminating causes of error.

REVIEW QUESTIONS

1. What is the purpose of MRP?

2. Where does MRP fit in with all the various production and inventory planning and control activities?

3. What information is required before the MRP can be drawn up?

4. How is the MRP different from the MPS?

5. Why do we distinguish between dependent and independent demand?

6. What are the main functions of MRP?

7. How could MRP be used in the service sector?

1. How does MRP simplify the planning of capacity and scheduling priorities?

2. Why is it suggested that safety stocks are necessary only for independent demand?

3. Is it true that the planning horizon for MRP must be equal to or greater than the sum of delivery and production lead times? Why or why not?

4. In a computerized company, why does MRP not always give the expected results?

5. Can MRP benefit every company?

6. Are the introduction of increasingly powerful computers and the decline in information-processing costs likely to make business planning obsolete?

7. How can the MPS guide managers in deciding whether to accept new orders from customers?

PROBLEMS AND CASE STUDIES

1. A company manufactures product B, with the following bill of materials (BOM):

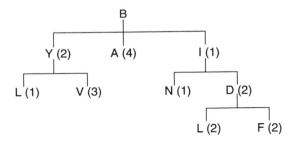

a) According to this BOM, what are the net requirements for part L, if sales of 1,000 units of B are forecast and the available inventory at all levels is zero?

b) Why do gross requirements not always equal net requirements?

c) Is this BOM adequate for a material-requirements explosion? Justify your answer.

2. The A.R. Turner company assembles products A, B and C, among others, from components 1, 2 and 3 and raw materials 4, 5 and 6.

    –   Product A requires one No. 2 unit and two No. 3 units.

    –   Product B requires two No. 1 units and five No. 5 units.

    –   Product C requires two No. 1 units, one No. 2 unit and two No. 3 units.

    –   Each of these components requires the following quantities of raw materials:

Component	Raw materials		
	4	5	6
1	0	1	2
2	1	0	2
3	3	2	1

    –   Inventory breaks down as follows:

Product	Quantity	Component	Quantity	Raw material	Quantity
A	0	1	10	4	40
B	20	2	20	5	0
C	40	3	30	6	50

    –   Delivery lead time is nil.

– Forecast demand for the next four weeks is:

Week	Finished products		
	A	B	C
1	10	20	20
2	10	20	0
3	0	10	20
4	10	0	10

a)   Explode the material requirements, using the above information.

b)   Give the BOMs for products A, B and C.

3.   The product line of a manufacturer of CD players consists of three different models. The MPS for the next four weeks (October) is as follows:

Model	Week			
	1	2	3	4
Do	160	220	280	110
Re	120	180	130	90
Mi	110	140	220	170

The company manufactures all the components and all the finished products, and obtains its raw materials from outside suppliers. However, following an unforeseen production surplus and the purchase of surplus raw materials justified by temporary price reductions on the market, the projected inventory in hand for the end of September is as follows:

	Inventory (units)	
Finished products	Do	40
	Re	37
	Mi	12
Components	1	15
	2	30
	3	120
	4	25
Raw materials	A	400
	B	250
	C	390

The delivery lead time for raw materials is one week, except for unit B, for which the lead time is two weeks. Suppliers are generally reliable. Once the inputs have been received, it takes one week to assemble the components.

a)   Prepare a BOM. Using this and assuming that the MPS begins in three weeks, draw up the MRP in keeping with the MPS, while maintaining the inventory level as low as possible.

b)   If the MPS came into effect immediately, what problem would the company have?

4.   A company that manufactures two products is having a very hard time planning production. You have been asked to help it in its MRP, based on the MPS it has just drawn up for the next eight weeks.

	Period							
	1	2	3	4	5	6	7	8
Product A	0	0	10	20	80	100	100	0
Product B	0	0	0	75	75	0	50	50
Component X	10	5	10	5	10	5	10	5
Component Y	0	0	50	50	0	0	50	50

In addition, you have been given the following information:

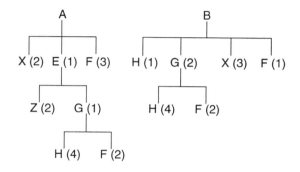

	Lead time (weeks)	Inventory available	Lot size
A	1	0	lot for lot
B	1	0	lot for lot
E	1	120	125
F	1	40	50
G	1	200	250
H	2	100	200
X	2	150	200
Z	2	0	lot for lot

a) Explode the company's material requirements.

b) What product is subject to dependent demand? To independent demand?

c) Why is it preferable to use the MRP method to prepare the material requirements plan?

d) Does the economic order quantity (EOQ) method apply in this context? Explain your answer.

5. The planning grid for Rheo Ltd. is shown below, for the next 10 weeks, for products A and B. You, as Planning Director, have to decide:

a) What are the BOMs for product A and product B?

b) According to these BOMs, how many X and Y are required to manufacture 100 A and 100 B?

c) The company has brought forward net requirements for raw material X by two weeks and net requirements for raw material Y by three weeks. What information is necessary to determine the offset time?

		Week									
		1	2	3	4	5	6	7	8	9	10
Product A											
Gross requirements									160	200	100
Inventory									(160)	(50)	
Net requirements									–	150	100
Offset requirements								150	100		
Product B											
Gross requirements*								100	–	50	–
Offset requirements							100		50		
Component K											
Gross requirements (A)								600	400		
Gross requirements (B)							200		100		
Total gross requirements							200	600	500		
Inventory							(100)				
Net requirements							100	600	500		
Offset requirements					100	600	500				

* An offset in gross requirements (rather than in net requirements) means that there will be no inventory available.

	Week									
	1	**2**	**3**	**4**	**5**	**6**	**7**	**8**	**9**	**10**
Component L										
Gross requirements (B)						100		50		
Offset requirements						100		50		
Component M										
Gross requirements (A)							300	200		
Gross requirements (B)						300		150		
Total gross requirements						300	300	350		
Offset requirements					300	300	350			
Raw material X										
Gross requirements (K)				300	1,800	1,500				
Gross requirements (L)						200		100		
Gross requirements (M)					300	300	350			
Total gross requirements				300	2,100	2,000	350	100		
Inventory				(300)	(1,600)					
Net requirements				–	500	2,000	350	100		
Offset requirements			500	2,000	350	100				
Raw material Y										
Gross requirements (L)						300		150		
Gross requirements (M)					600	600	700			
Total gross requirements					600	900	700	150		
Offset requirements		600	900	700	150					

6. The table below shows the net requirements for a component for the next 12 periods. It costs $100 to manufacture this component. Every setup costs $50. The carrying cost is 5% of the manufacturing cost.

    a) At present the company uses the lot-for-lot method to determine lot sizes. Is this recommended for this type of company? Why or why not?

    b) What other methods could the company use to determine lot sizes? Why?

    c) Apply these different lot-sizing methods. Which method do you think is best?

	Period											
	1	**2**	**3**	**4**	**5**	**6**	**7**	**8**	**9**	**10**	**11**	**12**
Component X	60	40	0	80	35	0	30	100	0	25	100	30

7. An industrial refrigerator manufacturer makes five models, each with a different production lead time. Forecast demand is constant every quarter. The table below summarizes the situation.

On January 1, the company has 40 employees who work eight hours every working day.

a) What equivalent unit should the company choose to have the smallest cumulative discrepancy, for the year, between available capacity and the requirements shown below?

b) In your opinion, does the company have enough workers? Justify your answer.

Model	Jan.–March	April–June	July–Sept.	Oct.–Dec.	Total	Hours per worker per unit
A	150	750	600	300	1,800	8
B	150	180	270	300	900	20
C	300	300	300	300	1,200	12
D	600	300	225	225	1,350	14
E	150	150	300	450	1,050	10

8. The GOP company makes two models of screwdriver. The BOMs given below are for these two models. The tables also contain other information you will need for your analysis.

Product/ part	Inventory on hand	Production/ assembly lead time	Procurement lead time
A	0	1.0	1
B	200	0.2	2
C	50	1.0	1
D	100	0.3	3
E	300	0.4	3
F	50	0.2	2

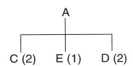

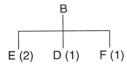

a) What are the net requirements for component D over the next six periods?

b) How many setups will there be?

c) What factors sometimes cause gross requirements to differ from net requirements?

		Period											
Requirements		1	2	3	4	5	6	7	8	9	10	11	12
A					35		95	60	75	20	50	10	50
B			20	30	10		65				45		35	105

9. Two product models (regular and deluxe) are to be manufactured over the next eight weeks. Each unit of the regular model represents two equivalent units, and each unit of the deluxe model represents three. Weekly production capacity is 1,500 equivalent units. Demand forecasts and confirmed orders for the next eight weeks, for each model, are given *in actual units* in the following table.

				Week				
	1	2	3	4	5	6	7	8
Regular model								
Forecast	200	200	200	300	300	400	400	400
Orders	220	170	150	200	140			
Deluxe model								
Forecast	250	250	400	400	250	250	300	300
Orders	300	200	200	300	250	300		

Initial inventory is 50 units of the regular model and 100 units of the deluxe model.

a) You have been asked to prepare an MPS to satisfy demand with no stockouts and conform to the weekly capacity. Complete all the rows of the chart for the two products. Assume that there is no setup time.

b) In preparing an MRP, you have to choose between the fixed-quantity lot (multiples of three units) and economic period methods. Ordering costs are $96 per order, and unit carrying costs are $0.48 per week. You must meet the following net requirements:

Assuming that there is no delivery lead time, draw up a schedule of planned launchings to meet requirements for the next 12 weeks, according to the two lot-sizing methods.

Which of the two methods has lower total costs (ordering cost + carrying cost)? How much less expensive is it than the other method?

						Week						
	1	2	3	4	5	6	7	8	9	10	11	12
Net requirements	40	10	0	0	60	50	0	40	15	10	35	40

10. A furniture manufacturer is offering a special promotion to all retailers, on condition that orders be placed immediately. The promotion applies only to two new types of furniture, for which there is no inventory at present. They are assembled in the week that components become available.

The orders resulting from the promotion are shown in the following MPS.

	Week		
	22	23	24
Type of furniture			
Traditional	60	90	100
Modern	20	70	50

The components and key raw materials are as follows.

Components/raw materials	Inventory	Lead time (weeks)
1	0	1
2	50	2
X	110	1
Y	300	2
Z	0	0

The product BOM is as follows for the key elements:

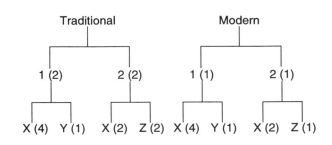

Draw up the MRP necessary to carry out the MPS shown.

---

11. The manager of a company that manufactures two finished products is having a hard time planning. She asks you to help with her MRP, based on the MPS that she has just prepared for the next eight weeks.

	Period							
Product	1	2	3	4	5	6	7	8
A	0	0	10	20	80	100	100	0
B	0	0	0	75	75	0	50	50

She also gives you the following BOM:

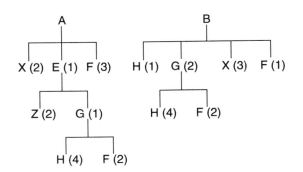

	Lead time (weeks)	Inventory available	Lot size
A	0	0	lot for lot
B	0	0	lot for lot
E	1	120	125
F	1	40	50
G	1	200	250
H	2	100	200
X	2	150	200
Z	2	0	lot for lot

Lead times, inventory and lot sizing for the finished products, components and raw materials are shown in the opposite table.

a) What products are subject to dependent demand? To independent demand?

b) Prepare the MRP.

12. Lightco makes two types of meters, AA and BB, for measuring home electricity consumption. They are assembled from subassemblies C and D and raw materials E and F, according to the BOM shown below.

In addition to complete meters, Lightco sells subassembly D and raw material E separately, since they are used for repairs and certain options. The quantities of D and E sold are added to the required quantities for assembling finished products AA and BB. The following orders have been received for the coming weeks:

	Period				
Product	9	10	11	12	13
AA				1,212	999
BB				800	808
D				650	669
E				325	239

The BOM for the products is as follows:

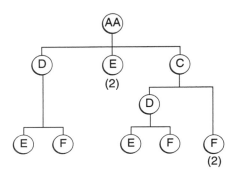 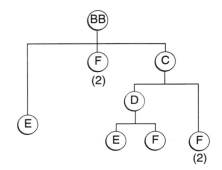

Numbers in parentheses show the quantity of lower-level elements in a higher-level element. The default quantity is (1).

The inventory file is as follows:

Prepare an MPS for AA and BB meters and an MRP for subassemblies C and D and raw materials E and F, using the lot-for-lot sizing method.

Product	Quantity on hand	Delivery or assembly lead time
AA	169	3
BB	42	2
C	21	1
D	118	1
E	11	1
F	539	1

13. The BOM for product F 414 is as follows:

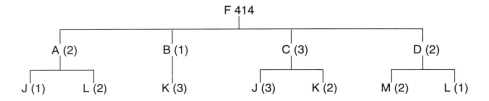

a) How many J, K and L components are needed to make 200 F414s, if there are none in inventory now?

b) When producing subassembly C, the average scrap factor when components J and K are welded is 5%. What quantities of J and K should be produced so that the necessary quantities of assembly C can be manufactured?

REFERENCES

1. BELT, B., *Cinq étapes pour la planification des capacités avec MRP*. Paris: Cabinet Bill Belt S.A., 1987.

2. BUFFA, E.S., and J.G. MILLER, *Production-Inventory Systems: Planning and Control*. Homewood, Ill.: Richard D. Irwin, 1979.

3. COX, J.F., and R.R. JESSE Jr., "An Application of Material Requirements Planning for Higher Education," *Decision Sciences*, Decision Sciences Institute, Georgia State University, April 1981, pp. 240-260.

4. DE VILLERS, M.-É., *Dictionary of Production and Inventory Management*. Montreal: Éditions Québec/Amérique, 1993.

5. FOGARTY, D.W., J.H. BLACKSTONE and T.R. HOFFMANN, *Production and Inventory Management,* 2nd ed. Cincinnati, Ohio: South Western Publishing, 1991.

6. ORLICKY, J., *Material Requirements Planning*. New York: McGraw-Hill, 1975.

7. STEINBERG, E., B.M. KHUMAWALA and R. SCAMELL, "Requirements Planning Systems in the Health Care Environment," *Journal of Operations Management*, August 1982.

8. TINCHER, M.G., "Master Scheduling: The Bridge between Marketing and Manufacturing," David W. Buker Inc., Illinois, 1980.

9. VOLLMANN, T.E., W.L. BERRY and D.C. WHYBARK, *Manufacturing, Planning and Control*, 3rd ed. Homewood, Ill.: Richard D. Irwin, 1992.

10. WIGHT, O., *Réussir sa gestion industrielle par la méthode MRP II*. Paris: CEP Éditions, 1984.

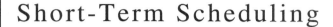

CHAPTER 7

Short-Term Scheduling

CLAUDE R. DUGUAY
JEAN NOLLET, *authors*

CONTEXT OF SHORT-TERM SCHEDULING

7.1   Definition and General Objectives

Short-term scheduling is the planning of production in the very short term, over a period of from one week or less for small and medium-size production runs, to several months for the production of a single item such as a ship or an aircraft. In the latter case, the approach used is closer to *project management*, which is the subject of Chapter 8.

More specifically, the purpose of short-term scheduling is to determine the *sequence* in which all the *work* involved in producing the good or providing the service will be done or in which orders will be processed. The schedule indicates where and when each task will be carried out. The output of this process is a detailed schedule of activities for the operations system in the coming periods.

In a service company such as a clinic or a garage, short-term scheduling consists of a series of activities that are not part of an aggregate planning and control system. In manufacturing (an industrial shop), on the other hand, short-term scheduling is one of the key aspects of production activity control (PAC), which in turn is part of the production and inventory planning and control (PIPC) system.

The main *objectives of short-term scheduling* are to:

- improve customer service in terms of quantities to be delivered, delivery deadlines and product quality;

- fill orders at the lowest cost while minimizing inventory, reducing in-process inventory, controlling priorities and optimizing the use of all available resources;

- take account at all times of the needs and well-being of employees.

Short-term scheduling is intended to help the company fill orders while meeting primary and sometimes secondary objectives. Performance criteria are used to measure the extent to which these objectives have been met. The company cannot hope to meet all its objectives at the same time, since some will conflict with others. Thus there are major trade-offs to be made, based on the firm's operations and corporate strategies.

For example, a company normally strives for a certain balance between low inventory, high efficiency and effectiveness, and satisfactory customer service. Low inventory reduces investments in raw materials, in-process inventory, finished products and storage space; consequently, production costs are lower, pushing down the price for the customer. However, the risk of stockouts can jeopardize efficiency and customer service. A shortage of raw materials or work in process can bring production to a halt (reduced efficiency) and lead to poorer customer service (delays in delivery), just as a stockout of finished products can jeopardize customer service. On the other hand, high efficiency minimizes inventory and improves customer service (on-time delivery). All in all, the key objective may be fast delivery, low prices or some other goal, and trade-offs will be made according to how they contribute to meeting this objective.

PRODUCTION ACTIVITY CONTROL (PAC)

7.2   The Role of PAC in the PIPC System

Production activity control (PAC), also called *shop floor control* when it applies to discontinuous production, comprises the various principles, approaches and techniques used by managers in planning, scheduling, controlling and evaluating the efficiency of production operations. In short, PAC is the control of the manufacturing activities defined earlier by means of the master production schedule (MPS), material requirements plan (MRP) and capacity requirements plan (CRP).

PAC is the execution or control step in the PIPC system. For PAC to work properly, and thus allow the company to meet its objectives, there must be sufficient information from the various steps in the planning phase (MPS, MRP and CRP), which are in fact the inputs to PAC. The MRP provides the information necessary to fill orders (what to produce, how much, and when, where and how), but does not consider the capacity of the system. Thus CRP is necessary to ensure that the MRP is realistic.

Once the required capacity has been determined, PAC can begin. Its three main phases are:

- *dispatching* (job orders) according to the MRP; the company must first ensure that the resources to be used (raw materials, labour, machines and tools) are available;
- *scheduling orders*, which includes allocating work to the workstations, drawing up reports on production activities and taking corrective action as necessary;
- *closing orders*.

More specifically, *dispatching* means that a job order must first be released and various documents assembled (routing sheet, orders for setups, drawings, etc.) to accompany the move ticket. The shop manager must ensure that the order can be filled on time, by checking the availability of materials, labour, machine time and tools, as well as other considerations.

Once the job order has been released, the shop manager monitors its progress and reports all information relevant to operations sequencing. Progress is measured with reference to the deadlines set in the MRP and is shown on the list of work to be done at each workstation. This list *schedules orders* by priority. According to scheduling principles such as the critical ratio, due date, etc. (section 7.8). The list of expected orders for the current period is a tool used in controlling the priorities initially set out in the MRP. The production activity controller must first strive to correct any problems in the planned progress of an order. If unable to do so, the production activity controller must report the delay in the anticipated delay report, which may result in the commitment of more resources to catch up or, as a last resort, changes in deadlines.

Once an order is completed, it is forwarded to customers or to inventory. Data must be complied on the quantity of products manufactured and defective products, as well as on actual manufacturing times as compared with standards. All this information is used to evaluate performance just before *the order is closed*. Significant discrepancies must be studied in detail and their causes identified.

Planning file	Control file
Parts	**Open orders**
— part number	— job order number
— part description	— quantity of products ordered
— manufacturing time	— quantity of products completed
— quantity in inventory	— quantity of products reserved
— quantity allocated for an order	— earliest delivery date
— quantity on order	— order priority
— lot size to be ordered	— quantity to be produced
Bill of operations	**Details of open orders**
— operation number	— operation number
— operation description	— actual setup time
— setup time	— actual manufacturing time
— manufacturing time	— quantity of parts completed
— special codes for distinguishing types of operations	— date required or available operations time
Workstations	
— workstation number	
— capacity of each station	
— replacement workstation	
— efficiency	
— use	
— waiting time	

Proper PAC relies on the accuracy of the data obtained in the preliminary planning stages. This accuracy in turn depends not only on how date are collected (section 7.11), but also on how they are stored, such as in a database.

The database may consist of two main sets of files: one for planning and one for control. The two are described in Table 7.1.[5] The information compiled in the database varies according to whether the company wishes to use it to monitor special orders, to keep track of production at all times, or, perhaps, to answer such hypothetical questions as: What would happen if we accepted such-and-such an order?[11]

7.3   Main Short-Term Scheduling Activities

Short-term scheduling is the final step in the production planning process. In fact, in some small and medium-sized businesses it will be the only step. Schedulers are constrained not only by all the decisions already made concerning the operations system, but also by the previous steps in the planning process. In the limited time frames of short-term scheduling it is not possible to rearrange production facilities or make significant changes in capacity.

The orders to be filled or tasks to be carried out consist of operations at production centres (factory, department, machine, doctor's or dentist's office, barbershop chair, garage, etc.). Production scheduling is based on all known and probable orders.

In a *static* approach under unchanging conditions, short-term scheduling is carried out only once per period (day, week, etc.) for all orders received. Any new order requires changes in scheduling, hence the need for accurate forecasting when the aggregate plan and the MPS are prepared (see Chapter 4). With a *dynamic* approach, all orders are taken into account whenever they arrive, but scheduling then becomes a very complex activity that draws on mathematics and advanced operational research, such as queuing theory and simulation.

When the company is dealing with confirmed orders, demand is known and no forecasting need be done. Major errors that occur when demand is calculated will have consequences for scheduling, and the costs of correcting them may be very high. For probable orders, proper forecasting reduces the cost of making changes to the manufacturing schedule. In any case, despite impressive progress in operations research, short-term scheduling decisions are still based more or less on judgement.[12]

There are six main steps in short-term scheduling, which can be combined into three phases: *planning*, *execution* and *control* (Figure 7.1). These steps require data from the planning phases of the PIPC system and the bills of operations that list the steps in manufacturing a product, in order. These bills of operations are in fact the basis for routing the work.

The first step in scheduling, *allocating tasks*, consists of distributing orders to the various workstations according to their relative efficiency. A company may either accept orders that will overload its production system or turn away orders that would cause it to exceed its theoretical operating capacity. The same choice applies to scheduling for workstations.

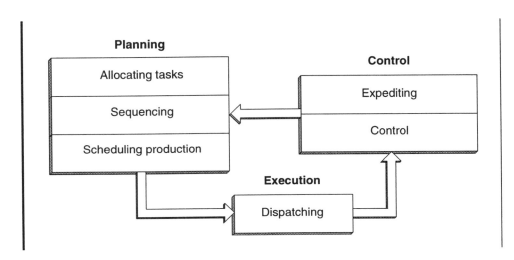

◄   **FIGURE 7.1**
Short-Term
Scheduling Steps

TABLE 7.2 ▶
Evaluating Main
Production
Objectives
According to
Certain
Performance
Criteria

Performance criterion chosen	Importance of objective			
	Cost	Inventory level	Utilization rate	Service level
Setup cost	X		X	
Amount of work in process	X	X		
Utilization rate of equipment			X	
Average lateness of orders				X
% of late orders				X

Management can use the *finite loading approach*, to determine the amount of work to be done by a given workstation, or the *infinite loading approach*, to identify bottlenecks by determining the actual workload of each workstation according to actual demand. Steps can then be taken to solve any problems caused by overloads in the system. However, the infinite loading approach will make the next scheduling step, sequencing, less realistic: the order established will most likely have to be changed, since it is known from the start that the sequence cannot be carried out as planned.

Standard manufacturing times are normally used to determine the processing times at each workstation. This principle also underlies the operations research technique called the *assignment method*, which consists of assigning a certain number of customers or orders to a corresponding number of workstations according to their relative efficiency. This technique is simple and gives optimal results.

The second step, *sequencing*, establishes the order in which the various jobs will be carried out or assigned to each workstation. This means that the complete range and length of the operations involved in filling each order must be known ahead of time.

Sequencing is done on the basis of a number of criteria—for instance, cost, inventory level, utilization rate of workstations, or customer service level. Table 7.2 shows some of these performance criteria and the significant variables that justify their use. Prioritizing these criteria makes for simple, systematic sequencing (section 7.8).

Short-term scheduling can just as easily be applied to the service sector, in which case the performance criteria will be the number of customers or transactions per hour and the utilization rate of points of service.

Many researchers have attempted to define an optimum sequence of internal orders (for inventory) or external orders (for customers). To optimize a given performance criterion, restrictive assumptions that greatly reduce the significance of optimality have often been applied. Most of the models have been developed in deterministic and static frameworks in which the quantity of orders is known. The real world, however, is dynamic and, to some extent, unpredictable. New orders may oblige managers to rework the established sequence. Some attempts have recently been made to evaluate scheduling situations in dynamic contexts, but few of them deal with actual situations.[4]

Actual operating conditions, in fact, show that sequences remain optimal only for brief periods. It is often better to develop a sequence that leads to satisfactory results under realistic conditions than to develop a sequence that gives an optimal result in theory but that is based on unrealistic assumptions.

To compensate for the problems arising when a single evaluation criterion is used, many multi-criteria sequencing approaches have been suggested. These techniques are, for the most part, complex, but some are surprisingly simple and effective. Computer simulation simplifies sequencing, since it can recreate actual situations. It quickly checks sequences by using certain performance criteria, such as the average number of late orders. Consequently, trade-offs can be made without necessarily having to be tested directly on the production system. Although the contribution of experience and intuition is a valuable one in scheduling, proven techniques and the role of computers should not be overlooked in the design of a sequencing system that can adjust to a company's characteristics and frequently changing priorities.

Once the orders have been allocated to each workstation and the sequence has been determined, the third step can be undertaken—which is to draw up the *production schedule*, assigning a date and even a time for releasing each operation to the corresponding workstation. Any variation in the range and duration of operations results in changes to the production schedule, and may even require changes in the first two steps.

Knowledge of the company's operations can speed up a scheduler's decision-making regarding the trade-offs needed in arriving at a satisfactory production schedule, an adequate level of service and efficient use of production capacity. These decisions also take into account the physical and psychological effects of specific sequences on employees.

The fourth step in short-term scheduling is *dispatching*, or releasing the orders to the workstations for processing.

Finally, the scheduling-control phase, which is actually an ongoing process, takes in the fifth and sixth steps, *control* and *expediting*. Progress is monitored by examining data collected on open orders (quantity of products completed, time available, setup time, quantity of defective products and so on). These data may be culled from many different reports, depending on control needs, such as system efficiency reports and exception reports (late orders, defective parts to be reworked), with a view to taking corrective action.[9] For instance, any delay in executing orders may be recorded in an anticipated delay report, to be used in the planning and scheduling phase to review production priorities.

The input-output report (in hours) is useful for controlling production activities. It compares actual and planned results and highlights any departure from the plan, and its importance. Managers can evaluate performance and make corrections in the plant (execution step) or in the planning phase of the PIPC system.

The importance of this third planning step was noted by Brucker *et al.*[1] in a study production-activity reports. The researchers found many benefits, including:

- review of errors of all operations;
- highlighting of problems at workstations;
- better scheduling and more efficient control of production flows;

–   up-to-date priority list of orders to be executed;

–   elimination of informal manual lists of late or emergency orders;

–   accurate delivery dates.

Any change to the short-term scheduling system may necessitate a review of the entire system. For example, what would happen if, on some very busy evening, a bank manager informed the customers waiting in line that those with the shortest transactions would be processed first?

It is a relatively simple task to draw up a suitable schedule when the production system is not used to full capacity. If the system is almost at maximum capacity, on the other hand, even a minor order may be difficult to fill within the required time. Ease of scheduling depends on the actual and forecast capacity, the setup and processing times for orders (or customers), the length of queues and processing deadlines.

Everything we have looked at so far in this section applies to four types of production system: continuous, flow (repetitive), discontinuous and project, which present different challenges at the scheduling stage. Figure 7.2 shows some key aspects of each type. All of these are discussed in the following paragraphs.

In a *continuous system*, the goal of short-term scheduling is uninterrupted production and low in-process inventory. Continuous production systems such as petroleum refining are designed with many steps, each dependent on the previous one. The first step directly determines what happens next, and, normally, co-ordinating the entire process poses few problems. Difficulties in balancing the steps of the process may arise, however, when problems occur at one step.

FIGURE 7.2 ▶
Importance of Different Aspects of Production Systems for Effective Scheduling

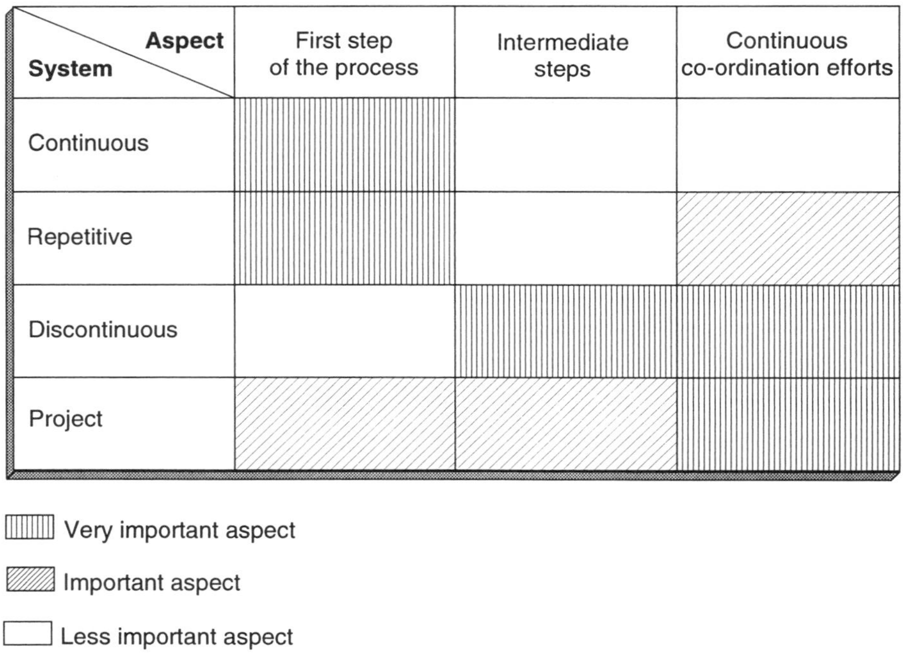

Aspect / System	First step of the process	Intermediate steps	Continuous co-ordination efforts
Continuous	Very important	Less important	Less important
Repetitive	Very important	Less important	Important
Discontinuous	Less important	Very important	Less important
Project	Important	Important	Very important

▓ Very important aspect

▨ Important aspect

☐ Less important aspect

A problem at one step almost immediately affects all the others in the system. It is not always possible or practical to accumulate inventory between the steps. Aluminum smelting is another industry in which this type of system is used. The molten metal proceeds from one step to the next and cannot be stocked—once the transformation process has started it cannot be stopped until the product is completed.

Flow shops include assembly lines and other systems in which the products follow the same main sequence. Once production has begun, the very nature of the operations eliminates the possibility of excessive work-in-process accumulation. Moreover, since these are not continuous production systems, interdepartmental coordination can prove difficult. These observations explain the choice of key aspects for this type of system, as shown in Figure 7.2.

Discontinuous production applies mainly to specialized job-shop systems. A clear example of discontinuous production is a system made up of workstations with queues of jobs or groups of people, all requiring different handling. Consequently, bottlenecks must be carefully monitored. Small production runs lead to a lower capacity utilization rate, because of the large number of setups required to prepare the machinery for the next job. As we saw in Chapter 4, the main trade-off is between the quantity and the value of the inventory carried. This value may be substantial, since orders or customers in such systems often spend more than 90% of their total time waiting!

Some circumstances make it more difficult to estimate the processing time required for scheduling purposes. Customers may interfere with the system by chatting with the clerk serving them. It is also a more complex matter to schedule special orders for which the processing time is unknown than items that have already been run many times over; in addition, in the latter case it is easy to know when another run should be begun, because the quantities on hand are easily monitored.

Finally, a *project system* is a series of co-ordinated activities designed to produce a single product or service, usually requiring many resources. Allocating human and material resources, while it takes available time into account, can present a daunting challenge. Short-term scheduling is an important step, and if poorly managed may increase not only the length of the project but also related costs.

7.4   The Production Controller and System Utilization

The director of Operations is usually responsible for controlling production activities, while subordinates deal with material management and operations supervision. The materials manager and the production controller are more aware of overall priorities. They must remain in constant touch and work closely with the plant manager and foremen. In addition, they are more familiar with the strengths and weaknesses of each workstation in carrying out the MPS. All in all, the materials manager and production controller are better placed to react quickly to any unexpected occurrences on the plant floor.[5]

The smaller the company, the more PAC will be decentralized, while in large companies control is centralized in the Materials Management function. These days, PAC tends to be a mixture of both approaches. Materials Management and Production Control managers determine the sequencing of orders and the production schedule, while the controller or foreman allocates each order to a workstation in accordance with the sequence and the schedule. The controller is also responsible for moving orders from one department to another as operations progress.[9]

In the latter case, a full-time employee may be responsible for allocating each order (a controller who reports to the materials manager) or this may be one of the foreman's tasks, in which case less time will be left for other duties.

As we saw in section 7.2, the person in charge of PAC must monitor the planned progress of orders, endeavour to carry out the plan and always keep with company objectives in mind. If for any reason this is not possible, the planners must be informed so that the necessary corrections can be made.

Young[12] emphasizes the importance of the PAC manager's role, listing the possible negative consequences of poor control: higher costs owing to production slowdowns in other departments where defective parts have been shipped, leading to a shortage of parts; higher costs because of overtime necessary to rework the parts and fill orders; dissatisfied and possible lost customers; and under-utilization of equipment and human resources.

The company can avoid these costly consequences by providing the PAC manager with training in proper planning of priorities, an overall view of the system, a written description of the work to be done, feedback (performance evaluation), and all the information required to do the job properly. The PAC manager must also have the authority to fall back on personal judgement and experience when necessary.[12]

The increased use of new tools such as computer software (Lotus 1-2-3, etc.) will allow the controller to reduce the time spent collecting data and checking the availability of inputs, which, according to Suri,[10] now take up 80% of the PAC manager's time. More time can be spent on considering the costs and consequences of the trade-offs among various scheduling options, a task that now receives only 20% of the PAC manager's attention. In an ideal world the proportions would be reversed.

Nevertheless, PAC control does not make the system infallible. One of the difficulties that the controller faces is an increase in the number of late orders, which is symptomatic of various other problems. This subject will be examined in the next section.

7.5   A Problem Specific to PAC: Growing Proportion of Late Orders

When a company finds that some of its orders are being filled late, it may be tempted to circumvent the formal system by expediting orders. While this may be a solution for specific orders, it will have long-term repercussions. The key is always to find the cause of a problem and attempt to remedy it; expediting should be considered only in exceptional circumstances.

Plossl and Wight[8] list three reasons for excessive queues and production lead times that may result in late orders:

- insufficient capacity;
- mismanaged order dispatching (inefficient and ineffective short-term scheduling);
- inflated manufacturing lead times.

Insufficient capacity and mismanaged order dispatching can cause orders to back up, thereby often increasing delivery lead times. Suppliers and retailers may be tempted to stockpile goods to gain more control over delivery lead times and improve customer service; however, carrying inventory is costly.[10]

Although there are reasons to carry inventory, suppliers and retailers do so as little as possible, since the resulting savings can be substantial. Lower inventory places pressure on those in charge of short-term scheduling, as well as on employees and the production system. Improved short-term scheduling can replace extra inventory, as can the use of more flexible equipment.

If the problem persists, and if the current volume of orders seems likely to continue, management will have to look at the costs and benefits of increasing capacity by adding machines or shifts. Deadlines promised to customers must also be reviewed to see that they are realistic, taking actual capacity and manufacturing lead times into account.

Manufacturing lead time consists of all processing, waiting, handling and preparation times for an order. Time saved at any of these points cuts the manufacturing lead time correspondingly and improves the service level. Minimizing manufacturing lead time is all the more important since competition in the '90s is not just a matter of quality, but also of time. Suri[10] reports that companies with lower lead times than their competitors are the leaders in their industries.

In order to estimate manufacturing lead time, the time allowed for an increase or decrease in the total number of orders is often added to or subtracted from the total manufacturing time of recently completed orders. This heuristic method takes into consideration neither priority rules nor order delivery dates. To reduce lead times, it is better to concentrate on waiting times than processing times. Vollmann et al.[11] note that processing time usually accounts for at most 10% of the total time an order spends in a plant. The Japanese just-in-time approach (Chapter 9) emphasizes this way of reducing waiting time.

Furthermore, it is not necessary for all the items of a given job to have passed through the first operation before transfer to the next is begun. Figure 7.3 illustrates the case of an order of 20 items for which manufacturing time is one hour at each step, for each item. In the first case, the products are not moved to the second workstation until they are all finished. However, each item is transferred as it is finished, rather than waiting for all of them to be finished. The second approach is simpler and more expedient, because reducing waiting time cuts production time and hence also in-process inventory. Note, however, that if manufacturing time at the various steps in the process is not essentially similar, one of the workstations may sit idle for too long.

Similarly, if the company has machines suited to more than one type of operation, or several machines capable of the same operation, a given job may be performed simultaneously on several machines (Figure 7.4). The amount to be manufactured is divided into small lots. An order can also be divided into suborders and processed in sequence. In this way the part of the order required first can be delivered immediately and the rest produced later.[9]

Because the manufacturing lead time is used to compute the delivery date promised to customers, arbitrarily lengthening the manufacturing lead time will invalidate a properly planned schedule and undermine efficient use of resources and good

▼ **FIGURE 7.3**
Impact on the Manufacturing Lead Time of an Immediate Transfer to the Next Operation

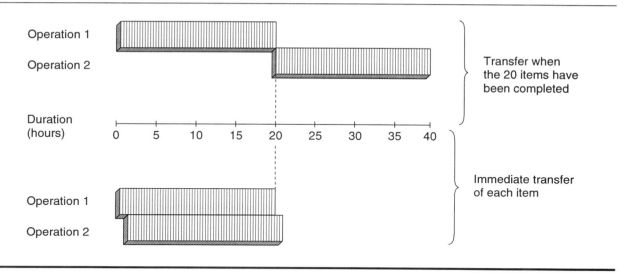

FIGURE 7.4 ▶
Impact on the Manufacturing Lead Time of Dividing up Operations or an Order

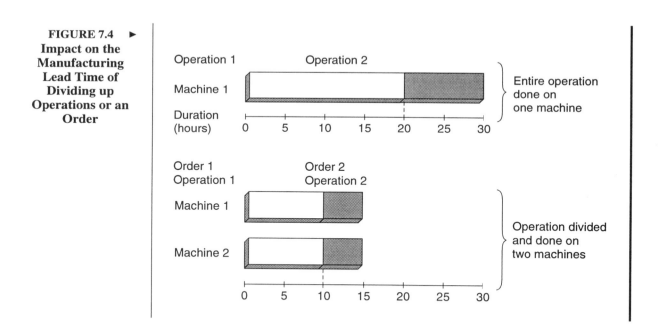

customer service. This effect will make it tempting to add jobs to the production schedule, on the assumption that planned lead times have in any event been inflated. The end result is a lack of internal and external confidence in forecast lead times. It will no longer be possible to use planned times cumulatively to determine actual order completion dates. Consequently, it will be difficult to know whether an additional order can be inserted, and the number of late orders is likely to grow.

When faced with such situations, production managers are strongly tempted to inflate the manufacturing lead times given to customers. When offered longer lead times, customers can either place their orders earlier than they would have otherwise, or change suppliers. This vicious circle can be avoided if the number of work orders released to the production department is carefully controlled. Figure 7.5 shows that with this approach, estimated and actual manufacturing lead times are shorter than they would be if the orders were not controlled.

Longer manufacturing lead times mean higher in-process inventories. It is a well-known fact that a high number of jobs and large amounts of work in process reduce output levels and increase lead times.[8] Accordingly, the control of jobs is not limited to the flow of the work, but also includes the volume of jobs accepted for production. Control should improve customer service.

The problem of late orders also applies to the service sector, and the queues of customers that form when a company cannot immediately adapt its resources (supply) to unexpected demand. Telephone companies, for instance, must handle calls that vary in numbers with the time of day, the day of the week and the season. Telephone operators' hours and, in the longer term, the capacity of the system, must be adapted to meet the volume of calls. Efficient demand forecasts are essential to ensure that production resources will be available when they are needed—particularly because it is next to impossible to stockpile them in this case.

Nollet and Haywood-Farmer[7] suggest these other means of balancing the supply of and demand for services in order to reduce customer waiting time:

- use two work shifts at the same time during peak periods;
- hire extra workers at peak times, or use a floating team, as is done in hospitals, to cope with unforeseen demand;
- make appointments; although this method allows orderly scheduling, it requires that various other factors be taken into consideration, such as emergencies, cancellations and customers who drop in without an appointment.

Other factors may cause queues. The "first come, first served" rule makes for longer service time, and consequently longer waiting time, but is the customer preference.[3]

Finally, a great deal of contact between supplier and customer results in queues, along with uncertainty about the length of time it will take to provide the service. This factor must be taken into account in short-term scheduling, which has to be flexible enough to allow different processing times.[7]

7.6   Rescheduling

Speeding up orders that are not progressing as quickly as stipulated in the production schedule is another simple solution to the problem of late orders. However, expediting these jobs does not necessarily solve scheduling problems, for some delivery dates will be met at the expense of others. This step might not be necessary if the entire production schedule were re-examined. Some jobs could most likely be delayed without causing a problem; for example, it does not make much sense to produce one part immediately when the other required parts will not be available at the scheduled time.

▼ **FIGURE 7.5**
Impact on Manufacturing Lead Times of Controlling the Jobs Released to the Production Department

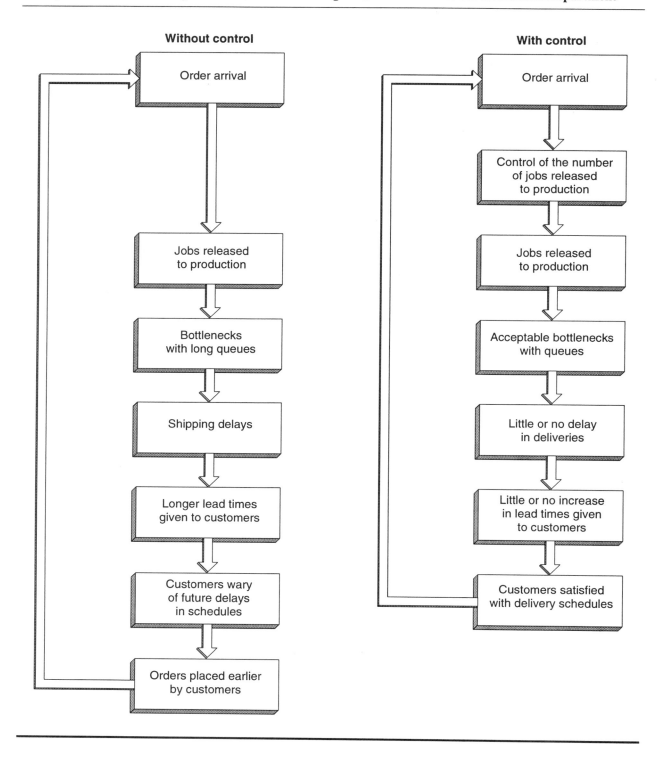

The concept of *rescheduling* implies that the scheduling system adapts to changes in both the internal and external environments of the organization. However, rescheduling negates the benefits of effective planning for resource allocation. Frequent changes can create confusion, reduce output and even result in a higher number of stockouts, despite efforts to establish appropriate schedules.

The concept of rescheduling also applies in the service sector. For example, although the average patient may wait several hours in a hospital emergency clinic before being treated, someone in critical condition will be seen immediately. As a result, all the other patients must wait longer.

Thus the frequency and extent of rescheduling should be kept to a minimum, and the more distant the time horizon, the more flexible the production schedule should be. Table 7.3 illustrates this choice, based on the time-fences principle discussed in Chapter 6. In the very short term, no changes are allowed. In other words, an order in process is never interrupted to produce another order that seems more urgent.

Number of days into the future	0–3	4–7	8 or more
Allowable changes	None	A few	Several

◄   **TABLE 7.3
Flexibility of a
Production
Schedule**

Despite the undeniable inflexibility of this approach, the underlying principle is important. Flexibility can be added by reducing the length of the time during which no change is authorized. This will obviously suit Marketing managers, but will usually intensify the problems faced by Production personnel.

Campbell[2] notes that most rescheduling results in additional costs, poor utilization of production capacity and probable confusion. In his experience, there are six major causes of rescheduling:

- required raw materials are not available;

- proper tools are not available;

- equipment has broken down;

- some customer specifications have changed since the order was placed;

- the number of orders accepted and in process is too high for the capacity of the plant or of a specific operation, causing a bottleneck;

- appropriate priority rules have been inadequately applied.

Everything we have looked at thus far shows that manufacturing lead times are actually much more flexible than they might seem. Nevertheless, a number of trade-offs are unavoidable if a large number of orders is to be filled quickly and simultaneously.

We will now describe certain basic techniques used to simplify scheduling: the Gantt chart, priority rules, Johnson's rule and the runout method.

BASIC SCHEDULING TECHNIQUES

The method described below applies once the schedule has been set up and production is underway. It allows managers to monitor changes in production over time.

7.7   Gantt Chart

The technique developed by Gantt makes it easy to visualize a given sequence and its corresponding times. A Gantt chart is not a sequencing method in itself; rather, it simplifies control because the situation can be visualized. This rigorous instrument allows managers to make better use of human and material resources, but it must be updated regularly if it is to remain useful. Time is indicated on the X axis and workstations on the Y axis. For every workstation, a line indicates the number of hours it takes to process each order. Figure 7.6 illustrates a Gantt chart applied to a tailor's problem. In this case, the total execution time is greater than 14 hours, from Monday at 7 a.m. to Tuesday between 2 and 3 p.m. This is longer than the sum of the execution times for the first operation, since the tailor must wait until each suit has been cut out and sewn before beginning the fitting and finishing work. This also explains the idle time between orders in the second step.

FIGURE 7.6 ▶
A Gantt Chart

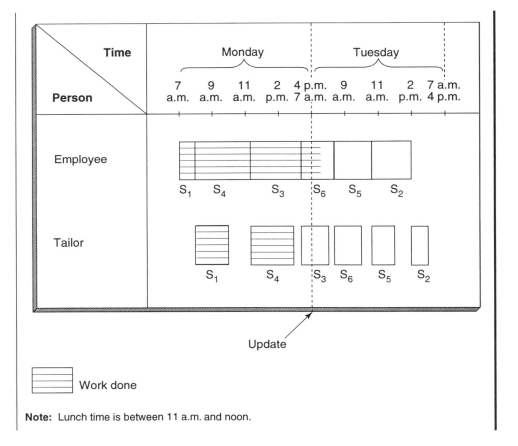

Note: Lunch time is between 11 a.m. and noon.

Although the Gantt chart is widely used in one form or another, it reflects reality only at a specific moment. For instance, what is done with new orders? How much processing time is assigned to each of the jobs? These are natural concerns of operations managers, but the Gantt chart simply points out the facts without providing any answers.

The planned and actual work completed can be compared quickly by referring to the update line. Figure 7.6 shows the work scheduled for completion by Monday at 4 p.m. and the actual work done by that time. If the update line is reached it means that the planned work has been completed. The chart shows that after eight hours the employee is ahead of schedule, whereas the tailor is slightly behind.

The Gantt chart is useful only if corrective measures are taken, yet the need for such measures becomes apparent only once the chart is updated. The update line is particularly useful when specific delivery dates must be respected or when the process consists of many operations. This technique is very effective in project management.

The next section explains various priority rules that can be useful in sequencing orders to be processed.

7.8   Priority Rules

A *priority rule* is simply a means of sequencing jobs by assigning a relative value to each one and then classifying them in increasing or decreasing order. This evaluation makes it possible to select the job-processing sequence that will best meet the performance criteria chosen. Much research and many simulations have been done to determine which priority rules are most effective in meeting the various performance criteria. Some rules, however, are based solely on experience.

A priority rule may give excellent results for one workstation but not necessarily for others, because processing time varies from one workstation to the next. Unless there are only a few key workstations, it is best to evaluate the effect of this rule on the plant's operations as a whole. However, it is not necessary to apply the same priority rule to all workstations, especially in job shops. A combination of priority rules weighted according to their importance can be used to sequence work at a particular workstation. It is important that the impact of the priority rule on the chosen performance criterion or criteria be studied.

Some production system characteristics, nevertheless, influence the impact of priority rules on important performance criteria. These characteristics include:

- the starting conditions of the production system (number and duration of orders in process, etc.);
- criteria used to evaluate the proposed short-term schedule;
- priority rules selected in relation to evaluation criteria;
- number of available workstations;
- capacity utilization of each workstation and of the company as a whole.

In addition, any sequencing method must first be an integral part of the organization's production system and must also consider cost and convenience.

The last factor to be considered is setup time. It is generally assumed that this is the same for all production sequences. However, this assumption does not apply to a paint manufacturer switching from black to white paint rather than the reverse, for instance. Different setup times, corresponding to the chosen sequence, have to be taken into account. In some situations, provided both internal and external demand are satisfied, minimizing setup times may be an important objective.

The multitude of studies on this subject have led to some interesting observations, the most significant of which are presented below. The most common rule in order sequencing is "change the rule": use one or more standard rules, but be prepared to modify the established sequence when new priorities arise. Here are two definitions.

- Operating time, or OT, for a given *operation*, includes setup time and processing time per unit. Operating time is generally set according to a given lot size.

- Execution time, or ET, for an *order*, is the interval between the moment when the order is released and the moment when it is completed. It includes operating time and waiting time for each operation involved in filling the order. Execution time for a standard-sized order generally corresponds to the manufacturing lead time for the product.

Table 7.4 shows some of the most common rules with their respective abbreviations. Each rule has its advantages and disadvantages.

TABLE 7.4 ▶
Common Priority Rules

Abbreviation	Priority rule
FCFS	First-come, first-served
SPT	Shortest processing time (at one or all centres)
DD	Due date (earliest due date)
DS/RO	Dynamic slack per remaining operation
RAND	Random
CR	Critical ratio Having the lowest critical ratio: $$\dfrac{\begin{bmatrix} \text{number of} \\ \text{days until} \\ \text{due date} \end{bmatrix} - \begin{bmatrix} \text{number of} \\ \text{processing} \\ \text{days required} \end{bmatrix}}{\text{number of days until due date}}$$
LWR	Least work remaining
NQ	Next queue The waiting line for the next operation is the shortest
COVERT	Cost over time The highest ratio for a given operation $$\dfrac{\text{Cost of delay}}{\text{Time required}}$$

Let us look at an example in which four orders are released at the same time.

Order number	1	2	3	4
FCFS sequencing	1	2	3	4
Operating time OT	8	21	15	3
Waiting time	0	8	29	44
Execution time ET	8	29	44	47

Average execution time AET:

$$AET = \frac{8 + 29 + 44 + 47}{4} = \frac{128}{4} = 32 \text{ hours}$$

Maximum waiting time = 44 hours, average waiting time = $81 \div 4 = 20.25$ hours.

To minimize AET, the *shortest processing time* (SPT) rule is applied. For this example, this gives:

Order number	1	2	3	4
FCFS sequencing	4	1	3	2
Operating time OT	3	8	15	21
Waiting time	0	3	11	26
Execution time ET	3	11	26	47

The total execution time remains the same, but the average execution time, AET, is minimized:

$$AET = \frac{3 + 11 + 26 + 47}{4} = \frac{87}{4} = 21.75 \text{ hours}$$

The maximum waiting time is 26 hours and the average waiting time is $40 \div 4 = 10$ hours.

Applying the SPT rule makes it possible to reduce both waiting time and average waiting time.

The FCFS rule appears to be equitable, and so is frequently used in most types of service firms such as banks and public transit systems. Yet it is actually one of the worst rules, regardless of the performance criterion used. FCFS results are no better than RAND results. The reason is simple: jobs or clients that require more processing time keep the others waiting, especially when the number of queues is the same as the number of service points. The appeal of FCFS lies in its simplicity, its democratic approach and the fact that it does not require that the servicing time for each client be estimated.

Banks are a particularly revealing example. Early on, managers noted that the FCFS rule appeared the most equitable for customers, yet customers became impatient waiting for others to complete lengthy transactions. A single queue with multiple wickets has partially corrected this situation, since when one wicket is busy for 10 or 15 minutes customers have access to other tellers. With the single-queue method, managers do not have to estimate transaction time in order to serve customers with shorter transactions more quickly. Given these observations about banking services, it is surprising that so few supermarkets have adopted the single-queue approach.

A number of studies agree that the SPT rule is the best for almost all performance criteria. Knowing the estimated processing time for each job is the only prerequisite. In addition to simplicity, the SPT rule has three other major advantages. First, it results in the lowest average number of late orders, which is a fundamental criterion in evaluating customer service. Second, it makes for the lowest average number of jobs in the system (Figure 7.7). As we have seen, fewer waiting jobs ensure better control. Lastly, the SPT rule gives the shortest operation time of all priority rules.

When the SPT rule is applied to the service sector, the same advantages are usually obtained. However, the SPT rule does not work well when customers themselves are the inputs to the system, because they do not usually take to being processed according to this rule. For instance, the customer with the most groceries will not be very happy seeing those with fewer items served first!

Note that although the SPT rule does not take the promised delivery date into account, it results in better service than rules that do. Because it deals first with those orders that take the least time to process, a high percentage of orders is ready on time. Orders with the longest lead times are the ones delayed.

The major disadvantage of this rule is the reason for its success: it neglects those orders that take the longest to process. Some orders could be delayed indefinitely if another rule, such as CR, were not used in conjunction with SPT. Also, the results of SPT are not as good when the required setup time is taken into consideration—an important factor when sequencing involves a workstation that is already heavily loaded.

Some authors suggest that a job sequence be established for each workstation, based mainly on the due date (DD).[8] This runs counter to the most common method, which is to release orders to the plant or shop as soon as possible. The DD approach makes it possible to foresee that a delay at one step will push back the delivery date of the entire order. It also reduces in-process inventory, since fewer items are started and so are less likely to be waiting to be used. This approach is very close to the zero-stock philosophy that will be covered in Chapter 9 and the MRP method discussed in Chapter 6.

Priority rules may also be applied by companies in the service sector, such as to determine the sequence in which patients at a hospital emergency clinic will be treated; in this case, priority will be given to those patients requiring the most urgent care.

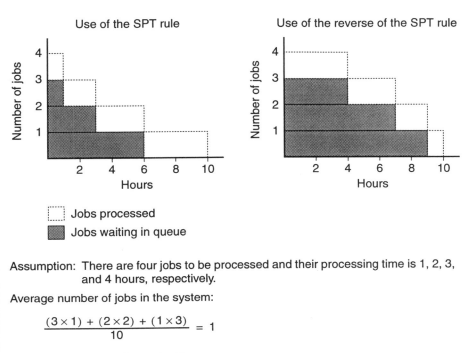

◄ **FIGURE 7.7**
Impact of the SPT
Rule on the
Average Number
of Jobs

Assumption: There are four jobs to be processed and their processing time is 1, 2, 3, and 4 hours, respectively.

Average number of jobs in the system:

$$\frac{(3\times1) + (2\times2) + (1\times3)}{10} = 1$$

$$\frac{(3\times4) + (2\times3) + (1\times2)}{10} = 2$$

where the multiplicand is the number of jobs and the multiplier, the number of hours during which this number of jobs is waiting.

An interesting experiment in the service sector continues to be a classic in the field. Kwak et al.[6] used priority rule as opposed to the SPT rule. They performed a simulation of the use of recovery rooms and the impact of their scheduled use on the personnel involved. The objective was to determine the number of beds required in the recovery room—there must be enough, but any excess capacity is extremely costly. Management also requested that the researchers identify a method for establishing a sequence of planned surgical operations, to minimize total daily use of the recovery room. Shorter recovery room hours would also mean a considerable decrease in overtime.

The authors took into consideration the close correlation between type of surgery and the average time patients spent in the recovery room. After testing various methods of establishing the sequence of surgical operations, they found that the best method consisted in starting with the longest operations and ending with the short ones not requiring the use of the recovery room. Consequently, recovery room staff were not needed as early in the morning, because the first patient was not transferred from the operating room to the recovery room until several hours after surgery had been begun. Recovery room staff could also finish earlier in the evening, because the last patients did not need recovery room care.

FIGURE 7.8 ▶
**Impact of a Change
in Scheduling
Methods on the Use
of a Recovery
Room**

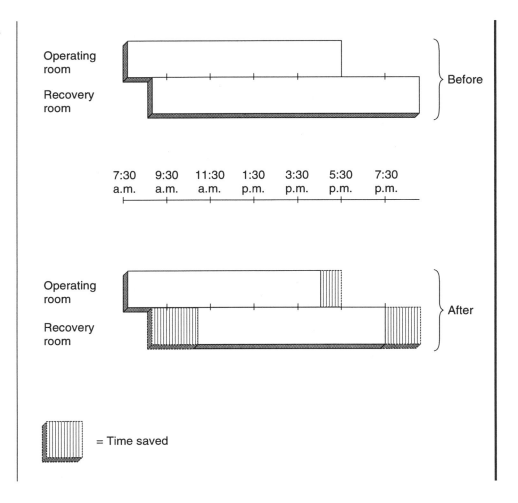

This method reduced recovery room use by an average of 2.4 hours a day and, at the same time, cut back on the total monitoring time required (see Figure 7.8).

The COVERT rule (Table 7.4), which has been the subject of many studies, is similar to the SPT rule but also considers the estimated cost of delaying each order. This rule gives priority to those orders that would be the most costly to delay, in view of the processing time required. While this is an attractive approach in theory, it is not always easy to assign a cost to delaying an order.

Many other priority rules can provide an organization with the tools to develop a short-term scheduling method, and thus to achieve its objectives. These methods vary greatly, according to the nature of the organization's operations and production systems. However, heuristic rules that have not been tested, even if they sometimes provide better results, should be regarded with caution. The ideal solution is a combination of a few simple rules, for in practice optimal results are not so important; user understanding is often more valuable, provided results are close enough to the optimal solution. In short-term scheduling, as elsewhere, priority rules must be applied with discretion.

In the following section we will look at another short-term scheduling method, based on one of the priority rules discussed above (SPT), for the case of two consecutive workstations.

7.9   Johnson's Rule

Johnson's rule establishes the sequence of jobs to be handled by two workstations in succession. Each job must be processed by the first workstation, then by the second, and not the reverse. The performance criterion is the shortest processing time for a batch of jobs. This can be reached using the SPT priority rule, but because there are two workstations this rule does not always give optimal results. Johnson's rule is based on a very simple principle, which is directly related to the SPT rule: the first workstation should process the shortest jobs first because the second one cannot begin work until the first one has finished. In order that the second step does not slow down the total job processing time too much, the last jobs executed at the second workstation must also be short.

Johnson's rule is easy to understand. When the above conditions are satisfied it also guarantees an optimal solution. However, other sequences can be optimal as well. Before using Johnson's rule, the controller must ensure that job processing times are independent of the possible sequences. The most restrictive assumption for service firms is that setup times between each job be equal, regardless of the order in which jobs are performed. Ultimately, judgement and experience determine whether the rule should be applied. Johnson's rule can be used for more than two workstations, but optimality cannot be ensured in such cases and the process becomes time-consuming, particularly if there are more than four workstations. A computer is almost indispensable in such situations. Johnson's rule comprises the steps listed in Table 7.5, which is followed by an example.

A Gantt chart can be used to graphically represent the sequence obtained. The following section discusses another scheduling method, which can be used when the same production resources are available for a group of products.

◀   **TABLE 7.5**
Steps in Johnson's Rule Applied to Two Workstations

1. Choose the job with the shortest processing time (SPT) from all the jobs. If the chosen time is for the first workstation, place the job at the beginning of the sequence, otherwise at the end.

2. Choose the SPT job from among the remaining jobs. If the time is for the first workstation, place the job behind the first job of the sequence, if there is one. Otherwise, place the job in front of the job (if there is one) at the end of the sequence.

3. Repeat step 2 being careful never to place jobs ahead of those at the beginning of the sequence or to place jobs after those already at the end of the sequence.

Example
■

A tailor must prepare six suits as quickly as possible. He is faced with a difficult situation; he urgently needs money and will not be paid until all suits are completed.

The number of hours required for each operation is as follows:

Operations	Orders					
	S_1	S_2	S_3	S_4	S_5	S_6
Cut and sew	1.3	2.2	3.1	3.0	2.5	1.9
Fit and finish	1.6	0.9	1.4	2.7	1.2	1.3

The work has been allocated as follows: the tailor prepares the second operation; an employee is responsible for the cut and sew operation.

What sequence minimizes total execution time?

Solution

	Sequence of execution
– The shortest time is 0.9 hours and occurs at the second operation; therefore, it goes to the end of the sequence	$\rightarrow S_2$
– The next shortest time is 1.2 hours (2nd operation); it will precede S_2.	$S_5 \rightarrow S_2$
– 1.3 hours applies to both S_1 and S_6; either S_1 or S_6 can be first. We choose S_1.	$S_1 \rightarrow \qquad S_5 \rightarrow S_2$
– S_6 follows.	$S_1 \rightarrow \qquad S_6 \rightarrow S_5 \rightarrow S_2$
– Likewise, S_3 goes to the end of the sequence; then S_4 immediately before.	$S_1 \rightarrow S_4 \rightarrow S_3 \rightarrow S_6 \rightarrow S_5 \rightarrow S_2$

7.10   Runout Method

The *runout method*, a heuristic planning method, allocates production so that those items whose inventories will run out first are manufactured first. It corresponds to the DD rule for orders and appears to result in very few stockouts. Naturally, the company must ensure that this technique does not lead to all its inventories running out at the same time.

The runout time is obtained using the following formula, all elements being expressed in machine hours:

$$\frac{\text{Equivalent time to produce inventory on hand + Available production time for the period}}{\text{Forecast demand for the period}}$$

This calculation is used to plan production runs so that the quantities on hand and the quantities manufactured will satisfy demand during the runout time, which is the same for each product.

The runout method is preferable when there is a *limited product mix* that uses the same equipment, *relatively stable demand and sufficient capacity*. Because the objective is to have the same runout time for all products sharing the same equipment, it is likely that some products, either those more in demand or those with a longer manufacturing lead time, will monopolize the available production time. The runout method is useful for making to stock, but not for making to order. It is used mainly in job shops (discontinuous system), although it can also be applied in other types of production systems. It does not take carrying costs or possible fluctuations in demand into consideration.

The following example will illustrate how the runout method works. Although economic order quantities (EOQs) are not taken into account here, trade-offs between the fluctuating demand for different products and economic EOQs are possible in practice.

Example ■

A bakery uses its main production line for four types of cookies. It often runs low on stock because of great fluctuations in demand for one type of cookie and because of large production runs set up by the production schedule established the previous week. The controller seeks a method that will be more adaptable to changes in demand, since in a few weeks demand is expected to slightly exceed the weekly capacity. One hundred hours of weekly production, excluding maintenance, are available. How can the risk of stockouts be reduced, considering the following data?

Type of cookie	On hand inventory ('000 kg)	Weekly demand ('000 kg)	Production time/ 1,000 kg	On hand inventory (machine-hours)	Weekly demand (machine-hours)
	(1)	(2)	(3)	(1) × (3) = (4)	(2) × (3) = (5)
Cream	7.0	7.5	6 hrs	42 hrs	45 hrs
Flat	12.0	6.0	2 hrs	24 hrs	12 hrs
Round	2.0	1.0	4 hrs	8 hrs	4 hrs
Thick	10.0	6.0	5 hrs	50 hrs	30 hrs
Total				124 hrs	91 hrs

$$\text{Total runout time} = \frac{124 + 100}{91}$$

$$= \frac{224}{91} = 2.461 \text{ weeks} \approx 2.46 \text{ weeks}$$

**Example
(*cont.*)
Solution**

Currently, 1.36 weeks of production in equivalent units are on hand (124/91). A week of production represents 1.10 weeks of demand (100/91). Since the runout method requires that stock levels be such that if demand occurs as planned the inventory of all products will run out simultaneously, the required inventory level equal to 2.46 weeks of demand must be determined.

Type of cookie	Required final inventory 2.46 × (2) = (6)	Quantity to produce (6) − (1) = (7)	Production hours (7) × (3) = (8)
Cream	18.45	11.45	68.70
Flat	14.76	2.76	5.52
Round	2.46	0.46	1.84
Thick	14.76	4.76	23.80
Total			99.86 hours* ≃ 100.00 hrs

*   Difference results from rounding 2.461 weeks to 2.46.

The four types of cookies must be produced within the specified number of hours, so that there will be sufficient stock to meet projected demand, for the same period, for each type of cookie. The choice of manufacturing sequence depends on the quantities on hand and the weekly demand, both of which factors are required to calculate the individual runout time of products on hand.

Type of cookie	Inventory on hand	Weekly forecasted demand	Runout time (weeks)
Cream	7.0	7.5	0.93
Flat	12.0	6.0	2.00
Round	2.0	1.0	2.00
Thick	10.0	6.0	1.67

The production sequence would be cream cookies, thick cookies, and then flat cookies or round cookies.

In all likelihood, quantities equal or similar to economic order quantities (EOQs) could be produced when the reorder point (Rop) is reached, in which case the bakery would have to ensure that no other product is out of stock during the production time. Generally speaking, economic lot-sizing is seldom used in conjunction with the runout method. Indeed, it is difficult to successively manufacture EOQs because this would probably lead to conflicts between optimal production times for each product. A company with a fairly flexible production system and low setup costs can put off deciding which products it will manufacture, and when. Because demand fluctuates, the decision on which product to manufacture next can even be made toward the end of a production run. The runout method, then, involves only determining—by calculating the runout time—the first product that would be out of stock if none were produced. The company can choose not to manufacture products at each cycle if there is a sufficient quantity on hand. The disadvantage of this method is the tendency to produce fairly high quantities in order to make full use of production facilities. The system's flexibility could be better used through an appropriate computer application.

REVIEW QUESTIONS

1. What is short-term scheduling? How is it integrated into the planning process?

2. What are the main steps in short-term scheduling? What is the purpose of each step?

3. What are the key trade-offs a manager must make in short-term scheduling?

4. Is it easier to schedule make-to-stock production or make-to-order production? Explain.

5. Describe the relationship between lengthy manufacturing lead times and late orders.

6. Under what circumstances can Johnson's rule be used?

7. What are the particular characteristics of short-term scheduling in the service sector?

DISCUSSION QUESTIONS

1. To what extent is the assumed trade-off between inventory, efficiency and service level really a trade-off?

2. Should a sequence be adjusted once it is planned? If so, under what circumstances?

3. To what extent can certain orders be expedited frequently? What factors influence this decision?

4. Under what circumstances is it recommended to release orders to the Production department as early as possible?

5. The SPT rule provides excellent results in relation to certain performance criteria. Give three examples in which the use of a priority rule other than SPT appears preferable.

6. Use an example from the service sector to illustrate the impact of a customer-oriented system on short-term scheduling.

7. Which short-term scheduling method, other than appointments, can be used in a dentist's or doctor's office?

8. Should a sequence be altered once it has been planned? If so, under what circumstances?

PROBLEMS AND CASE STUDIES

1. The main activity of the Medical Clinic for Executives Inc. is giving company executives their annual physical examinations. The clinic's reputation rests on its performing this task. The priority rule has always been "first come, first served." However, clinic management now realizes that two major problems result from this approach:

   – The doctors have too much idle time.

   – Senior managers arriving a few minutes after their lower-level colleagues often have to wait a long time before being examined.

   March 2 was a typical day: six executives from the H. Personnel Company had appointments at 8 a.m. to undergo tests and then be examined by a doctor. Because many executives prefer to come to the clinic in the afternoon, in the morning there is only one nurse on duty to administer tests and one doctor to examine patients.

   Following are some other details about this typical situation:

Executive*	Time required (minutes)		
	Tests	Examination	Arrival time
E_1	20	10	7:46 a.m.
E_6	5	25	7:50 a.m.
E_3	25	30	7:51 a.m.
E_5	35	15	7:57 a.m.
E_4	10	10	8:00 a.m.
E_2	40	5	8:05 a.m.

   * The number indicates the hierarchical level of the executive; E1 is the most senior manager in the group, E6 the lowest-level manager.

   a) What sequence would allow the doctor to finish examining all the patients in the shortest total time? Which performance criterion does this sequence use? At what time would each physical be completed?

   b) Using a Gantt chart, determine when the doctor would finish examining the last patient if the priority rule used were to test the most senior manager first and then work down.

   c) Which performance criterion or what priority rule would better satisfy:

      – clinic management?

      – the managers?

      Briefly explain your answer.

   d) What recommendations can be made to clinic management to solve their scheduling problems?

2. To plan next month's production, the Operations manager receives the following information from the various department heads.

   Marketing: "For next month, we project that demand for Product A will decrease to about 1,700 units and for Product B to about 1,300 units. This projection is predicated in part on the rise in our net selling price to $405 per unit for Product A and $360 per unit for Product B."

   Scheduling: "Departments I, II, III and IV will have a capacity of 17,500 person-hours (p-hrs), 21,000 p-hrs, 8,000 p-hrs and 9,000 p-hrs, respectively. Product A requires 7 p-hrs in I and II, 4 p-hrs in III and does not go to Department IV. Product B requires 5 p-hrs in I, 10 p-hrs in II, no p-hrs in III and 3 p-hrs in IV."

   Accounting: "Our forecasts of total manufacturing costs are as follows: $15 per p-hr for the use of Department I, $18 per p-hr for the use of Department II, $21 per p-hr for the use of Department III, $15 per p-hr for the use of Department IV."

   Personnel: "Given the tense situation between the company and the union, and to simplify negotiations for the next collective agreement, it would be best not to lay off any workers temporarily, and to make maximum use of the workforce on hand."

   Finance: "In two months we will be negotiating a large loan to pay for future expansion. One criterion the bank will be using to evaluate our financial statements is our profit margin/sales ratio. As a result, it may be necessary to distribute production orders to optimize this ratio."

After digesting this information, the Production manager arranges a meeting with the company president before making a final decision about the quantities of products A and B to run. Because the president always asks very pointed questions, the Production manager needs to know beforehand:

a) which production schedule uses the maximum workforce;

b) which schedule ensures the best profit margin/sales ratio;

c) whether Marketing department projections will be met;

d) the total number of unused p-hrs in a) and b);

e) what to advise the president to do, and why.

3. On the morning of September 1, a real estate promoter reviews his schedule to make sure he will meet the deadlines promised to his eight customers. In the sales contract, the promoter has guaranteed that his townhouses will be ready by an agreed date; otherwise he will have to pay a penalty equal to one monthly mortgage payment ($600) per day of lateness. He has eight units to complete, and the last two steps are finishing the floors and painting. The operation times (in days) are shown below.

Steps	C_1	C_2	C_3	C_4	C_5	C_6	C_7	C_8
Floors	2.1	1.5	2.9	2.4	1.9	2.0	2.7	2.9
Painting	1.6	2.0	2.15	1.85	1.6	2.1	1.4	1.6
Deadline	9/9	3/9	8/9	9/9	14/9	3/9	22/9	14/9

a) Which sequence would save the most time?

b) Will the promoter have to pay a penalty? If so, for which customer or customers? How much will he have to pay in all?

c) What recommendations would you make in this situation?

4. Over the last 30 years, Letterpress Inc., a small print shop in a metropolitan area, has carved itself out an enviable position in the market owing to its personalized service and rigorous respect for promised delivery schedules. The majority of the printer's customers are loyal and place orders on a relatively regular basis. The printer's operating system consists of two departments: preparation and printing, and finishing (cutting, folding, stapling, etc.). Because of technical restrictions, each department can handle only one job at a time.

The business hours of Letterpress Inc. are Monday to Friday from 8 a.m. to 5 p.m. No work is done between noon and 1 p.m. If necessary, two hours of overtime can be worked each day in the preparation and printing department, but because of union restrictions no overtime is possible in the finishing department. The company is always closed on the weekend. Generally, overtime is used only to cope with unexpected events.

Company policy is to give priority to regular customers. Whether the customer is considered regular depends on total annual sales and frequency of orders. This policy is applied only when deciding on delivery dates. Once an order has been accepted, a precise delivery date is set. From then on no distinction is made between regular and occasional customers. After 30 years of loyal service to the company, Mr. Bancroft, the Operations manager, knows practically all the regular customers and is able to set delivery dates quickly.

The Operations manager and his two foremen enjoy some latitude as to how they organize production. Their objective is to meet delivery schedules while using the equipment as efficiently as possible in each department.

The Sales manager, Mr. Rose, is not entirely satisfied with company policy. Promising the earliest delivery dates to regular customers is a valid way of maintaining good customer relations, he feels, but does nothing to increase the company's sales. He cites the remarkably high number of potential customers who, after learning the estimated promised dates, prefer to place their orders with competitors who can frequently offer earlier delivery dates.

Today, Tuesday, Financial Inc., a large finance company, places its first order with Letterpress Inc. However, the order is conditional: it must be completed by 5 p.m. on Thursday at the latest. According to the Sales manager, if this new customer is satisfied with the work, Letterpress Inc. could get the contract to print all its forms for the coming year. The contract would represent an increase of approximately 10% in annual sales volume, a significant amount.

This new order is divided into three printing and three finishing jobs. Mr. Bancroft has evaluated the work as follows:

Job	Preparation and printing department (D_1)	Finishing department (D_2)
A	6 hrs	3 hrs
B	3 hrs	1.5 hrs
C	3 hrs	2 hrs

The general manager of the print shop must decide today before 5 p.m. whether to accept the order.

Mr. Bancroft has asked his two foremen to analyse the situation in order to make a decision on this contract and the work schedule for the rest of the week. To date there are only five orders for which delivery dates have been scheduled, as follows:

Order	Department (D_1)	(D_2)	Promised delivery date
P_1	2 hrs	1.75 hrs	Thursday, noon
P_2	3 hrs	—	Tuesday, 4 p.m.
P_3	3 hrs	2.5 hrs	Wednesday, 5 p.m.
P_4	4 hrs	2.0 hrs	Thursday, noon
P_5	—	2.0 hrs	Friday, 5 p.m.

a)   What is the minimum processing time for Finance Inc.'s order, considered independent of the others?

Would it be possible to meet the requirements of Finance Inc. if its three jobs were

processed after the orders already scheduled? Explain.

b)   What is the minimum time required to complete all the orders (the five orders already accepted and the three jobs offered by Finance Inc.)?

Given the short-term schedule needed to complete all the orders, is it still possible to respect all the promised dates? Explain.

c)   What are the main advantages and disadvantages of accepting the Finance Inc. contract?

What would you recommend? Explain.

Prepare a schedule to back up your recommendation.

5.   Classic Flow has received five orders to be delivered within 40 days. Every order must be processed in the same sequence on machines M_1 and M_2.

	C_1	C_2	C_3	C_4	C_5
M_1	3	6	9	4	7
M_2	2	3	8	6	4

a)   What sequence should be used?

b)   Plot a Gantt chart for the suggested sequence.

c)   What is the latest setup date that can be used to produce these five orders and still respect the delivery date? Explain.

6.   A friend of yours who owns a garage tells you that next Monday will be a very busy day for him. He has to inspect five new cars and his colleague has to apply a rust-prevention treatment to each. The forecast operation times and the promised times are as follows:

Car	Inspection	Rust prevention	Time promised
A_1	45 min	30 min	noon
A_2	60 min	15 min	10:00 a.m.
A_3	75 min	45 min	10:30 a.m.
A_4	60 min	60 min	11 a.m.
A_5	75 min	75 min	1:30 p.m.

Your friend feels there must be a way for him to finish the work on each car more quickly. He tells you that he starts work at 8 a.m. and breaks for lunch between noon and 12:30, and that the inspection must be done before the rust-prevention treatment is applied.

a) Suggest a sequence for each of the two services that will let him deliver the cars by the promised time.

b) Suggest a sequence for the two services that will minimize execution time for both operations.

c) Comment on the results of *a)* and *b)*.

7. One of the electric arc furnaces at a large steel mill is used for the three products for which demand is highest: 12-metre billets, measuring 7.5 cm, 8.75 cm and 10 cm in diameter. It takes little time to switch from one type of production to another. The time available is 150 hours per week. At present, there are 1,800, 2,000 and 5,000 tonnes, respectively, in inventory for these kinds of billets.

Since this is a continuous process and the size of the billets is fairly constant from one time to another, hourly production of each kind of billet is 150, 200 and 250 tonnes. Weekly demand is relatively stable, at 9,000, 8,000 and 5,500 tonnes.

Draw up a manufacturing sequence using the runout method. Calculate the inventory available after the first week of production.

REFERENCES

1. BRUCKER, H.D., G.A. FLOWERS and R.D. PECK, "MRP Shop-Floor Control in a Job Shop Definitely Works," *Production and Inventory Management Journal*, 2nd quarter, Vol. 33, No. 2, 1992, pp. 43-46.

2. CAMPBELL, K.L., "Scheduling Is Not the Problem," *Production & Inventory Management*, 3rd quarter, 1971, pp. 53-59.

3. CHASE, R.B., and N.J. AQUILANO, *Production and Operations Management*, 6th ed. Homewood, Ill.: Richard D. Irwin, 1992.

4. GRAVES, S.C., "A Review of Production Scheduling," *Operations Research*, Vol. 29, No. 4, 1981, pp. 646-675.

5. HABLEWITZ, M.J., *et al.*, *APICS Training Aids, Shop Floor Control*. Milwaukee, Wis.: APICS Chapter, 1979.

6. KWAK, N.K., P.J. KUZDRALL and H.H. SCHMITZ, "The GPSS Simulation of Scheduling Policies for Surgical Patients," *Management Science*, May 1976, pp. 982-989.

7. NOLLET, J., and J. HAYWOOD-FARMER, *Services Plus*. Montreal: G. Morin Publisher Ltd., 1991.

8. PLOSSL, G.W., and O.W. WIGHT, "Capacity Planning and Control," *Production & Inventory Management*, 3rd quarter, 1973, pp. 31-67.

9. SMITH, S.B., *Computer Based Production and Inventory Control*. Englewood Cliffs, N.J.: Prentice Hall, 1989.

10. SURI, A.H., "Change Brought About by Time: What's the Impact on Planners and Schedulers?" *APICS*, Vol. 3, No. 1, January 1993, pp. 33-35.

11. VOLLMANN, T.E., W.L. BERRY and D.C. WHYBARK, *Manufacturing, Planning and Control System*, 3rd ed. Homewood, Ill.: Richard D. Irwin, 1992.

12. YOUNG, J.B., "Practical Dispatching," *American Production and Inventory Control Society, 1981 Conference Proceedings*, pp. 175-177.

Project Management

ROGER HANDFIELD, *main author*
MATTIO O. DIORIO, *contributor*

PROJECT AND OPERATIONS MANAGEMENT

8.1   What Is a Project?

Some operations systems are designed to turn out large quantities of a single product or product type. Taken to the extreme, some systems may do nothing else over their entire lifetimes. In such cases we speak of *continuous* or *process mass production* systems. An example would be an assembly line for standardized products, a blast furnace, or the complex equipment used in oil refineries. But operations systems are more often used to make a number of different products in varying quantities, sometimes on a cyclical basis. These are known as *job shop* or *mass production by lot* systems. An example would be a production line at a canning factory or in a factory making screws, bolts and nuts. Finally, operations systems may be set up to produce very small quantities of a given product, good or service, or even a single unit, such as building a hydro-electric station or sending a rocket to the moon.

This type of production is called a *project*, defined as a series of activities having the following characteristics:

1. The start and finish of the project are each marked by one or more of these activities (thereby excluding continuous processes).

2. Each activity has a clear-cut start and finish (thereby excluding processes in which one activity flows into the next, making it impossible to determine where one ends and the next one begins).

3. Some activities may be accomplished independently of others, while others may be *linked*, in that one activity cannot start until one or more of the others is completed.

4. Each activity takes time to complete, called its *duration* or *length*.

5. Completion of an activity calls for one or more *production resources* (labour, equipment, power, etc.) and its duration cannot be reduced without increasing the use of this resource, with an attendant rise in costs.

Project management implies that administrative decisions differ from those required in managing other production systems, or at least that they are made in a different context. The design of an operations system for a project takes on special dimensions, because of its limited duration (the system will disappear once the project is finished) and the unique nature of the product. The operations system established for a project must often function side by side with an operations system for continuous production, one involving varying quantities of products. The techniques described in chapters 5 and 7 do not apply to operations planning and control for projects. Special techniques have been designed for this purpose and we will take a brief look at some of these in sections 8.10 to 8.14.

Although project management calls for a system unlike the one used for managing a company's routine activities, it cannot stand entirely on its own. There remain fundamental links between the two types of management, and the decisions relating to one are sure to have repercussions for the other. A project may have to rely on labour or equipment that is ordinarily used in intermittent or continuous production, thereby altering the usual constraints in effect at various steps of operations planning (see Chapter 5). Furthermore, some features of a project may create a demand for products from the company's continuous or intermittent production systems. For instance, manufacture of a steam turbine may require huge quantities of specific parts. These can be manufactured by the company itself, using special equipment operating continuously or intermittently, to satisfy internal or external demand. This would be the case if the company manufacturing the turbines had a shop that could constantly turn out the mountains of rivets needed for the turbine.

There are links between all facets of project management and the corresponding subsystems involved in normal operations management. Carrying out a project often requires raw materials or equipment purchased or leased from external suppliers. Except for very large-scale projects (such as Montreal's Olympic Stadium, the James Bay hydro-electric dams or international turnkey projects), the creation of a procurement department devoted to the needs of a single project cannot be justified; the company's central procurement department will purchase or lease everything needed for the project. Nevertheless, before deciding whether all goods and services should be acquired by the central department, managers must consider the advantages and disadvantages of centralized and decentralized procurement. If a project is to be carried out far away from the firm's headquarters, for example, it may make sense to assign responsibility for certain acquisitions to managers on site, who are directly involved in the project.

This question also arises for other aspects of operations management such as inventory control, equipment maintenance and product quality. We will return to this point in section 8.7, and discuss some means of resolving such organizational and management issues.

8.2   Project Management Objectives

The main objective of project management is to ensure that the company's projects are completed within the established deadlines and budgets, while maintaining its standards of quality. This objective is often very difficult to achieve, because of conflicts among time cost and quality. For instance, it may be impossible to meet deadlines without incurring cost overruns (a well-known example is Montreal's Olympic facilities), or quality may have to be sacrificed to meet time constraints. When it is not feasible to satisfy all three criteria, some trade-offs will be necessary. Ideally, these will make it possible to balance deadlines, costs and quality.

To simplify such trade-offs, set specific objectives for project management:

1. Set up a strong organization, so that every responsibility is assigned to a specific person in the company.

2. Ensure that the work of all members of the organization is co-ordinated, particularly in cases where relationships are complex.

3. Plan the progress of operations by drawing up a schedule for main activities and secondary activities (procurement, hiring, obtaining the necessary permits, etc.).

4. Ensure that progress is monitored constantly and the appropriate authorities are informed as soon as possible of all delays, possible cost overruns and difficulties meeting standards of quality, so that they can take the proper steps.

Each of these specific objectives must be reached in turn, for failure at one step will make it difficult or impossible to meet the next.

8.3   Operations Management Projects

Many managerial tasks or initiatives are best approached as projects. Tasks that are complex, involving a lengthy decision-making process and many decision-makers, and that must meet budgets and deadlines, should use the project management approach. Here are examples of such tasks:

- choosing and implementing a new production process or new technology;
- introducing new products;
- implementing flexible automation and robotics;
- carrying out any plan intended to increase the capacity of production facilities;
- restructuring production units;
- systematically implementing organizational techniques and methods;
- introducing computerized decision-support systems for POM;
- designing and perfecting major changes to the existing control system;
- shifting from batch production to just-in-time production;
- adopting and implementing a total-quality approach;
- establishing a preventive maintenance program for equipment;
- designing a systematic plan for measuring productivity;
- taking whatever steps are necessary to give the company world-class production facilities.

STEPS IN PROJECT MANAGEMENT

8.4   Identifying Main Activities and Their Order of Execution

While this first step may seem obvious, in practice it often does not receive all the attention it deserves. Proper care at this point will make it much easier to carry out the following steps and to avoid many pitfalls. It is at this stage that the operations manager will most likely seek assistance from various different experts (e.g., engineers, architects and technicians) familiar with all the technical requirements of the activities in question.

Each activity in a project must form a homogeneous unit, with a well-established beginning and end, and for which it is possible to estimate the duration and resource requirements. One of the problems in identifying the parts of a project consists in deciding on the appropriate degree of detail. For instance, an expansion project for a factory may be broken down into preparing the plans, obtaining the necessary permits, preparing the site, excavating, erecting the building, and fitting out the new premises. Listing only these first-level activities makes the project seem easy to manage, but this simplicity comes at the expense of precision in the definition of each activity, which may in fact be broken down in turn into a number of sub-activities. For instance, preparing the plans includes identifying the need for new space, developing the concept, choosing an architectural firm, studying constraints, producing renderings and preliminary plans, and completing the plans. A general description may make it difficult, if not impossible, to realistically estimate the duration of activities, the resource requirements and the budget. On the other hand, an overly detailed description may well cause the project to become bogged down in planning and control minutiae.

The general rule in project management is to define activities at a level of detail sufficient to bring out the individual nature of each, although it may be linked with others, and at which the use of resources remains constant. Thus activities will be properly defined if each constitutes a whole to be completed without interruption, requiring the same quantity of each resource for its duration. Until this criterion is met, planners must continue breaking down activities into sub-activities.

Determining the *order* in which activities are to be carried out calls for sequencing. This used to be limited to those *immediately preceding* the activity in question. Some managers prefer to identify *immediate successors* (activities that can start as soon as the activity in question is completed), to arrive at the same result. Today, with the availability of planning software, managers have much more flexibility in determining the order of execution. In addition to the traditional sequence, often termed *start-finish*, programs offer such sequences as *start-start* (an activity can start only when another has also begun), *finish-finish* (an activity can end only when another is completed), *partial overlap* (an activity can start only when a given percentage of another activity is completed) or *waiting* (an activity can start only when a certain period has elapsed after another has been completed, e.g., to allow concrete to set). We will use the traditional order of *start-finish* for the purposes of this chapter.

8.5   Determining Durations, Resources and Direct and Indirect Costs

Project planners must determine—through forecasts and budgets at the planning stage and through appropriate monitoring at the control stage—the duration of activities, resource requirements and direct and indirect costs. Once again, operations managers will want to call on experts in various fields.

At the planning stage, *durations* can be determined by means of two approaches, corresponding to two major project management techniques. With the *critical path method* (CPM), the duration of each activity is specified deterministically (e.g., activity A will last 20 days). This approach was developed in the late 1950s by the DuPont company, to assist in planning and control of a maintenance project for its chemical plants.[4] It applies particularly well to projects made up of activities for which there is plenty of past experience and that are to be carried out under foreseeable or controllable conditions, thus making it possible to set a specific duration.

In other cases, either because of the experimental nature of the project or because the duration of activities may depend greatly on conditions such as temperature, moisture, soils, etc., it is preferable to use a probabilistic estimate of durations. The *Project Evaluation and Review Technique* (PERT) was developed in 1958 by the U.S. Navy for the development of its Polaris submarines[4] and is well suited to this context. In this approach, the duration of each activity can be defined by some probability distribution, although most users rely on a specific type of statistical distribution called the *beta distribution* (β). This is a unimodal distribution, meaning that it has a single peak value with finite and non-negative end points, and is not necessarily symmetrical. With PERT, planners set three possible values, which is a particularly suitable technique for planning projects consisting of activities with a probabilistic duration. The *optimistic* duration indicates the time required by each activity if all conditions are favourable. The *most probable* or *realistic* duration assumes that there will be the usual combination of favourable and unfavourable conditions. The *pessimistic* duration applies when an activity is carried out under entirely unfavourable conditions. Experience shows that in most cases the difference between the optimistic and most probable durations is less than the difference between the most probable and pessimistic durations. In this distribution, the expected duration (mathematical expectancy) is slightly greater than the most probable duration.

We will discuss the PERT approach in greater detail in section 8.13. Let us now concentrate on the CPM approach.

Estimating the duration of each activity in a project is a vital task for management. The estimation of costs, allocation of resources and planning and control efforts depends on the various expected durations; if there are many errors in their estimates, the resulting plans will be largely useless.

Those responsible for the various activities in a project often inflate time estimates somewhat in order to give themselves a cushion in case of unforeseen difficulties. These unrealistic time estimates, whether they have been inflated deliberately or not, lead managers and workers to use all the allotted time to complete most of their tasks, and this can affect adverse scheduling and budgets. Underestimating durations, on the other hand, can also cause many problems: it may be impossible to respect deadlines and budgets, making it necessary to transfer labour and equipment and to resort to overtime and subcontracting.

Resource requirements for each activity must be determined as accurately as possible, starting at the planning stage. For all direct resources, planners generally use resource utilization rates (e.g., such-and-such an activity requires a foreman, three labourers, two cranes, a truck, etc., for each working day). For indirect resources, they can estimate the daily cost of the project, regardless of the activities performed every day, or give an estimate for the project as a whole.

At this point it is also essential to identify those activities whose duration depends on the resource utilization rate. Some activities can be expedited by using more resources. For instance, six workers might be able to accomplish in eight days what it would take three workers 16 days to do. This is not always the case, however; the duration of some activities remains constant regardless of the resource utilization rate. This distinction will have a key influence on the subsequent steps in project management.

Various sources of information are used at the planning stage to determine *direct costs* and *indirect costs*: internal accounting data showing standard costs of resources, wage scales, prices listed in catalogues or tenders from suppliers. The penalties payable for exceeding the project deadline must also be included in indirect costs, as well as bonuses offered for completing work ahead of schedule.

Once the project is underway, it is essential that the manager have ready access to information on actual work status, the resources used and actual costs incurred. A good accounting system and computer systems are invaluable for this purpose.

8.6   Project Planning

Project planners must consider the four main variables, time, resources, costs and quality, all at the same time. As we have seen, there may be a good many trade-offs. We will now briefly describe the main considerations in the first three project planning variables. As for quality, the principles and techniques in Chapter 9 are perfectly suited to project planning.

Time planning

The first task in project planning is to determine how activities will be performed over time. Planners will have to:

- accurately determine all the necessary activities, their respective durations and their sequence;
- calculate a certain number of variables for each activity:
  - the earliest start and finish dates,
  - the latest start and finish dates, when there is a deadline for the project,
  - the number of days by which the start and finish of a project can be pushed back without affecting the planned completion date of the project as a whole (which represents the *total slack* for each activity) or the start date for any subsequent activity;
- identify critical activities—that is, those for which the total slack is equal to the difference between the deadline set for the project and the earliest date for finishing the last activity in the project; a series of these critical activities, from the start to the finish of the project, makes up a *critical path*;
- if it is impossible to come up with a plan for completing the project within the scheduled deadline, re-examine the structure of the project, if possible, to make the necessary changes.

Resource planning

With few exceptions, every activity calls for one or more production resources. In a complex project, those activities that require the same resources may be carried out simultaneously. If there are limited overall quantities of some resources, allocation problems will occur. Even if there are no specific limits, project managers prefer that resource utilization be as balanced as possible, for significant fluctuations in the use of a given resource can lead to such additional costs as unused equipment, idle labour or the need to lay off workers and then hire them back.

Resource planning comprises the following steps:
- for resource requirements, the compilation of resources based on deadlines set at the previous planning stage;

- for resource requirements that exceed the limits imposed, steps will have to be taken to reduce requirements (which may call for changes to the original schedule);
- for all resources, planners must endeavour to reach the best possible balance in their use (which once again may call for changes to the original schedule).

The techniques for solving problems that arise in resource requirements planning for project management are often complex, and some are difficult to implement. An overview of these techniques will be given in section 8.11.

Cost planning

The first task in cost planning is to compile all costs, both direct and indirect, involved in a project, according to the plans prepared at the previous steps, so as to draw up budgets for the various steps.

The second task is to determine the total cost of the project according to the various possible durations. We have seen that the duration of some activities could be reduced by using greater quantities of resources in the same period, but with a corresponding rise in direct costs, since the marginal cost of additional resources may well exceed the average unit cost of the resources. However, by reducing the duration of some activities in this way, it may be possible to shorten the overall length of the project, reduce certain indirect costs or avoid penalties for failing to meet the deadline, or even earn a bonus for completing the project ahead of time. Cost planning, therefore, must include identifying those activities that could most profitably be shortened, in terms of total costs, and drawing up a curve to represent the total project cost, depending on its duration. This curve will generally show an optimal duration for the project, one that corresponds to the lowest total cost. The techniques for plotting a curve showing the total cost and an example are included in section 8.12.

In closing, we emphasize the close links among the four variables (time, resources, costs and quality) in project planning. Any change to one of these variables may make it necessary to modify the other three. Project planning must be considered a single administrative task that takes all these variables into consideration.

8.7   Project Organization and Management

Depending on the size of a project in terms of the firm's overall activities, it may be appropriate to make changes to the company's organization. At the beginning of this chapter we discussed the distinctive nature of projects, noting that they are often conducted simultaneously with the company's regular activities. If projects are carried out only occasionally, very few organizational changes will be necessary. In a company with a functional organization, for example, each functional authority takes responsibility for those aspects of the project related to his or her position, as part of their normal activities. For instance, the Procurement manager will handle the purchasing required for project purposes.

If, on the other hand, a large proportion of the company's production is carried out by means of projects, it may be in its interest to consider something called *matrix organization* (Figure 8.1). Each project is run by a different project manager. The project managers, in turn, report to a general project manager, who reports directly to the president and CEO of the company. This project "branch" operates in parallel to the company's regular organization.

▼ **FIGURE 8.1**
Matrix Organization for Projects

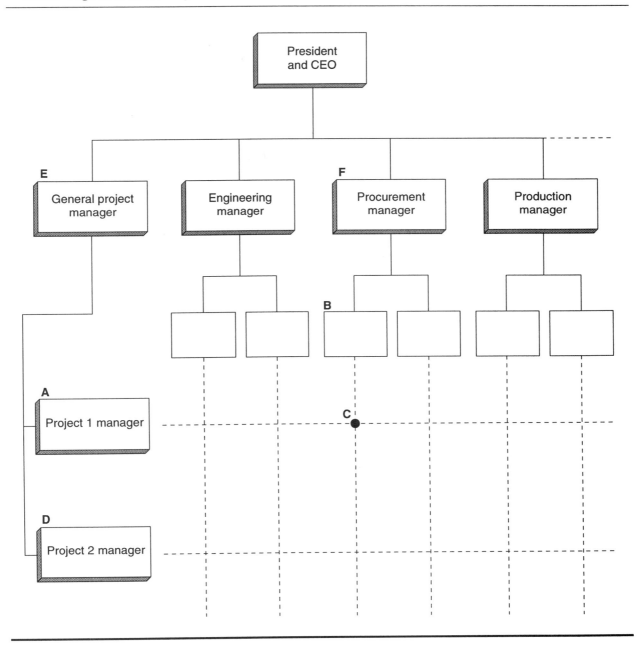

Figure 8.1 is a rudimentary illustration of one of many possible forms of matrix organization. If the company is involved in other production activities at the same time, the managers of the various functions (engineering, procurement, manufacturing, etc.) are entirely responsible for these activities. However, all the activities related to projects come under the dual control of these managers and of the project managers. The success of this type of organization requires a clear-cut definition of the responsibilities allocated to each manager for each decision, and co-operation among them.

To illustrate this sharing of responsibilities, let us take an example from procurement. A key raw material, cement, is needed for project 1. The project manager assumes responsibility for procuring the proper quantities of cement for the date it is required. The Procurement manager assumes responsibility for quality, choice of supplier, price and execution. They must co-operate closely if this order is to be filled and meet their respective objectives (complete project 1 within the deadlines set and the constraints established, for the project manager; run an efficient procurement department within budgetary standards, for the Procurement manager). Tables 8.1 and 8.2 summarize the respective advantages and disadvantages of functional and matrix forms of organization as they apply to project management.

Adequate planning and an appropriate organization alone are not enough to guarantee the success of a project. The other management functions (direction, co-ordination and control) also have important roles to play. We will return to the subject of project control in the next section. As for the other management functions, the reader may consult the many books and articles dealing with project management in the list of references at the end of this chapter.

TABLE 8.1 ▶ Functional Organization

Advantages	Disadvantages
– clearly defined reporting relationships; each employee has a single supervisor	– every aspect of project monitored by the department responsible, but no one responsible for overall project; difficulty in tracing cause of problems quickly and taking appropriate steps
– simple manpower planning within each department	
– motivated employees, because of stable relationships with other department members	– tendency of functional managers to favour the objectives of their own departments, at the expense of project
– simplicity of evaluating a department's personnel and management (training and development)	– lack of interdepartmental co-ordination
	– specialists tend to emphasize quality at any cost
– department head entirely responsible for department's performance	
– improved skills in different specialities or functions	

Advantages	Disadvantages
– a single person appointed to head up each project; all information on given project available from one source; control greatly simplified; problems and their causes quickly identified and promptly corrected	– project manager lacks direct authority over all employees working on project; in the event of conflict, functional manager may attempt to protect his or her own employees
– company allocates sufficient resources to each project	– difficult for project manager to make technical changes to reduce costs and expedite project; major source of conflict between project manager and functional manager
– employees more motivated, given more diversified tasks alongside employees of other departments	
– formal horizontal relations (Figure 8.1):	– poorly defined lines of authority between project manager and functional manager
A/C conflict: settled by B	
A/B conflict: settled by E/F	– possible insecurity of employees assigned to a project for a relatively long period, away from their regular departments
E/F conflict: settled by President & CEO	
– optimal use of project management techniques	– management difficulties
– improved skills	

◄   **TABLE 8.2**
Matrix Organization

8.8   Project Control

Once the project is underway, it must be monitored. Controls apply to the four planning variables: time, resources, costs and quality. Please consult Chapter 9 for a discussion of the principles and techniques of quality control.

With regard to *time*, activities must be monitored to ensure that they are keeping pace with the schedule planned at the first step. If any delay exceeds the allowable slack, planning for the rest of the project must be adjusted and reports issued on the consequences of these delays or corrective steps taken to make up for lost time. The status of activities along the critical path must be closely monitored. If the start is delayed or if activities take longer than planned, the entire project may be delayed. In such cases, production resources must be shifted to activities along the critical path as soon as any delay is detected.

Resources are controlled by comparing the quantities actually used with those planned. All kinds of events may disrupt a project and distort the planned use of resources: lack of planned resources, equipment breakdowns, work stoppages (owing to bad weather or strikes) or lack of required raw materials. The maximum resources foreseen at the planning stage might be unavailable once the project actually gets underway, in which case the project manager must be informed as soon as possible so that appropriate corrections can be made.

Costs are controlled by ensuring that the amounts actually spent do not exceed those budgeted. Cost control calls for timely and accurate accounting. Project managers can quickly collect data and accurately allocate actual costs using project-management software. The principles of management accounting make it possible to identify discrepancies and determine their causes. For a well-informed comparison of actual and budgeted costs, managers will have to examine the status of the project. If expenses by a given date are 10% higher than planned, but activities are actually 20% ahead of schedule, the value of the extra work performed easily accounts for the additional costs. However, if the work is 20% behind, there is cause for alarm. As soon as a cost overrun is identified, the project manager must determine the cause, take corrective steps and anticipate a possible cost overrun for the entire project.

Project control is a significant challenge for the project manager. It calls for a systematic and simultaneous examination of results obtained in terms of time, resources and costs. Section 8.14 offers a brief overview of the techniques used for this purpose.

8.9   Computers and Project Management

Project management involves the collection, processing and storage of large amounts of data relating to many variables. This step frequently calls for a multitude of calculations, most of which are repetitive. Moreover, the results must be obtained quickly and then sent promptly to everyone concerned. Project-management software fits the bill perfectly. The enormous demand for this type of software and the popularity of microcomputers, including portable ones, have led software designers to offer a wide range of specialized programs.

Project management is the sector of operations management where specialized computer programs are most heavily used. These range from very simple versions that perform only basic calculations for time planning, to very complex ones that can assist managers in all aspects of project management.

The many functions offered by the more sophisticated programs include the following:

- storing, updating and retrieving project-management information, in particular for large-scale projects that may involve hundreds of activities and extend over several years;
- performing all calculations for dates, costs and resource requirements for project planning;
- viewing on screen or on paper all diagrams, tables and reports desired (networks, Gantt charts, resource bar charts, etc.);
- applying algorithms or heuristic methods for balancing resources or calculating optimal durations;
- entering monitoring data and quickly making the comparisons required for control purposes;
- sorting activities according to status (whether critical, whether completed) or according to start or finish dates, the amount of slack or the resources used; sorting resources by scheduled use or by compliance with maximum budgeted quantities, etc;
- subdividing large-scale projects (particularly useful when parts are contracted out) or linking interdependent projects;
- carrying out cross-analyses between variables essential for project control.

Some of the most popular project-management programs on the market today are Microsoft Project for Windows, Harvard Project Manager, Primavera, Project Planner, Quicknet, Super Projet Plus, Time Line, Project Scheduler 4, Project Workbench and MacProject. One of the attractive features of software designed for a Windows environment or the equivalent is that changes may be made directly on screen, using a mouse. Wood[8] provides an excellent summary of the use of computers in project management.

PROJECT PLANNING AND CONTROL TECHNIQUES

8.10 Time Planning

Once the previous two steps (identifying and sequencing the main activities and determining durations, resources and direct and indirect costs) have been completed, the major remaining planning steps will be:

- drawing up the project graph;
- calculating dates and slack;
- determining critical paths.

Preparing a project graph

Three main types of graphs, or *networks*, are used in project management: that of Kelley and Walker,[2] in which project activities, or jobs, constitute the arrows on the graph and events (start or finish of activities) form the nodes; that designed by Levy, Thompson and Wiest,[3] which inverts these assignments (activities=nodes, events=arrows); and, finally, the Gantt chart, in which each activity is represented by a separate line of varying length, according to the duration of the activity. The Gantt chart, although it provides an excellent view of the status of activities (which is why most project-management programs offer it as an option), is not well suited to manual processing of calculations in anything other than the simplest of projects. The Levy, Thompson and Wiest version, although it has the advantage of avoiding the need for dummy activities (see the Kelley and Walker method, below), has slipped in popularity with the introduction of project management software, which tends to work better with the Kelley and Walker graph. Consequently, we will use this latter version in our discussion.

The Kelley and Walker method, when used for manual calculations, consists of the following:

- *activities* are represented by *arrows* pointing in the direction of time flow;
- *events* are represented by *nodes* (where the arrows begin or end) on the graph;
- each event (node) is identified by a *successive whole number* and each *activity* is identified by a pair of numbers representing the events that form the start and finish of the activity (for any activity, the initial node must always be assigned a whole number lower than that of the terminating node; to comply with this rule, never assign a number to a node until the initial node of any predecessor activity has been numbered);

- when two or more activities have certain common *immediate predecessors* (meaning that they must be completed just before these activities can begin) and others that are specific to them, *dummy activities* (with a length of zero) must be inserted in the graph to properly represent successor relationships;
- similarly, when two or more activities start at the same event and finish at another common event, dummy activities must be inserted.

Calculating times and slack

Times and slack are calculated according to the following rules:

1. The *start time* for the project, represented by S (a calendar date of 0 can be used if the time is calculated according to the cumulative number of work periods required, an option we will apply in our example).
2. The *earliest start date* for each activity (ES)—i.e., the date on which all immediate predecessor activities, which themselves started on their respective *ES*, have just been completed. Here we are working with the *as-soon-as-possible (ASAP)* rule.
3. The *earliest finish date* for each activity (EF), when the activity begins on its earliest start date (if the duration of an activity $= T$, then $EF = ES + T$).
4. The *earliest finish date* for the entire *project* (EPF), which is equal to the *EF* of the last activity to finish in the project.
5. The *latest finish date* for each activity (LF)—i.e., the date that will allow the project to finish as early as possible (EPF) or on any other scheduled deadline (SPF) if $EPF \le SPF$; otherwise the project cannot be completed within the allocated time (*LF* being equal to the earliest of the latest finish dates of the immediate successor activities).
6. The *latest start date* for each activity (LS) such that it will respect the *LF*, thus $LS = LF - S$.
7. The *total slack* (TS) for each activity, equal to the maximum by which the start of the activity can be delayed from its *ES* without delaying the scheduled completion of the project ($TS = EF - ES = LF - LS$ for each activity).
8. The *free slack* (FS) for each activity, equal to the maximum time by which an activity can be delayed without the *ES* of each subsequent activity being delayed ($FS = \min [ES$ of immediate successors$] - EF$, and *FS* necessarily $\le TS$).

Note that the earliest dates must be calculated from the start of the project, whereas the latest dates are calculated backwards, from the end of the project. For each activity, and by convention, the six times calculated are shown on the appropriate arrow of the project graph in the form:

$$\frac{FS \text{ (activity code: duration) } TS}{ES, LS; EF, LF}$$

Determining critical paths

The critical path consists of a series of activities extending from the start to the finish of the project, each of which has a minimal slack time. There may be one or more critical paths for a given project, but they will all have the same length. In all cases where the earliest finish date for the project corresponds to the deadline set (EPF = SPF), an assumption on which project management is often based, the total slack (and hence the free slack) of activities on the critical path is equal to 0.

The board of directors of a stockbroking firm is thinking of moving its offices closer to downtown. If they decide to go ahead with this project, you will be the person in charge. The eight activities involved in the project, and their duration, successor relationships and required labour are all shown in Table 8.3.

Example ■

Activity	Description	Duration	Predecessors	Labour
A	Plans for new offices	14 d	–	1
B	Selecting a moving company	7	–	1
C	Packing of less important documents	4	A,B	7
D	Electrical and other facilities	18	A,B	8
E	Packing of frequently used documents	3	C	6
F	Storage of little-used documents	2	C	1
G	Audit	1	D	1
H	Moving	2	E, F, G	8

◄ **TABLE 8.3 Relocation Project**

You have been asked to draw up the plans. You begin with time planning.

The first step is to make a graph (Figure 8.2). Note that all the rules discussed above are respected:

– each activity corresponds to an arrow on the graph, reaching from a node represented by a whole number to another node represented by a higher value;

– because of the need to distinguish between activities with the same predecessors (A and B; E and F), two dummy activities of zero duration (2, 3 and 6, 7) were created.

The times have also been calculated according to the rules we have covered. Let us look at activity C, for example, which is to last four days:

– its earliest start date (ES) corresponds to the earliest finish date (EF) of the last of the predecessor activities (A and B) to be completed, or 14 days (for A);

– its earliest finish date (EF) is equal to $ES + T$ ($14 + 4 = 18$);

– its latest finish date (LF) corresponds to the earliest LS of the successor activities, or 30 days for activity E;

$\longrightarrow$

Example
(*cont.*)

FIGURE 8.2 ▶
Graph for
Relocation Project

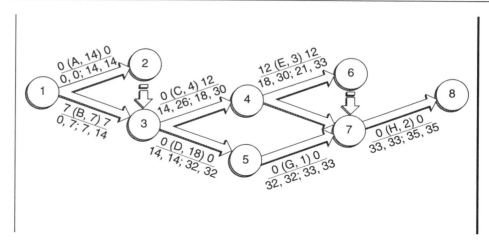

- its latest start date (*LS*) is equal to $LF - T$ ($30 - 4 = 26$);

- its total slack time is calculated as $LS - ES = LF - EF$, or $26 - 14 = 30 - 18 = 12$;

- its free slack time is the difference between the earliest *ES* of the immediate successors and its own *EF*, or 18 (for E or F) - 18 = 0.

The critical path of the project is made up of activities with a *TS* of 0, or A, D, G and H. The earliest finish time for the whole project will be 35 days, or the *EF* date for activity H.

8.11 Resource Planning

The techniques for balancing the use of resources for the duration of a project or for respecting the maximum quantities budgeted are still rather rudimentary, and are in fact particularly inefficient when used to plan the use of various resources at the same time for several activities. While optimization approaches were initially supported by researchers,[5,6] it was later found that they had serious limitations when applied to complex projects.

Today, the preference is heuristic approaches, which are often incorporated in specialized software. Generally speaking, these are based on a set of simple priority rules. In case of a conflict among several activities for the use of a limited quantity of the same resource, critical activities receive priority. Next in priority are activities of the shortest duration or with the highest resource utilization rate, the least free slack, the greatest number of critical successors or the most successors of any kind. These methods usually work on two levels, with a first rule for making the choice and a second one for breaking ties. Other, more complex approaches using branching methods and successive constraints have also been proposed, but these have received little acceptance.

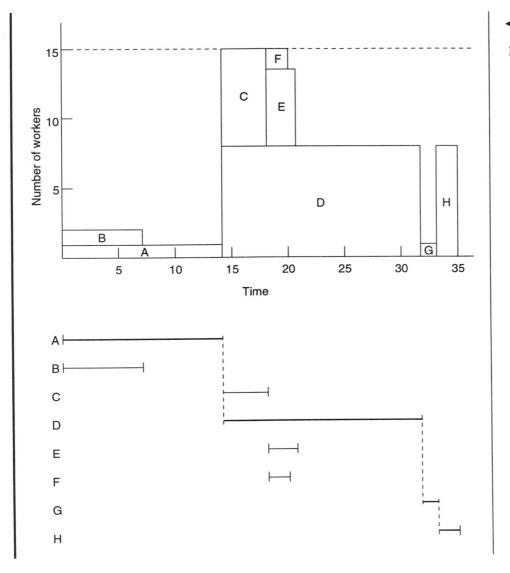

If it is not possible to solve a problem by delaying certain activities, another solution is to extend the duration of some of the activities competing for the same resource.

An activity can often be carried out with fewer resources, although it will take longer. Thus an activity that requires 10 workers per day for 12 days can just as easily be carried out in 20 days using only six workers a day. However, the manager who takes this approach will have to avoid complicating the schedule in trying to solve resource planning problems.

To return to the example in the previous section, the labour requirements bar chart and the Gantt chart for the process, according to the original plan, will be as shown in Figure 8.3.

If no more than 14 workers are available, the original plan will not be feasible. The problem occurs on days 18 and 19, when activities D, E and F are to be carried out simultaneously and require a total of 15 workers. This dilemma can easily be solved by delaying the start date of E or F by the appropriate number of days, which can be done within their respective slack times of 12 and 13 days. It is more difficult to solve the problem that arises on days 14 to 17. Activity D is on the critical path, and so cannot be delayed without delaying the project as a whole. Activity C has no free slack and total slack of 12 days. In any case, it will have to be delayed by at least 18 days so that it does not conflict with D. On the other hand, if C can be accomplished with only six workers at the expense of taking one day extra, the problem can be solved by extending C. It remains within the allowable slack, and so does not delay the project finish date. Figure 8.4 shows the new labour requirements bar chart and the modified Gantt chart.

FIGURE 8.4 ▶
Modified Labour Requirements Bar Chart

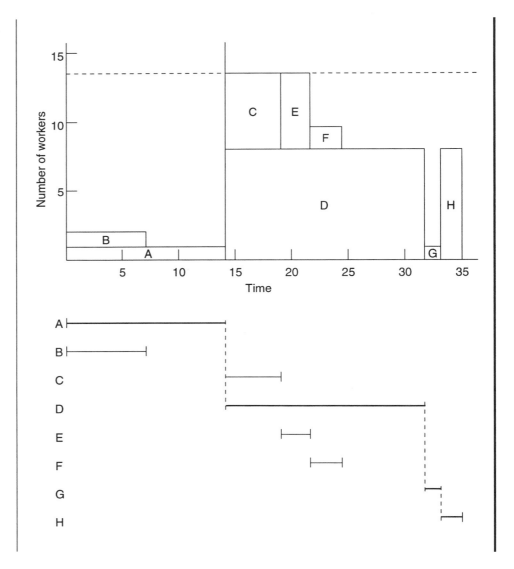

8.12 Cost Planning

Cost-planning techniques are used to calculate the optimal duration of a project when some activities can be shortened, although the direct costs related to these activities will rise. These increased costs can be justified if they permit the duration of the entire project to be shortened, with a resulting reduction in indirect costs. Cost-planning techniques provide planners with a curve showing the total cost of the project as a function of its duration. The following example illustrates their use.

Example
■

A project consists of four activities corresponding to those in the graph below; the time values have already been calculated.

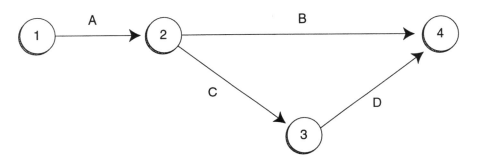

The duration of each activity can be reduced, with the following costs:

Activity	Normal duration (in days)	Minimal duration (in days)	Cost, per day, of reducing the duration of the activity
A	3	1	$800
B	7	3	200
C	4	2	800
D	5	2	400

A minimal duration has been assigned to each activity, since it is generally impossible to shorten them beyond some point determined by technical considerations, regardless of any additional costs the company is ready to assume. The indirect costs are $900 for each day of the project. Costs vary linearly.

Assuming the most probable duration for all the activities, the project graph shows that the critical path comprises activities A, C and D, and that the project duration will be 12 days. The indirect costs in this case are $10,800.

⟶

Example
(cont.)

To reduce the project duration from 12 to 11 days, we will have to reduce the duration of activity A, C or D, on the critical path. If we choose the least costly activity in terms of additional direct costs, activity D, and reduce it by four days, direct costs rise by $400. Since this step will reduce indirect costs by $900, it will produce overall savings of $500.

Similarly, to reduce the total project length from 11 to 10 days, once again we can produce savings of $500 by reducing the duration of activity D. Note, however, that by reducing activity D to three days, paths A-B and A-C-D also become critical.

To reduce the project duration from 10 to 9 days, we will have to shorten both critical paths, either A alone (with an increase in direct costs of $800), or both B and C (combined increase in direct costs of $1,000) or both B and D (combined increase in direct costs of $600). It is least costly to reduce B and D, and the resulting reduction of $900 in indirect costs leads to an additional saving of $300.

By proceeding systematically in this way, we arrive at the following table:

Project duration (in days)	Activities shortened	Net gain (or net loss)
12	None	$ 0
11	D	500
10	D	500
9	B and D	300
8	A	100
7	A	100
6	B and C	− 100
5	B and C	− 100

The project cannot be reduced to fewer than five days, because all activities will then reach their minimal duration. The above table of net gains (or losses) shows that the optimal duration, which will minimize total costs, is seven days, since the net gain becomes a net loss after that point. The total cost curve (indirect costs plus increases in direct costs) in Figure 8.5 confirms this conclusion.

For a relatively complex project, however, this is not an efficient approach. Algorithms such as that suggested by Fulkerson[1] are very efficient when calculated by computer.

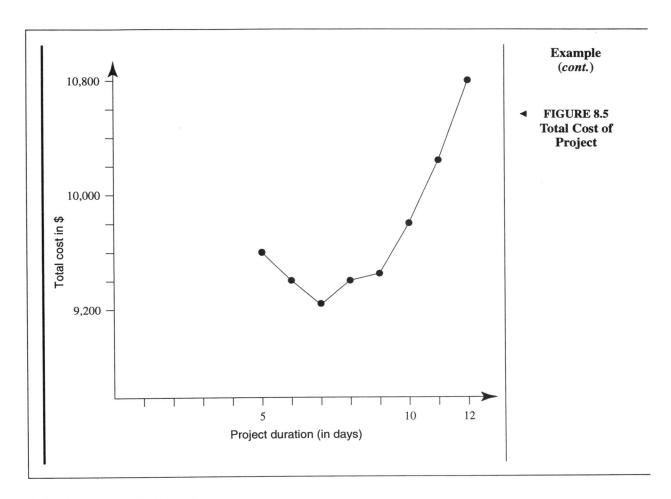

Example
(*cont.*)

◄   **FIGURE 8.5**
Total Cost of
Project

8.13 The PERT Method

We saw in section 8.5 that the PERT method is particularly well suited to managing projects for which the duration of activities is difficult to predict and where a proba-bility distribution is preferable. Rather than producing precise project durations and values of variables, the PERT method allows planners to determine the statistical data relating to these values (mathematical expectancy, standard deviation, confidence in-terval, etc.).

Most studies based on this method assume that the individual duration of each activity has a β-type continuous distribution characterized by three parameters (Fig-ure 8.6):

t_o = optimistic time—that is, the predicted duration of the activity if all the circum-stances are particularly favourable;

t_m = most probable time—that is, the forecast duration of the activity if favourable and unfavourable circumstances are balanced;

t_p = pessimistic time—that is, the forecast duration of the activity if all circumstances are particularly unfavourable.

FIGURE 8.6 ▶
Example of β
Distribution

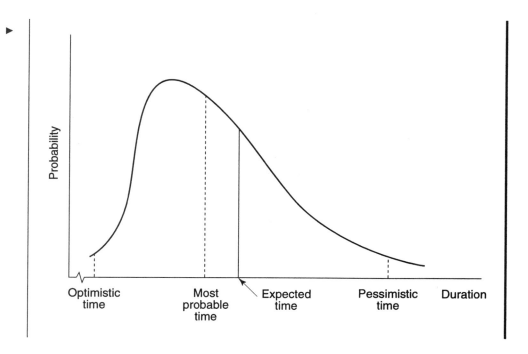

With these values and the following formulas it is possible to estimate the mathematical expectancy and the standard deviation of the duration of each activity:

$$E(t_i) = \frac{t_{o_i} + 4t_{n_i} + t_{p_i}}{6}$$

where $E(t_i)$ = expected duration of activity i.

$$\sigma_i = \frac{t_{p_i} - t_{o_i}}{6}$$

where σ_i = standard deviation of the duration of activity i.

The PERT analysis can then be conducted in two ways.

In the first approach, each activity is considered to have a deterministic duration equal to $E(t_i)$. The time values for the project and the critical path can then be found using the CPM techniques described previously. Once the critical path has been established, the duration of the project is determined by adding all the $E(t_i)$ of the activities along this path. Assuming that distribution of the duration of each activity is independent, the standard deviation of the project duration may be considered equal to the square root of the sum of the variances of the durations of each activity on the critical path. Finally, the central limit theorem allows us to consider that the project duration is normally distributed, with the mean and standard deviation calculated above. We can then calculate the confidence intervals for the project duration, or the probability that it will be completed by a set deadline, using a normal distribution.

Take a project for which we have calculated: **Example**
                                                                                  ■

$T_e =$ expected project duration = 20 months,

$S_T =$ standard deviation of the project duration = 3 months.

Statistical theory tells us that the probability of the actual project duration falling within one standard deviation of the mean is 68%, and 95% for it falling within two standard deviations. This gives us the following two confidence intervals:

   Pr { 17 months ≤ project duration ≤ 23 months } = 0.68

   Pr { 14 months ≤ project duration ≤ 26 months } = 0.95

Now, we can determine the probability of the project lasting two years (24 months) or less with the following calculation:

$$Z = \frac{24 - T_e}{S_T} = \frac{24 - 20}{3} = 1.33$$

The normal distribution table indicates that the desired probability is 0.91.

The PERT approach can produce faulty results, nevertheless, because it does not take account of near-critical paths—that is, those slightly shorter than the critical path when all activities are assumed to have their most probable duration but that can become critical if some of the activities along them take their pessimistic duration.

Because of this phenomenon, a second PERT approach, using simulation, can provide better results. The planner chooses a specific duration for each iteration of the simulation, depending on the distribution of the duration of each activity, and applies the CPM technique to the project obtained in this way. Thus for each iteration there is a project consisting of activities for which the probability of their duration being equivalent to the optimistic or pessimistic duration is 1/6, and 4/6 for their being equal to the most probable duration. Following a sufficient number of iterations (a properly programmed PC can do them in a few seconds), it is possible to calculate accurate estimates of the mean, standard deviation and confidence intervals for the projet duration, as well as the probability that each activity will be on the critical path (this probability is called the *criticality index*).

8.14 Project Control

Project control first calls for simultaneous monitoring of progress, the amounts of resources used and the costs actually incurred. At this step, the techniques are based on graphs (designed by Wiest and Levy[7]) showing the budgeted and actual costs of the project to date, the value of the work done to date, the percentage of cost overruns (negative if actual costs are lower than budgeted costs) and whether the project is ahead of or behind schedule, and by how much. Figure 8.7 is a typical example of such a graph, for a project that started in January 1993 and was scheduled to be completed in March 1994.

▼ **FIGURE 8.7**
Project Control Graph

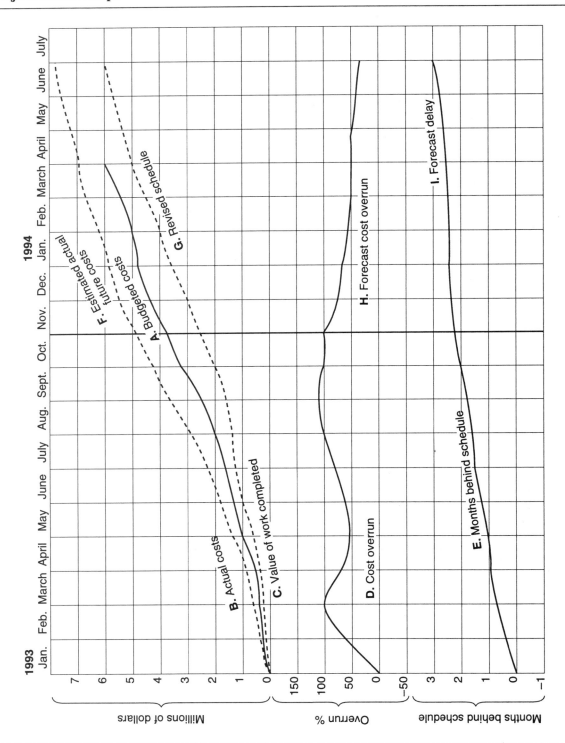

A comparison of curve A (budgeted costs) and curve B (actual costs) and of curves C (value of work completed) and E (months behind schedule) shows that by late October 1993 the work actually completed had fallen progressively behind schedule, while the actual costs had considerably exceeded budgeted costs and were equivalent to twice the value of the work completed (curve D, cost overrun).

An analysis of this graph reveals that project management, by late October 1993, had proved totally inefficient, necessitating immediate drastic measures to avoid a disaster. This is the purpose of the second step in project control: determining the causes of departures from the plan. The last step is to choose and implement the appropriate corrective measures. For these final two steps, managers must fall back on their experience and consult engineers, architects, accountants and other experts. All the possible types of corrective action cannot be listed here. In any case, the appropriate steps depend on the type of difficulty and its cause, as well as the remedies available. These may include exercising tighter control over expenditures, using overtime, changing the structure of activities, devoting more resources to the project, contracting out, or negotiating with suppliers or authorities.

To return to our example, it can be seen that two aspects must be corrected: the cost overrun and the delay in executing the work. It is rarely possible to correct both these problems at the same time. The company must come up with a compromise, or sacrifice one for the other. Curves F, G, H and I in Figure 8.7 show the foreseeable results of taking steps to reduce the cost overrun at the expense of delaying the work. If everything proceeds as planned for the rest of the project, these measures should reduce the cost overrun to about 30% by the end—but the project will be completed three months behind schedule.

In a complex project, this kind of graph can be used not only for controlling the project as whole, but also for monitoring each of its main components.

REVIEW QUESTIONS

1. How are projects different from job-shop or continuous production systems?

2. Name three kinds of operations activities that can be considered projects.

3. What are the main steps in project management?

4. What are the immediate *successors* or *predecessors* of activities in project management?

5. Name the three essential variables in project planning.

6. What type of organization is particularly well suited to managing several projects at once?

7. Name the main activities in project control.

8. What is the difference between the CPM and PERT methods?

9. How are the time values for activities calculated in project planning?

10. What does a critical path consist of? Why is it so important for project managers?

11. What is the difference between *total slack* and *free slack*?

12. What is meant by *direct costs* and *indirect costs* in project management?

13. What are the available options for ensuring compliance with the limits set in resource-requirements planning?

14. List the main steps in project control.

DISCUSSION QUESTIONS

1. "Operations managers rely to an increasing extent on project-management approaches and techniques." Comment.

2. Discuss the role of the POM manager in identifying the activities that make up a project.

3. Explain why direct and indirect costs vary differently with the duration of a project.

4. Compare the advantages and disadvantages of functional and matrix organizations as they apply to project management.

5. Discuss the contribution of computers to project management.

6. "Project management can be particularly useful for service companies." Do you agree? Why or why not?

7. Is it really useful to have two different methods (CPM and PERT) for project management? Shouldn't one of them be abandoned?

8. How can a systems approach help to ensure that projects proceed as planned?

PROBLEMS AND CASE STUDIES

1. A production manager wishes to set up a preventive maintenance program. Before it is implemented, the activities opposite must be carried out.

   a) Plot a graph for the project; calculate the dates and slack and show the critical path.

   b) Briefly explain the significance of the dates and slack for activity E.

   c) You learn after a few days that it will now take 30 days instead of 22 to carry out activity H. Will this delay the scheduled completion date? What would happen if it were to take 40 days? Explain your answers.

Activity	Preceding activity	Duration (days)
A	—	16
B	—	22
C	—	37
D	A	36
E	B	28
F	B	45
G	B	52
H	C	22
I	D, E	25
J	G, H	35

2. A consultant has just completed the list of important activities for his first project. The requisite information for the project is shown in the table below.

Activity	Preceding activity	Normal duration Number of days	Normal duration Direct costs	Expedited duration Number of days	Expedited duration Direct costs
A	—	30	$1,500	25	$2,100
B	A	50	900	40	2,100
C	A	40	2,400	25	2,800
D	A	50	1,700	40	2,700
E	B	30	1,200	10	4,400
F	C	35	3,100	15	5,200
G	D	60	4,300	40	3,700
H	E, F	45	800	20	2,900

a) Plot a graph illustrating this project and calculate the times necessary, based on the most probable durations.

b) Find the critical path and scheduled project duration, based on the normal durations of activities.

c) If asked to reduce the total project duration to 125 days, while minimizing additional costs, how should a consultant proceed? What would be the new cost for the total project?

3. A children's hospital wishes to expand and add a new wing for short-term care. You are appointed to head up the project, and must submit a planning report to management. Because it is impossible to foresee exactly how long activities will take, you decide to use the PERT method. You base your calculations on the table below.

a) Plot a project graph.

b) Assuming that the optimistic, most probable and pessimistic durations for each activity have a β-type distribution, calculate the average duration of each activity and plan the project on this basis.

c) Identify the activities on the critical path and calculate the expected average duration of the project, as well as the 90% and 95% confidence intervals.

d) From the plan drawn up in *b)*, design a labour-requirements bar chart for the project. Make the necessary changes to the plan in order to use at most 15 workers.

Activity	Description	Duration (weeks)			Immediate predecessor	Number of workers
		Optimistic	Most probable	Pessimistic		
A	Project development	3	4	5	None	2
B	Fund-raising	3	3.5	7	None	3
C	Locate suppliers	4	5	6	B	5
D	Approve equipment	2	3	4	A, C	4
E	Build new wing	6	10	14	B	7
F	Financial review	7.5	8.5	12.5	B	6
G	Purchase and delivery of equipment	4.5	6	7.5	E	3
H	Electricity, plumbing, wiring	5	6	13	E	3
I	Install equipment	2	2.5	6	D, G	3
J	Interior finishing	4	5	6	F, H	2

4. A construction project can be broken down into nine activities. The durations of the activities and their immediate predecessors are shown below.

Activity	Immediate predecessor	Duration (in days)
A	—	4
B	—	2
C	A	5
D	A	4
E	B	5
F	C	2
G	D, E	7
H	D, E	5
I	H	3

a) Calculate the duration of the project as well as the total slack and free slack for each activity; determine the critical path.

b) If activity E lasted six days rather than five, how would this affect the project as a whole?

c) Because of technical problems, the start of activity C or activity D must be delayed by two days. Which one should be delayed, and why?

5. You are to plan the execution of work for the project described in the following table:

Activity	Immediate predecessor	Duration (in days)	Number of workers needed
A	—	5	9
B	A	6	4
C	A	12	8
D	A	10	5
E	D	5	6
F	C	6	10
G	C	3	4
H	B	5	7
I	F	6	7
J	G, E	4	6
K	I, J	4	5

a) Plot the project graph. For each activity, calculate the earliest and latest start and finish dates, and total and free slack. What activities lie along the critical path?

b) Plot a graph to show the labour utilization rate as the project proceeds.

c) The maximum number of workers available at any given time is 16. Will this limit interfere with the project schedule? If so, when, and what activities will be affected?

6. A television antenna is to be set up on Mount Royal in Montreal, entailing the following activities:

Step	Duration (in days)	Predecessor
A	4	—
B	11	—
C	8	—
D	10	A
E	11	B
F	7	C
G	10	D
H	6	E, F, G

Find the critical path by plotting the complete project graph. Will it be possible to complete the project in 28 days?

REFERENCES

1. FULKERSON, D., "A Network Flow Computation for Project Cost Curves," *Management Science,* Vol. 7, No. 2, January 1961, pp. 167-178.

2. KELLEY, J.E., and M.R. WALKER, "Critical Path Planning and Scheduling," *Proceedings of the Eastern Joint Computer Conference*, Boston, 1959, pp. 160-173.

3. LEVY, F.K., G.L. THOMPSON and J.D. WIEST, "The ABCs of the Critical Path Method," *Harvard Business Review*, September-October 1963, pp. 98-108.

4. MEREDITH, J.R., and S.J. MANTEL, *Project Management: A Managerial Approach*. New York: John Wiley & Sons, 1985.

5. MOHRING, R.H., "Minimizing Costs of Resource Requirements in Project Networks Subject to a Fixed Completion Time," *Operations Research*, January-February 1984, pp. 89-120.

6. STINSON, J.P., E.W. DAVIS and B.M. KHUMAWALA, "Multiple Resource-Constrained Scheduling Using Branch and Bound," *AIEE Transactions*, September 1978.

7. WIEST, J.D., and F.K. LEVY, *A Management Guide to PERT/CPM*, 2nd ed. Englewood Cliffs, N.J.: Prentice-Hall, 1977.

8. WOOD, L., "A Manager's Guide to Computerized Project Management," *Manufacturing Systems*, Vol. 7, No. 8, 1989, pp. 18-24.

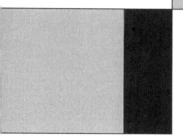

The Just-in-Time Approach

MATTIO O. DIORIO, *main author*
JEAN NOLLET, *contributor*

INTRODUCTION

9.1   A History of the JIT Approach

Some authors claim that the just-in-time (JIT) approach to inventory management was devised by the Japanese shipping industry 30 years ago.[22] Most (except Ohno[18]) agree, however, that the basic idea was developed into a highly sophisticated an innovative operations management system by Toyota starting about 1970 (or, according to Ohno, about 1955). JIT concepts became widely popular in Japan starting in 1975 (or, as per Ohno, in the 1960s), and by the late 1970s (or again according to Ohno, by the early 1980s) in North America and Europe, where the system was known as *kanban*, one of the elements of JIT. We will discuss kanban later.

Today, JIT continues to attract enormous interest and has been adopted in many companies, since it allows for the production of high-quality goods, at the same time enhancing productivity and eliminating waste. The widespread interest in JIT has led to some confusion, however, for authors refer to the concept by various names or confuse it with other concepts such as kanban, zero defects, zero stock, stockless production, world-class manufacturing, continuous improvement, value-added manufacturing, total quality control (TQC) and flexible manufacturing. These many different concepts are all indicative of the systematic and strategic nature of JIT, an approach that involves all functions of the company and is implemented as part of a series of consistent decisions that give it a competitive advantage.

9.2   Cornerstones of the JIT Philosophy

Simply defined, JIT is a system that produces and delivers finished goods just in time to be sold, subassemblies just in time to be assembled into finished goods, fabricated parts just in time to go into subassemblies, and purchased materials just in time to be transformed into fabricated parts.[24] More specifically, JIT is a management system built around a simple philosophy based on two principles.[31] The underlying philosophy is the continuous improvement of quality and productivity in the pursuit of excellence at all steps in the manufacturing cycle, from identification of customer needs to product design and manufacturing, right up to delivery to the customer. The two principles applied in putting this philosophy into practice, are *elimination of waste* and *respect for the whole person*.

Waste is defined as anything that adds absolutely no value to the product, be it machinery, materials, space, activities or time, within or outside the company. The idea of eliminating waste was originated by Henry Ford. It was expanded on by Taiichi Ohno, who listed and described the seven most common types of waste:[6]

1. **Waste of overproduction:** occurs when more is manufactured than is necessary to meet demand, leading to excess inventory and additional requirements in terms of labour, materials, machines, space, handling, transactions, etc. This type of waste can be eliminated by producing only the minimum necessary, reducing setup times, synchronizing demand and machine-time planning, and modifying plant layout.

2. **Waste of waiting:** caused by unwanted interruptions and stoppages in resources, labour, machines and materials. This type of waste can be

eliminated by making it visible. For instance, rather than making to stock, halt production and re-balance workloads with more versatile or flexible man-machine resources.

3. **Waste of handling or transportation:** caused by excessive distances and inadequate layout. Can be eliminated by combining or eliminating handling, rationalizing the physical layout and maintaining order and cleanliness in the plant. This type of waste is also caused by over-division of tasks. For instance, a worker who receives a delivery at the receiving dock asks a worker in the warehouse to come and get the merchandise, who in turn asks another worker to deliver the merchandise to the operations centre.

4. **Waste of processing:** is generally linked to the process itself; for example, a poorly adjusted mould causes rough edges that must eventually be eliminated, templates may be poorly adjusted, work methods may be inappropriate. This type of waste can be eliminated by designing failsafe processes, using foolproof templates, etc.

5. **Waste of stocks:** is one of the greatest culprits, leading to inefficiency and ineffectiveness. Stocks increase production costs, require additional space, handling and transactions, represent high carrying costs, become damaged and worn out, etc. When stocks are reduced, other problems they have been hiding suddenly become visible: inadequate planning, machine breakdowns, defective parts, overhandling, unbalanced assembly lines, problems linked to purchasing, absenteeism, communication difficulties, lengthy setup periods, disorder and uncleanliness, neglect, etc. This type of waste can be eliminated by reducing setup times and the different types of lead times, improving management of supply and demand, and improving flows and technical and human skills.

6. **Waste of motion:** is any movement that does not add value, and must therefore be eliminated. A motion study makes it possible to eliminate some movements, simplify others and combine still others.

7. **Waste of making defective products:** that must be corrected, reworked or rejected, not to mention the manufacturing delays and waiting they cause; if these products have already been delivered to the customer, replacement, transportation and repair costs are incurred. To eliminate this type of waste, total quality concepts must be applied. However, it should be pointed out that the process must be designed so as to prevent these defects from the outset and detect them quickly when they occur. Many JIT and TQC concepts and methods are similar and complementary[15]: both emphasize the cost of quality and role of employees, customers and suppliers; both call for employee involvement in problem-solving; both use techniques such as poka-yoke, Pareto analysis, etc.; and both encourage continuous improvement. In short, total quality and JIT are two sides of the same coin.[22]

Respect for the whole person, the second principle in the JIT philosophy, values employees not only for their muscles, but also for their mental, intellectual and creative skills. This emphasis on the whole person goes against the traditional approach of dividing up and specializing tasks, so that each worker performs only one part of an activity, without worrying about the links and interrelationships with others, and so that, consequently, everyone refuses to accept responsibility for problems that arise. In a JIT system, workers are trained to be versatile; they take part in decision-making,

▼ **FIGURE 9.1**
Key Elments of JIT

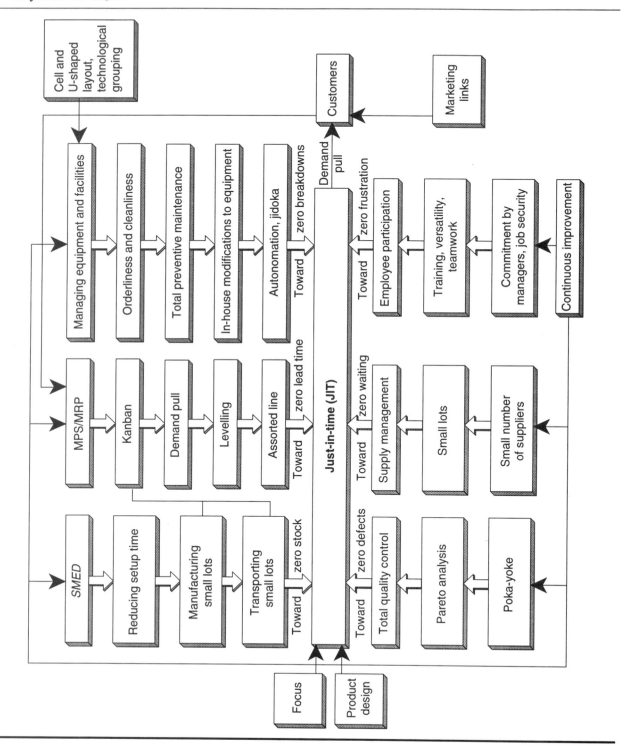

are kept informed of the company's business and, when a problem occurs, contribute to its solution. This approach calls for changes in the structure and organization of a company, including a flatter and more flexible hierarchy, more flexible classification of tasks, more egalitarian management methods, forms of job security, both top-down and bottom-up communications, and fostering of a team spirit.

These JIT fundamentals of continuous improvement, elimination of waste and respect for the whole person combine to link operations activities to the competitive factors of quality, costs, certainty and reliability. To put these principles into practice, however, companies must use a whole series of techniques, some recent but most having been used in the past in different contexts and with much less rigour.

Authors, researchers and consultants interested in JIT do not all agree on the number of is key features. Some elements are drawn from a review of well-known works,[31] while others are taken from surveys of companies[13]; some are combined, while the inclusion of still others depends on the breadth of the definition of JIT used; finally, some elements are included implicitly. Figure 9.1 shows the key elements of JIT that will be discussed in the sections that follow.

KEY ELEMENTS OF JIT

9.3 Small Lots

Reducing lot size makes the system more fluid and also ensures continuity in operations. In this section we will look at three related ideas: reducing setup time, manufacturing small lots and transporting small lots.

Reducing setup time makes it easier to adopt most of the other methods. Rather than using the principles of economic order quantity (EOQ) or economies of scale to minimize the disadvantages of long setup times, JIT simply concentrates on reducing this time, which until recently was considered fixed time or overhead. This concept is embodied in the phrase "single-minute exchange of dies" (SMED), which represents the goal of reducing all setup times to less than 10 minutes (single-digit times). Cutting down on setup times or costs also reduces the size of the lots to be manufactured and ordered, with a corresponding decline in inventory, carrying costs and the total costs of inventory management (Figure 9.2).

This reduction in setup time, as one might expect, eliminates most of the causes of waste mentioned earlier. For this purpose, Shingo[25] proposed SMED, an approach for minimizing setup time; Suzaki[26] cites companies that have cut setup times from 4 hours to 3 minutes, from 9.3 hours to 9 minutes, from 6 hours or more to 10 minutes, from 1.25 hours to 3 minutes, and from 50 minutes to 2 minutes.

Reducing setup time is essential, for it reveals waste and allows the company to apply certain JIT-related techniques. Taken to the extreme, the ideal setup time of zero corresponds to an ideal lot of one; capacity is increased because there is no setup, allowing more productive use of machines; production diversity, in which one model of a product follows another, is possible with no loss of time; production can be planned to suit demand, leading to a demand-pull system; flexibility is increased because of changes in schedule, volume and variety, thereby helping to smooth out the workload; with inventory reduced, any defects are immediately obvious, making it

FIGURE 9.2 ▶
Effects on Lot Size
of Reducing Setup
Costs

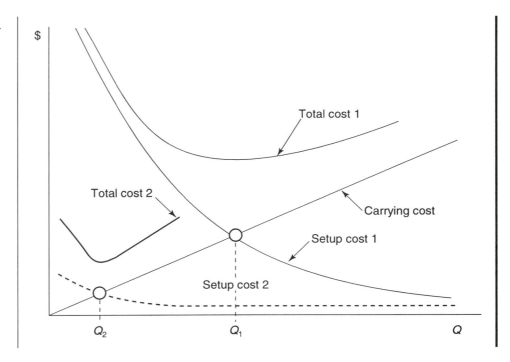

possible to improve quality; manufacturing lead times and waiting times are reduced; and small lots can be manufactured and transported, allowing frequent deliveries.

Manufacturing in smaller lots is possible for it is no longer necessary to spread overhead costs relating to setup over a large quantity of products. This has certain advantages:[20] inventories of work in process and finished products shrink; customer service improves; delivery lead times are reduced for new or existing products; faster detection of defective products limits the number of rejects and reworks; overall visibility of operations and of each workstation is improved; and storage space requirements in the plant and warehouse are reduced.

Transportation and *handling of small lots* are simplified because products are being manufactured in smaller lots, offering improved synchronization of upstream and downstream workstations. Manufacturing smaller lots also simplifies production planning.

9.4   Production Planning

Production in a JIT system is planned essentially as described in chapters 5 and 6 for three- to six-month horizons, but with monthly and sometimes weekly reviews and with variations specific to JIT. Since lead times are reduced, plans can be based on confirmed orders rather than forecasts, and the planning interval can be reduced. If production takes place in response to demand, it is essential that the sum of procurement, waiting, manufacturing and shipping lead times be less than the delivery time guaranteed to the customer, and the operations system must be efficient. No breakdowns or defects can be tolerated and it must be possible to standardize the workload.

Standardizing or *levelling* the daily workload is an essential characteristic of JIT, since one of its objectives is to ensure a constant flow of materials and work throughout the plant, when there is a *varied product line*. For this purpose, the master production schedule (MPS), revised and confirmed for one month, will be divided by the number of working days to obtain this constant standard workload.

For instance, the MPS may show, for a given month of 20 days, orders for quantities of 12,000 A, 9,000 B, 6,000 C and 3,000 D, each letter representing a product model. In traditional manufacturing by lots, the production schedule would show eight consecutive working days for A, six for B, four for C and two for D, in order to reduce the number of setups. In JIT manufacturing, in which setup time is negligible, the daily load could then be 1/20 of each model, or 600 A, 450 B, 300 C and 150 D, and this load could even result in 50 runs of 12 A, nine B, six C and three D. The "levelling out" of production reduces inventories of in-process work and finished products; it also protects against stockouts for a varied product line, because each run corresponds to a proportion of the independent demand for each product. In addition, these runs of varied products make work less monotonous and repetitive and eliminate the need to remember details of each product because of the long period between manufacturing runs.[5] If standardized planning is done downstream (final assembly), it is possible to obtain this levelling out in upstream processes and institute a demand-pull system.

In a traditional system, orders are assigned to the first appropriate workstation on the basis of a priority rule. Once the work is completed at that workstation, the order is shifted to the next step, the queue of waiting orders is once again resolved by a priority rule and so on. Every order is pushed to the following step and handled according to the availability of the machine: the system is controlled from *upstream*.

In a JIT system, work at a given workstation is triggered when the stock at the following workstation is depleted. In fact, this is similar to a double-bin system: when the first bin is empty, more stock is ordered, and there are enough parts in the second bin to meet production needs until the new components arrive. Thus it is the following workstation that signals the previous workstation to provide certain components: the system is controlled from *downstream*.

Since the system is "pulled" by the downstream workstation rather than "pushed" by the upstream workstation, at all steps in the manufacturing process, from beginning to end, the system is termed a *demand-pull* process—i.e., one that carries little or no inventory and in which all processes leading up to the last one (final assembly) keep pace with the production rate of the last process. To simplify this synchronization, cards or sheets, called *kanban* (meaning "card" in Japanese), are used to trigger operations.

The *kanban* is a valuable tool in a production and inventory planning and control (PIPC) system run on JIT principles. However, the kanban makes it possible to control quantities and lead times not only within the different segments of a production process, but also with *other* companies and suppliers[16]; accordingly, it acts as an information system for "pulling" the necessary parts from each operation, as required. The kanban is similar to a "traveller" card or a job order for a lot of parts.[31]

The kanban system may use one or two control cards. There are many variants. The following example briefly describes a two-card system.

Example

■

For each part or component, a specific type of container is designed to hold a preset number of units. For each container there are *two cards*, or kanbans, on which are noted the part number, the capacity of the container and other information. One of the cards, the *production (P) card*, is used by the department that produces the component or part. The other, the *conveyance (C) card*, is for the department that uses the component or part in question (Figure 9.3).

FIGURE 9.3 ▶
Two Types of Kanbans

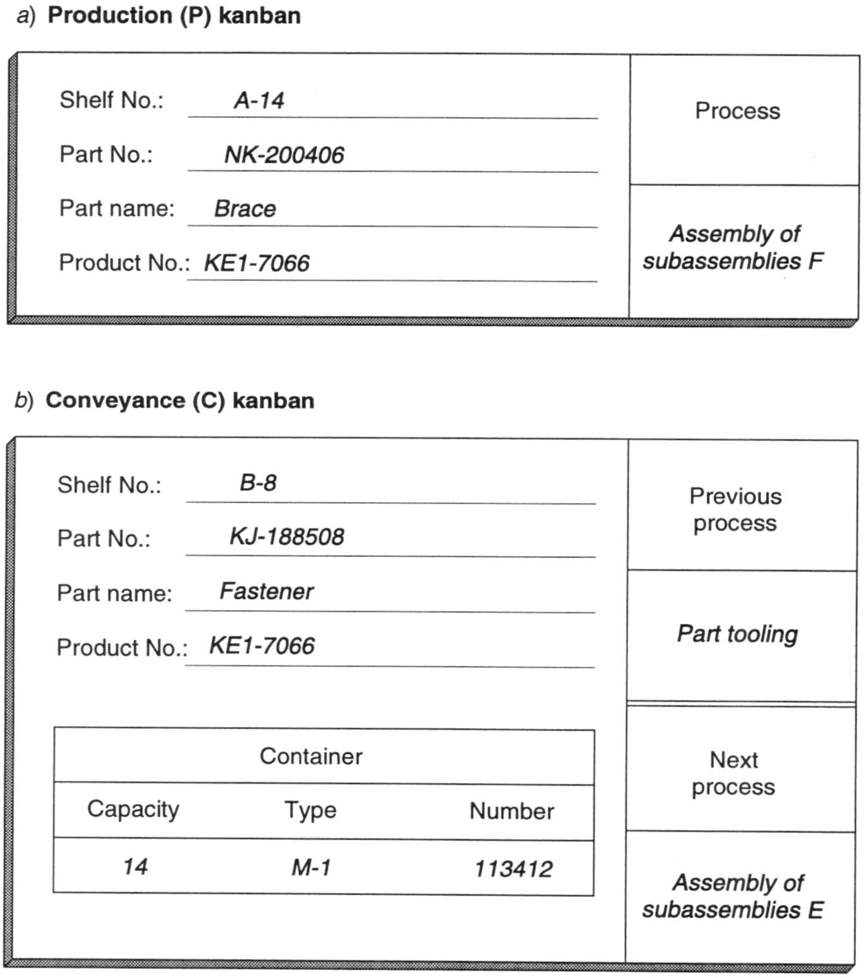

a) **Production (P) kanban**

Shelf No.: A-14	Process
Part No.: NK-200406	
Part name: Brace	Assembly of subassemblies F
Product No.: KE1-7066	

b) **Conveyance (C) kanban**

Shelf No.: B-8	Previous process
Part No.: KJ-188508	
Part name: Fastener	Part tooling
Product No.: KE1-7066	
	Next process

Container			Assembly of subassemblies E
Capacity	Type	Number	
14	M-1	113412	

The system works as follows:

Step 1: The "alternator E" assembly is part of the engine assembled in assembly department A. The department has a specific number of specially designed containers, each holding a given number of subassembly E. Each container also holds a conveyance card.

Example
(*cont.*)

Step 2: As soon as department A receives an internal or external order for an engine that requires an alternator assembly, one of these assemblies is taken from the appropriate container (Figure 9.4, step 1). Once the container is completely empty, a worker from department A takes it to department B, where these assemblies are produced (step 2). The worker then removes a full container in which there is a production (P) card, checks that the details noted on the P and C cards are correct, places the C card in the full container and leaves the P card at the appropriate counter in department B (step 3). Then the worker takes the full container back to department A (step 4).

Step 3: In department B, the production cards left by the worker from department A or any other department are picked up; department B produces the alternator assemblies to meet the demand signified by the number of accumulated production cards, multiplied by the capacity of each container. One P card is placed in each container filled by department B, which can use only specially designed containers for alternator assemblies. It cannot produce the assemblies unless it has the proper P cards, which are given to it whenever one of these containers is removed.

▼ **FIGURE 9.4**
Operation of the Kanban System

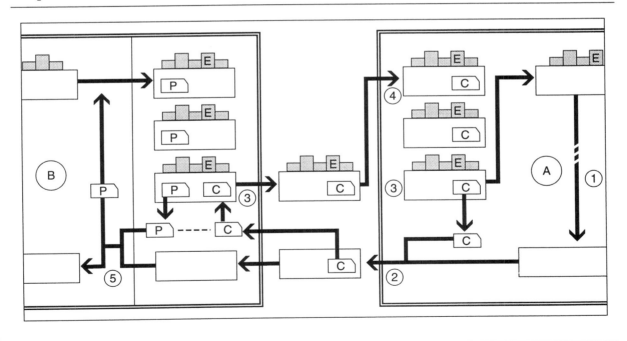

Example
(*cont.*)

Step 4: The same process takes place between department B and the upstream department C for the coil subassemblies required for alternator subassemblies. In fact, similar steps take place between the first production step and receiving, between receiving and the supplier, between the last production step and shipping, and between shipping and the distributor (Figure 9.5).

▼ **FIGURE 9.5**
Overall Kanban System

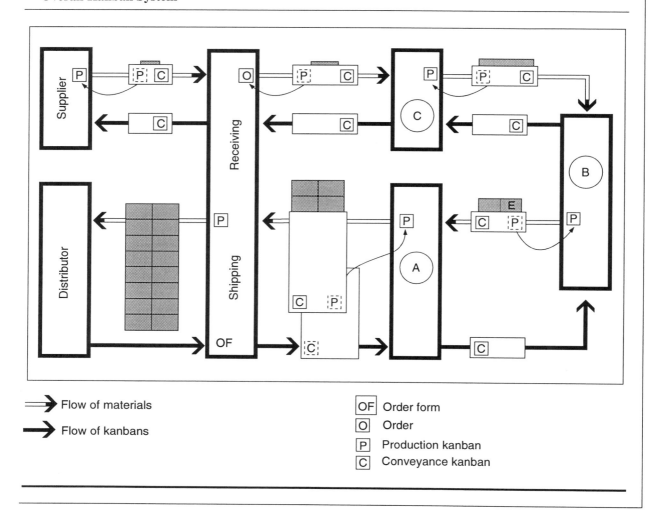

➡ Flow of materials
→ Flow of kanbans

OF	Order form
O	Order
P	Production kanban
C	Conveyance kanban

Note that the number of containers, and hence the number of P and C cards, is determined by operations managers. This number determines the production rate and the inventory required. Although a zero-stock system is being used here, the inventory is not actually zero, but simply kept to a minimum that generally stands at 10% of daily production.

The following formula can be used to calculate the number of kanbans:[7]

$$K = \frac{D\,(T_A + T_P)\,(1 + X)}{Q}$$

where K = number of cards or containers; the sum of all P and C cards,

D = production rate by time unit,

T_A = average waiting time per container or cycle time for C cards; the time it takes a C card to make a complete cycle between the source of the part and the point where the part is used,

T_P = average operating time per container or the time necessary for a P card to make a complete cycle in the workstation where the part is manufactured, including setup time, manufacturing time, inspection and materials-preparation time,

Q = quantity of parts (u) placed in each standard container,

X = safety factor: corresponds to a time period or safety stock; this factor must be closely monitored and does not generally exceed 10%.

Example
■

The demand from a workstation is D = 2,424 u per day; the contents of a container is Q = 20 u; the average waiting time (T_A) is 12 minutes; the average operating time (T_P) is six minutes; a safety factor of 10% (X) is built in. One work day corresponds to eight hours. Determine the number of containers or kanbans.

Solution

To solve this problem, you must begin by converting to standard units:

$$K = \frac{\dfrac{2424\ u/d}{8\ h/d}\left(\dfrac{12\ min}{60\ min/h} + \dfrac{6\ min}{60\ min/h}\right)(1 + 0.1)}{20\ u/\text{container}}$$

$$K = \frac{303\,(0.2 + 0.1)\,(1 + 0.1)}{20} = 5 \text{ kanbans or containers}$$

The simplicity of the manual kanban system is remarkably simple compared with a computerized MPS-type system. The kanban system can be computerized in some cases, however. In addition, the JIT and MPS systems can be used together.

Unlike centralized planning, a demand-pull system—with the visibility of kanban techniques—allows workers to initiate and synchronize operations throughout the entire operations system, reduces inventory and encourages teamwork. Nevertheless, the system does have a weakness,[14] in that it requires nearly zero-defect, zero-shortage and zero-breakdown conditions.

9.5   Managing Equipment and Facilities

Depending on the operations strategy used, equipment and all facilities must correspond to the needs of workers, the organization, the process, products and the market. Four generally accepted aspects of the JIT system relate to equipment and facilities: cleanliness and orderliness, preventive maintenance, in-house equipment modification and autonomation.

Orderliness and cleanliness are unusual essential elements, yet they help eliminate all kinds of waste and contribute to respect for employees. Orderliness and cleanliness directly influence worker morale and the work atmosphere, as well as quality, proper operation of machines, material flows and inventory levels, for how can the JIT approach be applied with mislaid tools, dirty machines, unavailable parts and crowded aisles?

Preventive maintenance is closely related to orderliness and cleanliness. It is indispensable in a continuous demand-pull system, for, since there are no more safety stocks, a machine breakdown may cause bottlenecks. In addition, the level of quality required does not tolerate defects or poorly adjusted machines. The new tendency is to design a total preventive maintenance program,[21] which some authors term a total *productive* maintenance program,[3, 13, 31] to highlight the link between production volumes and the availability of machines. Total preventive maintenance concepts cover the usual preventive maintenance factors, with the following additions:

-   train and empower machine operators to perform maintenance tasks such as cleaning and lubricating, and to suggest improvements;
-   in the statistical control program, include processes that will provide the necessary data to detect incidents and discrepancies;
-   for each machine, prepare a permanent log of the most frequent problems, breakages, breakdowns, or adjustments;
-   progressively eliminate these breakdowns by using a Pareto-type analysis, which will help to identify the most common problems;
-   consider each breakdown as a source of information that will lead to the eventual elimination and prevention of breakdowns and improvement of the machine;
-   conduct proactive or predictive maintenance, by replacing certain parts at set intervals to prevent them from breaking or causing problems;
-   select operating rates (usually less than the maximum possible) that reduce stress on mechanisms and thus the probability of breakdowns.

Nakajima[17] suggests the following features, in order of importance, of a successful total productive maintenance program: the main goal is to maximize machine productivity; preventive maintenance must continue over the entire life of each machine; the program must be implemented by engineering, operations and maintenance staff; the concept of total preventive maintenance must be properly understood by all employees; the concept of teamwork in small groups must extend all the way to maintenance activities, with team members interested in improving quality.

The idea of in-house improvements and manufacture of equipment is closely linked to the concept of preventive maintenance. Japanese companies devote 60% of capital expenditures to improving existing equipment, while North American companies spend 75% of their investments on replacing equipment and adding to capacity.[10]

Improving equipment in-house is less costly. It also helps workers to understand the workings of the machines, simplifies their operation and maintenance and allows them to be adapted to the company's needs without needless contrivances. In addition, it makes it possible to include poka-yoke and autonomation devices.

Poka-yoke, roughly translated as "mistake-proof," is an error-prevention device that simplifies the operator's work by making it impossible to overlook steps in the process, and it protects the operator by automatically halting the machine if an error occurs.

Autonomation, or *jidoka*, is a means of improving and operating a machine without moving to full automation. The supply, positioning, processing and output of parts are automated, as are the measurement of variances and the detection of anomalies; if an error occurs, the machine is automatically halted by a poka-yoke device, and a visible or audible warning signal (*andon,* in Japanese) is activated. The system is not automated, for it does not correct its own mistakes or start up again by itself. Autonomation costs less than automation; in addition, the machine requires little or no human monitoring; it can work without an operator, or a single operator can oversee several machines at once.

Poka-yoke and autonomation eliminate waste, since they reduce the need for the human supervision that adds no value to the product; and by detecting errors, halting production and making it possible to correct errors and defects, they reduce waste even further and improve quality.

9.6   Supply Management

In the industrial sector, the cost of supplies accounts for about 60% of a company's revenue; the importance of this figure in a JIT context makes it a very attractive target, not only because of the amount of expenditure involved but also because of its impact on quality, lead times and synchronization of needs. This section will deal only with those aspects of supply management that are related to JIT.

At least eight supply activities in a JIT context call for specific attention to permit continuous improvement of quality and productivity.[1]

1. Purchasing in small lots, delivered frequently in the quantities and with the lead times stipulated in the purchaser's MPS, allows the purchaser to integrate the supplier into its operations and to benefit from stable operations, reduced average inventory, rapid identification of defects, high quality and, very often, lower costs. The main inconvenience of ordering small lots may be the transportation costs of frequent deliveries. There are a number of ways of circumventing this problem: purchasing from local suppliers, encouraging the supplier to set up near the purchaser's plant, combining purchases from several suppliers in the same area so that they can use the same truck, or including only type A or B articles (as we saw in the ABC, or Pareto, analysis) in purchases of small lots.

2. Dealing with a small number of suppliers, preferably a single one for each category of purchase, allows the company to set up structural long-term procurement arrangements rather than depending on fluctuating short-term procurement. Ideally, the supplier will also introduce a JIT system. Under

such agreements, the supplier may also contribute to product design and suggest modifications that would allow it to produce better-quality supplies at a lower cost.

3. The selection and evaluation of suppliers is crucial. The company must consider the supplier's ability to consistently provide high-quality goods, the likelihood of a long-term co-operative relationship, the supplier's ability to consistently provide a small but precise quantity of the product on time, its proximity and whether its price structure is competitive. The company should undertake "supplier development"—that is, help the supplier develop the technical and operating capabilities necessary to meet JIT requirements.

4. Quality-control inspections must be carried out at the source, in the supplier's plant; once confidence is established, the supplier can be left to do the inspections itself. The purchaser may insist that the supplier obtain quality certification and submit to periodic inspections.

5. The product and its specifications are developed. Once the supplier is assured of a contract for a considerable future volume, it may invest in research and development (R&D), improving its process and its product so as to offer better quality, lower prices and superior product features.

6. The competitive process of *repeated tendering* with new prices no longer applies, since the relationship is a long-term, structural one. The purchaser no longer awards the contract to the lowest qualified bidder, although the contract is renewable annually.

7. Traditional boxes and crates are replaced by standard containers designed for specific small quantities of a given product; this allows fast recognition (kanban), simplifies transactions, helps avoid errors, reduces costs and eliminates waste and paperwork.

8. Paperwork is greatly reduced, for everything is eliminated, reduced, standardized or synchronized.

Note that suppliers who do not adopt a form of JIT may be obliged to carry considerable inventory, with the attendant high costs, so as to be able to supply the purchaser frequently with small lots.[9]

One exploratory study[19] on JIT supply and the *marketing relationship* from the supplier's point of view adds a number of assumptions about JIT, and confirms others, although the conclusions remain unconfirmed and are limited in scope:

- The *long-term relationship* between JIT suppliers and purchasers is considered to last longer than it does in a traditional context, and *customer selection* is more rigorous, since the investment, risk and costs of change are greater.

- A larger number of the supplier's functional units *participate* in its relations with the customer: quality-assurance services, materials management and production management expand and support marketing activities; interaction between the functional units is more *frequent*; marketing, customer service, design engineering, quality assurance, materials management and production management play a greater part in the interorganizational exchange process.

- Suppliers say that they enjoy *more open communications with the customer*, which results in their receiving more information on the customer's short- and long-term plans and needs; suppliers offer better support services for product design and technical assistance in terms of quality, standardization and value analysis.

JIT therefore implies major changes, both systematic and strategic, in the purchaser's procurement activities and the supplier's marketing activities. The selection of the supplier by the customer, and vice versa, must be carefully considered, for the links between customers and suppliers in a JIT system are closer to a marriage than dating, and they will be interdependent over the long term.

9.7   Continuous Improvement and the Human Factor

Continuous improvement (*kaizen*, in Japanese) is the underlying philosophy of JIT, while the *human factor*, combined with the elimination of waste, contributes to respect for workers.

Continuous improvement is a gradual and endless process, rather than a finite program, and is intended to refine the product, the process and every activity, from design to use, in order to attain the ideal of perfection. The process is gradual because it consists of small, progressive, ongoing improvements, rather than major innovations. Continuous improvement is based on the factors that go into the learning curve. Progressive improvement comes from setting a target or a goal. Whenever a target is reached, it is superseded by a new one. For instance, in its continuous-improvement efforts, a Canadian company progressively reduced its setup time from 14 hours to fewer than four hours, in five months.[26]

Such improvements stem not from massive investment, but from the constant efforts of well-trained and respected individuals. The most overlooked potential source of improvement is the shop floor, where 80% of employees spend 99% of their time. Senior managers represent only 2% of a company's staff and spend perhaps 1% of their time in the plant; middle managers and technical specialists represent 15% to 16% of staff and spend 5% and 25%, respectively, of their time, in the plant.[30] To implement JIT, the company must devote considerable time to training, changing attitudes and modifying the roles of the various parties involved.

Workers become more versatile with JIT, for they are called upon to operate several machines at once. They learn to work as a team, for they must solve problems that they and their co-workers have detected; they maintain their machines; they plan and control quality and quantity; and they contribute to continuous improvement. Middle managers, foremen and technical specialists will see their roles change as workers come to play a larger part and as their responsibilities increase. They will help workers solve problems, train them in their new tasks, and become group leaders, motivators and co-ordinators rather than auditors, inspectors and disciplinarians. Senior managers have the important job of effecting these changes, convincing everyone involved of the need for them, and creating a climate of trust. They must invent new policies, methods and procedures that will encourage workers to be creative, while assuring them that the improvements they make will not eventually steal their jobs away. Trust and mutual understanding are the basis of respect for employees, and it is up to senior management to lead the way.

9.8   Other Elements of JIT

Researchers and practitioners list other elements of JIT, which are implicit in the features we have seen above or in other chapters.

Layout: In the JIT context, facilities must be arranged so that components and products can flow or be depleted smoothly. Specific attention must be given to eliminating stocks, handling and queues, and to reducing distances between operations. In other words, the goal is to minimize waste in order to maximize operations that add value, through linear or U-shaped layouts. A cellular layout, as opposed to a functional one, organizes small groups of workers, or machines and workers, to produce a line of similar components or products; the machine/worker group is designed to suit the range of operations involved. A cellular layout, in which operations and setups are automated, becomes a flexible manufacturing system. A cellular layout, or manufacturing cell, is an integral part of the technological group, a manufacturing and engineering design philosophy wherein similar parts and components are grouped together and coded so that they can easily be recognized and are manufactured in the cells. Very often cells can be set up only in part of the plant.

A cellular layout is also a type of focussed plant intended to reduce all complexity: overly large product lines, excessive numbers of technologies or processes, a bureaucratic organizational structure, etc. Such complexity is reduced by means of simplification, standardization, grouping, repetition and experience.

Product design: Often mentioned as a key element of JIT, product design is intended to ensure not only customer satisfaction, but also improved production and supply activities. A well-designed product eliminates steps in manufacturing and assembly, and reduces setup time, supply and production lead times and inventory levels.[23] Product design also has a decisive effect on quality, for it determines product parameters and costs, and ease of quality control.[8]

9.9   JIT Applications

The philosophy of continuous and progressive improvement of quality and productivity, and the two principles of eliminating waste and respecting the whole person, apply in any type of firm. Every manager, in whatever position or whatever company, aspires to zero stock, zero stockouts, zero defects, zero breakdowns and zero lead time. However, some elements of JIT, in particular those dealing with PIPC, are more difficult to apply when demand fluctuates widely.

Ideally, JIT, with or without the kanban system, works very well with the PIPC of a company for which demand is relatively stable and repetitive, and where products are fairly similar so that there can be a constant flow—i.e., in a balanced system in which the workload is levelled and synchronous. If there are wide fluctuations in lead times, quantities or product models, however, this type of system can be slow to react and can lead to rising costs and increased inventory and lead times.

The JIT system is compatible with an MPS-type system, but four aspects of JIT require some explanation as to their use with the MPS.

1. Since JIT is a demand-pull system, it reduces and even eliminates the facets of scheduling related to shop control in an MPS. This activity is done with kanbans, which pull the materials required to the next step.

2. Because JIT ensures continual flow, and intermediate stocks are reduced or eliminated, the product bill of materials (BOM) can be designed with fewer levels, using "phantom" BOMs. Note, however, that the material requirement planning (MRP) BOM, although it may be reduced, remains useful for determining all the components needed to carry out the MPS and for determining the manufacturing release or stock order dates for these components.

3. Since the production cycle in JIT planning is shorter—because lead times are eliminated—it is often of no use to offset material requirements in a previous period.

4. Since stocks are low and quality is almost perfect, calculations for determining net requirements from gross requirements are unnecessary.

Karmarkar[12] suggests hybrid PIPC systems, in which selection of the control method depends on the type of production process. The rows in Figure 9.6 show four types of operations systems, ranging from a continuous flow system (i.e., a pull system), where there is little variability in production lead times, to a make-to-order system (push system) with great variability in production lead times. The columns show three types of PIPC activities: MRP, order release control and shop control. The numbered boxes are the choices to be made, and the numbers in each box are the reference points for the following explanations.

In a *continuous flow system*, the production process is dedicated to one or several similar products. Production is continuous and level, so that the lead time for production is uniform and predictable. Example: an assembly line: (1) materials can be delivered to the process using a JIT approach, since the production rates are uniform and predictable; (2) with level production, it is sufficient to specify the production rate, since the production order is unnecessary; (3) since the process is predictable, the flow of materials is uniform and is controlled by JIT-kanban.

In a *repetitive batch system*, parts of the process may resemble a continuous flow system while others involve products manufactured in batches. Lead times are constant and predictable. The range of products is relatively stable, with possible monthly variations. Example: production of parts and components for high-volume end products such as cars or electronics: (4) some parts and materials that are used uniformly can be delivered using a JIT approach, whereas for those requiring long lead times MRP is required to plan procurement, delivery and co-ordination between plants; (5) since lead times are predictable, MRP works well, but pull methods are less expensive; MRP may be necessary for master scheduling; inventory must be managed and operations co-ordinated; (6) since the flow is uniform, a demand-pull system may be used to move work on the shop floor.

In a *dynamic batch system* production is carried out by lots, and the output mix and volume can vary depending on customer orders. This makes for variability in the process and loads, bottlenecks, stockouts and lead times. Example: parts and product manufacturers supplying several customers, or factories supplying retail outlets with multiple parts: (7) MRP is appropriate for dealing with the great diversity of parts and operations and for co-ordinating activities in the different shops; (8) MRP, with its

FIGURE 9.6 ▶
Comparison of JIT
and MRP Systems
According to
Variability of Lead
Times

		Materials planning	Order-release control	Shop-floor control
Low ↑ Lead time variability ↓ **High**	**Pull: continuous flow**	JIT `1`	Rate-based `2`	JIT-pull `3`
	Hybrid push-pull: batch—repetitive	JIT-MRP `4`	Pull or MRP `5`	Pull `6`
	Hybrid push-pull: batch—dynamic	MRP `7`	MRP `8`	Pull or order scheduling `9`
	Push: custom engineering	MRP `10`	Order scheduling `11`	Operations scheduling `12`

Source: Adapted from a figure by Karmarkar.[12] Reproduced by permission of the President and Fellows of Harvard College; copyright 1989, all rights reserved.

forecasting skill and ability to control quantities, stocks and needs, is essential; (9) for operations with high part volumes, a pull system could be useful; however, work orders are necessary to create an MPS with MRP to control purchasing, parts, subassemblies and finished products and to match them with customer orders.

In a *custom engineering system*, low-volume complex products make for high variability in production partners. The loads or work quantity in each department, queues, bottlenecks and lead times are significant. Example: machine-tool manufacturers and producers of custom equipment: (10) MRP is indispensable as a management information tool, given the variety of parts, long lead times in obtaining components, etc.; (11) the plant runs on work orders generated by MRP, which maintains information about availability of materials and co-ordinates work among shops. However, MRP cannot ensure timely deliveries with such variable lead times and bottlenecks; (12) this type of production calls for extensive monitoring and follow-up; the appropriate scheduling systems, such as OPT (Optimized Production Technology) are sophisticated but costly.

Note that JIT, as a management philosophy, is indispensable for all types of operations. However, planning and control aspects must be suited to the type of manufacturing. When used properly, it promises very impressive benefits.

9.10 Advantages, Disadvantages and Implementation of JIT

Many studies confirm the benefits to be enjoyed by various companies implementing JIT systems. It is difficult to quantify the successes reported, however, because of the variety of methods used to measure the benefits, the methodology itself, the number of respondents, the number of years of JIT use and the number of JIT elements implemented. Vollmann et al.[27] report the advantages of JIT based on a study by Plossl.[21]

Table 9.1 gives the results for a group of companies, with improvements expressed as a percentage; Table 9.2 shows the benefits of JIT as reported by the 108 automobile companies with the most JIT experience, all members of the Automotive Industry Action Group (AIAG).

Although these two tables are not comparable, they offer complementary information, while all the benefits reported correspond, on the whole, to the elements of JIT. Other research results on the benefits of JIT have been published as well. Crawford et al.[4] examine the reasons for implementing JIT and list the resulting advantages, and also identify some implementation problems. Voss and Robinson[29] report on the results of research in the UK, while Bartezzaghi et al.[2] report on the Italian experience. Finally, Piper and McLachlin[20] discuss the use of JIT by 13 firms in Quebec and Ontario.

	Improvement		◄ TABLE 9.1 Summary of JIT Benefits
	Aggregate % (3 to 5 years)	**Annual %**	
Reduction of manufacturing cycle time	80 to 90	30 to 40	
Inventory reductions:			
– Raw materials	35 to 70	10 to 30	
– Work in process	70 to 90	30 to 50	
– Finished goods	60 to 90	25 to 60	
Reductions in labour costs			
– Direct	10 to 50	3 to 20	
– Indirect	20 to 60	3 to 20	
Reduction in space requirements	40 to 80	25 to 50	
Reduction in cost of quality	25 to 60	10 to 30	
Reduction in cost of materials	5 to 25	2 to 10	
Source: Adapted from a table by Vollmann et al.[27]			

TABLE 9.2 ▶
Benefits of JIT in
the Automobile
Industry
According to 108
Companies

	Percentage of companies
Reduced inventory	56
Better customer relations	45
Improved quality	44
Successful JIT deliveries	34
Better supplier relations	30
Improved productivity	33
Reduced setup costs	23
Better employee relations	22

Source: Adapted from a table by Celly *et al.*[3]

These reports are interesting in that they cover a variety of companies, in different countries, using various criteria. Despite the differences, JIT does offer the desired features. Nevertheless, everything is not perfect in the world of JIT. A number of problems and drawbacks have been reported.

The major drawback of JIT is that some people consider it a systematic and strategic management philosophy, while others see it as simply a toolbox containing a multitude of techniques to be applied as necessary. This makes it difficult to make full use of JIT and to benefit fully from its potential.

Along with the benefits of JIT, some companies have discovered an unexpected consequence: stress.[11] Many workers are not prepared to handle the constant pressure resulting from four particular aspects of the JIT philosophy:

–   Speed of the line: a steady pace must be maintained, for there are no anticipation inventories and there is no undesirable down time. Workers must adapt quickly to all changes, and this leads to stress. In addition, some workers have trouble handling the responsibility of being able to stop the assembly line if there are problems.

–   Reduced inventory: the company no longer has safety stocks to tide it over should unforeseen problems arise; furthermore, this reduction in inventory is intentional, designed to bring problems to light. Once a problem is corrected, a new target is set with a view to continuous improvement; this makes for a stressful system and stressed workers.

–   Reduced setup time: increases the frequency of changes and facilitates the continuous improvement that is designed to constantly reduce this time, thereby creating a double source of pressure.

–   Flexibility: makes it possible to enhance workers' tasks—for instance, by placing an operator in charge of a dozen machines instead of one; for some this is a challenge, while others find it stressful.

In short, every advantage can become a disadvantage or a problem if implementation is carried out improperly or if expectations are too high. Table 9.3 shows that 62% of respondents had problems with schedule changes or delivery lead times imposed by customers, and that 5% of companies then solved these problems. Poor internal and external quality, although improved by 10% and 13%, remained a major problem. It is worth noting that commitment on the part of workers and senior managers grew significantly, however, which suggests that constant efforts lead to continuous improvement.

Despite the fact that many problems and disadvantages remain, the spectacular benefits of JIT suggest that its proponents have the right idea.

Voss and Robinson,[29] in their study of JIT in the UK, found that of the 57% of respondents ($n = 132$) who were implementing or planning to implement certain JIT features, only 16% were doing so as part of a formal program. This study also shows that companies were adopting JIT features in a piecemeal fashion, without seeing any system-wide effects; for instance, only 3.2% of respondents had opted for a zero-defects plan, and 4.1% for kanban techniques. This research indicates that while industry leaders are familiar with the JIT philosophy, they are reluctant to implement it fully, preferring to begin with the simplest aspects, albeit not the most profitable ones. Nevertheless, if they decide to implement other JIT elements, it will simply confirm the continuous-improvement dimension of JIT.

	Percentage of respondents who say:		
	Was a problem	**Is still a problem**	**Is now under control**
Customer schedule changes	62	57	5
Poor supplier quality (external)	59	49	10
Poor production quality (internal)	57	44	13
Inability to change paperwork systems	57	46	11
Shortage of critical parts	57	44	13
Supplier inability to deliver JIT	57	49	8
Lack of employee commitment	49	31	18
Inability to reduce setup time	48	36	12
Inadequate equipment and tooling	45	31	14
Surplus of non-critical parts	44	33	11
Lack of senior management commitment	43	28	15
Labour contract problems	35	26	9
Source: Adapted from a table by Celly *et al.*[3]			

◄   **TABLE 9.3**
    JIT
Implementation
    Problems

There is no magic recipe or implementation guide for JIT. Everything depends on the state of the company, its strengths and weaknesses, its competitors, its suppliers and, above all, its employees. According to Voss,[29] Japanese managers use the following techniques to implement JIT in British firms:

-   establish order and cleanliness in the plant;
-   eliminate obvious waste by identifying and correcting methods and processes that produce defects and scrap;
-   train managers in information management;
-   encourage teamwork to foster interaction among managers and workers;
-   practise preventive maintenance;
-   implement statistical quality control;
-   train workers in order to elicit their participation;
-   study material flows and start reducing setup times;
-   simplify handling techniques, including the selection of kanban containers;
-   establish objectives and performance criteria; make the results visible and change the target whenever it is reached;
-   change the layout, the work rules, and the type and means of information.

REVIEW QUESTIONS

1. Why are the JIT philosophy and its central principles so important in POM?

2. Why is worker participation indispensable to the implementation of JIT?

3. What is the difference between a push system and a pull system?

4. Describe the kanban system.

5. How does supply in a JIT context differ from the traditional approach?

6. What precautions must be taken to ensure the smooth implementation of JIT?

DISCUSSION QUESTIONS

1. "If authors and researchers cannot agree on the number of elements that relate to JIT, it is because JIT is not yet universally understood." Do you agree or disagree? Why?

2. "All this talk about respect for workers is simply a clever ruse to get more out of employees." Do you agree or disagree? Why?

3. How are JIT and TQC two sides of the same coin?

4. What requirements are necessary to obtain progressive and continuous improvement?

5. What are the advantages of JIT for the customer?

6. What are the advantages of JIT for the company?

7. What are the advantages of JIT for the supplier?

8. Are JIT techniques applicable to the service sector?

9. Is the manufacturer who applies the JIT philosophy simply forcing its suppliers to carry inventory in its place?

10. Why are quality and productivity considered inseparable features of JIT?

11. Give everyday examples of poka-yoke or error-prevention devices.

12. Is it true that JIT replaces PIPC systems such as MRP?

PROBLEM

1. How many kanbans will be necessary if the weekly production rate is 15,868 units (distributed uniformly over time), there are 16 parts per container, the average waiting time is 14 minutes, the workstation can produce 480 units per hour and there is a safety factor of 10%, assuming that the company operates eight hours a day, five days a week?

REFERENCES

1. ANSARI, A., and B. MODARRESS, "JIT Purchasing as a Quality and Productivity Center," *International Journal of Production Research,* Vol. 26, No. 1, 1988, pp. 19-26.

2. BARTEZZAGHI, E., F. TURCO and G. SPINA, "The Impact of the Just in Time Approach on Production System Performance: A Survey of Italian Industry," *International Journal of Production Management*, Vol. 12, No. 1, 1991, pp. 5-17.

3. CELLY, A.F., W.H. CLEGG, A.W. SMITH and M.A. VONDEREMBSE, "Implementation of JIT in the United States," *International Journal of Purchasing and Materials Management*, (National Association of Purchasing Management Inc.) Vol. 22, No. 4, Winter 1986, pp. 9-15.

4. CRAWFORD, M.K., J.H. BLACKSTONE and J.F. COX, "Study of JIT Implementation and Operating Problems," *International Journal of Production Research*, Vol. 26, No. 9, 1988, pp. 1561-1568.

5. CROSBY, L.B., "The Just in Time Manufacturing Process: Control of Quality and Quantity," *Production and Inventory Management*, 4th quarter, 1984, pp. 21-33.

6. HALL, R.W., *Attaining Manufacturing Excellence*. Homewood, ILL.: Dow Jones-Irwin, Homewood, Illinois, 1987, pp. 22-27.

7. HALL, R.W., *Zero Inventories*. Homewood, ILL.: Dow Jones-Irwin, 1983.

8. HANDFIELD, R., "Quality Management in Japan Versus the United States: An Overview," *Production Inventory Management*, 1989, pp. 30-32.

9. HARRISON, A., and C. VOSS, "Issues in Setting Up JIT Supply," *International Journal of Production Management*, Vol. 10, No. 2, 1990, pp. 84-93.

10. HAYES, R., and S.C. WHEELWRIGHT, *Restoring our Competitive Edge: Competing through Manufacturing*. New York: John Wiley & Sons, 1984.

11. INMAN, R.A., and L.D. BRANDON, "An Undesirable Effect of JIT," *Production Inventory Management Journal*, 1st semester, 1992, pp. 55-58.

12. KARMARKAR, U., "Getting Control of Just in Time," *Harvard Business Review*, September-October 1989, pp. 122-131.

13. KIM, G.C., and S.M. LEE, "Impact of Computer Technology on the Implementation of Just in Time Production Systems," *International Journal of Production Management*, Vol. 9, No. 8, 1989, pp. 20-39.

14. LEE, L.C., "A Comparative Study of the Push and Pull Production System," *International Journal of Production Management*, Vol. 9, No. 4, 1988, pp. 5-18.

15. McARTHUR, D., Implementing TQM and JIT in a Factory Environment, American Productivity and Quality Center, case No. 79, November 1990.

16. MONDEN, Y., *Toyota Production System: A Practical Approach to Production Management*. Norcross, Ga.: Industrial Engineers and Management Press, 1983.

17. NAKAJIMA, S., *Introduction to Total Preventive Maintenance*. Cambridge, Mass.: Productivity Press, 1988.

18. OHNO, T., *Workplace Management*. Cambridge, Mass.: Productivity Press, 1988, p. 78.

19. O'NEAL, C., "JIT Procurement and Relationship Marketing," *Industrial Marketing Management*, No. 18, 1989, pp. 55-63.

20. PIPER, C., and R. McLACHLIN, "Just in Time: Eleven Achievable Dimensions," *Operations Management Review*, Vol. 7, No. 3-4, 1990, pp. 1-8.

21. PLOSSL, G.W., *Just in Time: A Special Roundtable*. Atlanta: George Plossl Educational Services, 1985.

22. SANDRAS, W.A., Jr., "Total Quality Control: The Other Side of the JIT Coin," *Just in Time Reprints*, ref. ed., APICS, 1989.

23. SCHONBERGER, J.R., *World Class Manufacturing: The Lessons of Simplicity Applied*. New York: Free Press, 1986.

24. SCHONBERGER, J.R., *Japanese Manufacturing Techniques: Nine Hidden Lessons in Simplicity*. New York: Free Press, 1982.

25. SHINGO, S., *A Revolution in Manufacturing: The SMED System*. Cambridge, Mass.: Productivity Press, 1985.

26. SUZAKI, K., *The Manufacturing Challenge: Techniques for Continuous Improvement*. New York: Free Press, 1987.

27. VOLLMANN, T.E., W.L. BERRY and D.C. WHYBARK. *Manufacturing, Planning and Control Systems*, 3rd ed. Homewood, Ill.: Richard D. Irwin, 1992.

28. VOSS, C.A., "International Perspectives on Just in Time Manufacturing," Symposium at the Annual Meeting of the Academy of Management, New Orleans, August 1987.

29. VOSS, C.A., and S.J. ROBINSON, "Application of Just in Time Manufacturing Techniques in the United Kingdom," *International Journal of Production Management*, Vol. 7, No. 4, 1987, pp. 46-52.

30. WANTUCK, K.A., *Just in Time for America*. Milwaukee, Wis.: The Forum, 1989.

31. WHITE, R.E., and W.A. RUSH, "Composition and Scope of JIT," *Operations Management Review*, Vol. 7, No. 3-4, 1990, pp. 9-18.

Tables

TABLE 1
Area under the Cumulative Standard
Normal Distribution

TABLE 2
Cumulative Poisson Probability
Distribution

TABLE 3
MIL-STD.105D (BNQ 9911-105),
Letter-codes Table and Single and
Normal Sampling Table

TABLE 4
Random Numbers

▼ TABLE 1
Area under the Cumulative Standard Normal Distribution

z	0.00	0.01	0.02	0.03	0.04	0.05	0.06	0.07	0.08	0.09
0.0	0.5000	0.5040	0.5080	0.5120	0.5160	0.5199	0.5239	0.5279	0.5319	0.5359
0.1	0.5398	0.5438	0.5478	0.5517	0.5557	0.5596	0.5636	0.5675	0.5714	0.5753
0.2	0.5793	0.5832	0.5871	0.5910	0.5948	0.5987	0.6026	0.6064	0.6103	0.6141
0.3	0.6179	0.6217	0.6255	0.6293	0.6331	0.6368	0.6406	0.6443	0.6480	0.6517
0.4	0.6554	0.6591	0.6628	0.6664	0.6700	0.6736	0.6772	0.6808	0.6844	0.6879
0.5	0.6915	0.6950	0.6985	0.7019	0.7054	0.7088	0.7123	0.7157	0.7190	0.7224
0.6	0.7257	0.7291	0.7324	0.7357	0.7389	0.7422	0.7454	0.7486	0.7517	0.7549
0.7	0.7580	0.7611	0.7642	0.7673	0.7704	0.7734	0.7764	0.7794	0.7823	0.7852
0.8	0.7881	0.7910	0.7939	0.7967	0.7995	0.8023	0.8051	0.8078	0.8106	0.8133
0.9	0.8195	0.8186	0.8212	0.8238	0.8264	0.8289	0.8315	0.8340	0.8365	0.8389
1.0	0.8413	0.8438	0.8461	0.8485	0.8508	0.8531	0.8554	0.8577	0.8599	0.8621
1.1	0.8643	0.8665	0.8686	0.8708	0.8729	0.8749	0.8770	0.8790	0.8810	0.8830
1.2	0.8894	0.8869	0.8888	0.8907	0.8925	0.8944	0.8962	0.8980	0.8997	0.9015
1.3	0.9032	0.9049	0.9066	0.9082	0.9099	0.9115	0.9131	0.9147	0.9162	0.9177
1.4	0.9192	0.9207	0.9222	0.9236	0.9251	0.9265	0.9279	0.9292	0.9306	0.9319
1.5	0.9332	0.9345	0.9357	0.9370	0.9382	0.9394	0.9406	0.9418	0.9429	0.9441
1.6	0.9452	0.9463	0.9474	0.9484	0.9495	0.9505	0.9515	0.9525	0.9535	0.9545
1.7	0.9554	0.9564	0.9573	0.9582	0.9591	0.9599	0.9608	0.9616	0.9625	0.9633
1.8	0.9641	0.9649	0.9656	0.9664	0.9671	0.9678	0.9686	0.9693	0.9699	0.9706
1.9	0.9713	0.9719	0.9726	0.9732	0.9738	0.9744	0.9750	0.9756	0.9761	0.9767
2.0	0.9772	0.9778	0.9783	0.9788	0.9793	0.9798	0.9803	0.9808	0.9812	0.9817
2.1	0.9821	0.9826	0.9830	0.9834	0.9838	0.9842	0.9846	0.9850	0.9854	0.9857
2.2	0.9861	0.9864	0.9868	0.9871	0.9875	0.9878	0.9881	0.9884	0.9887	0.9890
2.3	0.9893	0.9896	0.9898	0.9901	0.9904	0.9906	0.9909	0.9911	0.9913	0.9916
2.4	0.9918	0.9920	0.9922	0.9925	0.9927	0.9929	0.9931	0.9932	0.9934	0.9936
2.5	0.9938	0.9940	0.9941	0.9943	0.9945	0.9946	0.9948	0.9949	0.9951	0.9952
2.6	0.9953	0.9955	0.9956	0.9957	0.9959	0.9960	0.9961	0.9962	0.9963	0.9964
2.7	0.9965	0.9966	0.9967	0.9968	0.9969	0.9970	0.9971	0.9972	0.9973	0.9974
2.8	0.9974	0.9975	0.9976	0.9977	0.9977	0.9978	0.9979	0.9979	0.9980	0.9981
2.9	0.9981	0.9982	0.9982	0.9983	0.9984	0.9984	0.9985	0.9985	0.9986	0.9986
3.0	0.9987	0.9987	0.9987	0.9988	0.9988	0.9989	0.9989	0.9989	0.9990	0.9990

NOTE: These probabilities range from $-\infty$ to z. Areas for negative values of z are obtained by symmetry.

▼ **TABLE 2**
Cumulative Poisson Probability Distribution

λ or np \ c	0	1	2	3	4	5	6	7	8	9	10	11	12	13	14	15
0.02	0.980	1.000														
0.04	0.961	0.999	1.000													
0.06	0.942	0.998	1.000													
0.08	0.923	0.997	1.000													
0.10	0.905	0.995	1.000													
0.15	0.861	0.990	0.999	1.000												
0.20	0.819	0.982	0.999	1.000												
0.25	0.779	0.974	0.998	1.000												
0.30	0.741	0.963	0.996	1.000												
0.35	0.705	0.951	0.994	1.000												
0.40	0.670	0.938	0.992	0.999	1.000											
0.45	0.638	0.925	0.989	0.999	1.000											
0.50	0.607	0.910	0.986	0.998	1.000											
0.55	0.577	0.894	0.982	0.998	1.000											
0.60	0.549	0.878	0.977	0.997	1.000											
0.65	0.522	0.861	0.972	0.996	0.999	1.000										
0.70	0.497	0.844	0.966	0.994	0.999	1.000										
0.75	0.472	0.827	0.959	0.993	0.999	1.000										
0.80	0.449	0.809	0.953	0.991	0.999	1.000										
0.85	0.427	0.791	0.945	0.989	0.998	1.000										
0.90	0.407	0.772	0.937	0.987	0.998	1.000										
0.95	0.387	0.754	0.929	0.984	0.997	1.000										
1.00	0.368	0.736	0.920	0.981	0.996	0.999	1.000									
1.1	0.333	0.699	0.900	0.974	0.995	0.999	1.000									
1.2	0.301	0.663	0.879	0.966	0.992	0.998	1.000									
1.3	0.273	0.627	0.857	0.957	0.989	0.998	1.000									
1.4	0.247	0.592	0.833	0.946	0.986	0.997	0.999	1.000								
1.5	0.223	0.558	0.809	0.934	0.981	0.996	0.999	1.000								
1.6	0.202	0.525	0.783	0.921	0.976	0.994	0.999	1.000								
1.7	0.183	0.493	0.757	0.907	0.970	0.992	0.998	1.000								
1.8	0.165	0.463	0.731	0.891	0.964	0.990	0.997	0.999	1.000							
1.9	0.150	0.434	0.704	0.875	0.956	0.987	0.997	0.999	1.000							
2.0	0.135	0.406	0.677	0.857	0.947	0.983	0.995	0.999	1.000							
2.2	0.111	0.355	0.623	0.819	0.928	0.975	0.993	0.998	1.000							
2.4	0.091	0.308	0.570	0.779	0.904	0.964	0.988	0.997	0.999	1.000						
2.6	0.074	0.267	0.518	0.736	0.877	0.951	0.983	0.995	0.999	1.000						
2.8	0.061	0.231	0.469	0.692	0.848	0.935	0.976	0.992	0.998	0.999	1.000					
3.0	0.050	0.199	0.423	0.647	0.815	0.916	0.966	0.988	0.996	0.999	1.000					

▼ TABLE 2
Cumulative Poisson Probability Distribution (*cont.*)

λ or np \ c	0	1	2	3	4	5	6	7	8	9	10	11	12	13	14	15
3.2	0.041	0.171	0.380	0.603	0.781	0.895	0.955	0.983	0.994	0.998	1.000					
3.4	0.033	0.147	0.340	0.558	0.744	0.871	0.942	0.977	0.992	0.997	0.999	1.000				
3.6	0.027	0.126	0.303	0.515	0.706	0.844	0.927	0.969	0.988	0.996	0.999	1.000				
3.8	0.022	0.107	0.269	0.473	0.668	0.816	0.909	0.960	0.984	0.994	0.998	0.999	1.000			
4.0	0.018	0.092	0.238	0.433	0.629	0.785	0.889	0.949	0.979	0.992	0.997	0.999	1.000			
4.2	0.015	0.078	0.210	0.395	0.590	0.753	0.867	0.936	0.972	0.989	0.996	0.999	1.000			
4.4	0.012	0.066	0.185	0.359	0.551	0.720	0.844	0.921	0.964	0.985	0.994	0.998	0.999	1.000		
4.6	0.010	0.056	0.163	0.326	0.513	0.686	0.818	0.905	0.955	0.980	0.992	0.997	0.999	1.000		
4.8	0.008	0.048	0.143	0.294	0.476	0.651	0.791	0.887	0.944	0.975	0.996	0.996	0.999	1.000		
5.0	0.007	0.040	0.125	0.265	0.440	0.616	0.762	0.867	0.932	0.968	0.986	0.995	0.998	0.999	1.000	
5.2	0.006	0.034	0.109	0.238	0.406	0.581	0.732	0.845	0.918	0.960	0.982	0.993	0.997	0.999	1.000	
5.4	0.005	0.029	0.095	0.213	0.373	0.546	0.702	0.822	0.903	0.951	0.977	0.990	0.996	0.999	1.000	
5.6	0.004	0.024	0.082	0.191	0.342	0.512	0.670	0.797	0.886	0.941	0.972	0.988	0.995	0.998	0.999	1.000
5.8	0.003	0.021	0.072	0.170	0.313	0.478	0.638	0.771	0.867	0.929	0.965	0.984	0.993	0.997	0.999	1.000
6.0	0.002	0.017	0.062	0.151	0.285	0.446	0.606	0.744	0.847	0.916	0.957	0.980	0.991	0.996	0.999	1.000
6.2	0.002	0.015	0.054	0.134	0.259	0.414	0.574	0.716	0.826	0.902	0.949	0.975	0.989	0.995	0.998	0.999
6.4	0.002	0.012	0.046	0.119	0.235	0.384	0.542	0.687	0.803	0.886	0.939	0.969	0.986	0.994	0.997	0.999
6.6	0.001	0.010	0.040	0.105	0.213	0.355	0.511	0.658	0.780	0.869	0.927	0.963	0.982	0.992	0.997	0.999
6.8	0.001	0.009	0.034	0.093	0.192	0.327	0.480	0.628	0.755	0.850	0.915	0.955	0.978	0.990	0.996	0.998
7.0	0.001	0.007	0.030	0.082	0.173	0.301	0.450	0.599	0.729	0.830	0.901	0.947	0.973	0.987	0.994	0.998
7.2	0.001	0.006	0.025	0.072	0.156	0.276	0.420	0.569	0.703	0.810	0.887	0.937	0.967	0.984	0.993	0.997
7.4	0.001	0.005	0.022	0.063	0.140	0.253	0.392	0.539	0.676	0.788	0.871	0.926	0.961	0.980	0.991	0.996
7.6	0.001	0.004	0.019	0.055	0.125	0.231	0.365	0.510	0.648	0.765	0.854	0.915	0.954	0.976	0.989	0.995
7.8	0.000	0.004	0.016	0.048	0.112	0.210	0.338	0.481	0.620	0.741	0.835	0.902	0.945	0.971	0.986	0.993
8.0	0.000	0.003	0.014	0.042	0.100	0.191	0.313	0.453	0.593	0.717	0.816	0.888	0.936	0.966	0.983	0.992
8.5	0.000	0.002	0.009	0.030	0.074	0.150	0.256	0.386	0.523	0.653	0.763	0.849	0.909	0.949	0.973	0.986
9.0	0.000	0.001	0.006	0.021	0.055	0.116	0.207	0.324	0.456	0.587	0.706	0.803	0.876	0.926	0.959	0.978
9.5	0.000	0.001	0.004	0.015	0.040	0.089	0.165	0.269	0.392	0.522	0.645	0.752	0.836	0.898	0.940	0.967
10.0	0.000	0.000	0.003	0.010	0.029	0.067	0.130	0.220	0.333	0.458	0.583	0.697	0.792	0.864	0.917	0.951
10.5	0.000	0.000	0.002	0.007	0.021	0.050	0.102	0.179	0.279	0.397	0.521	0.639	0.742	0.825	0.888	0.932
11.0	0.000	0.000	0.001	0.005	0.015	0.038	0.079	0.143	0.232	0.341	0.460	0.579	0.689	0.781	0.854	0.907
11.5	0.000	0.000	0.001	0.003	0.011	0.028	0.060	0.114	0.191	0.289	0.402	0.520	0.633	0.733	0.815	0.878
12.0	0.000	0.000	0.001	0.002	0.008	0.020	0.046	0.090	0.155	0.242	0.347	0.462	0.576	0.682	0.772	0.844
12.5	0.000	0.000	0.000	0.002	0.005	0.015	0.035	0.070	0.125	0.201	0.297	0.406	0.519	0.628	0.725	0.806
13.0	0.000	0.000	0.000	0.001	0.004	0.011	0.026	0.054	0.100	0.166	0.252	0.353	0.463	0.573	0.675	0.764
13.5	0.000	0.000	0.000	0.001	0.003	0.008	0.019	0.041	0.079	0.135	0.211	0.304	0.409	0.518	0.623	0.718
14.0	0.000	0.000	0.000	0.000	0.002	0.006	0.014	0.032	0.062	0.109	0.176	0.260	0.358	0.464	0.570	0.669
14.5	0.000	0.000	0.000	0.000	0.001	0.004	0.010	0.024	0.048	0.088	0.145	0.220	0.311	0.413	0.518	0.619
15.0	0.000	0.000	0.000	0.000	0.001	0.003	0.008	0.018	0.037	0.070	0.118	0.185	0.268	0.363	0.466	0.568

▼ **TABLE 3**
MIL-STD.105D (BNQ 9911-105)—Letter-codes Table

Lot size			Special inspection levels				General inspection levels		
			S-1	S-2	S-3	S-4	I	II	III
2	to	8	A	A	A	A	A	A	B
9	to	15	A	A	A	A	A	B	C
16	to	25	A	A	B	B	B	C	D
26	to	50	A	B	B	C	C	D	E
51	to	90	B	B	C	C	C	E	F
91	to	150	B	B	C	D	D	F	G
151	to	280	B	C	D	E	E	G	H
281	to	500	B	C	D	E	F	H	J
501	to	1,200	C	C	E	F	G	J	K
1,201	to	3,200	C	D	E	G	H	K	L
3,201	to	10,000	C	D	F	G	J	L	M
10,001	to	35,000	C	D	F	H	K	M	N
35,001	to	150,000	D	E	G	J	L	N	P
150,001	to	500,000	D	E	G	J	M	P	Q
500,001	and above		D	E	H	K	N	Q	R

Source: Bureau de Normalisation du Québec, "Standard (S1)—Sampling Plans and Procedures for Inspection by Attributes," BNQ 9911-105, p. 11, Government of Quebec, 1980.

▼ **TABLE 3**
MIL-STD.105D (BNQ 9911-105)—Single and Normal Sampling Table

Acceptable quality level (normal Inspection) — each cell shows "Ac Re" (Ac = Accept, Re = Reject). ↓ = use the first sampling plan below the arrow; ↑ = use the first sampling plan above the arrow.

Letter-codes	Sample Size	0.010	0.015	0.025	0.040	0.065	0.10	0.15	0.25	0.40	0.65	1.0	1.5	2.5	4.0	6.5	10	15	25	40	65	100	150	250	400	650	1000
A	2	↓	↓	↓	↓	↓	↓	↓	↓	↓	↓	↓	↓	↓	↓	↓	↓	0 1	1 2	2 3	3 4	5 6	7 8	10 11	14 15	21 22	30 31
B	3	↓	↓	↓	↓	↓	↓	↓	↓	↓	↓	↓	↓	↓	↓	↓	0 1	1 2	2 3	3 4	5 6	7 8	10 11	14 15	21 22	30 31	44 45
C	5	↓	↓	↓	↓	↓	↓	↓	↓	↓	↓	↓	↓	↓	↓	0 1	1 2	2 3	3 4	5 6	7 8	10 11	14 15	21 22	30 31	44 45	↑
D	8	↓	↓	↓	↓	↓	↓	↓	↓	↓	↓	↓	↓	↓	0 1	1 2	2 3	3 4	5 6	7 8	10 11	14 15	21 22	30 31	44 45	↑	↑
E	13	↓	↓	↓	↓	↓	↓	↓	↓	↓	↓	↓	↓	0 1	1 2	2 3	3 4	5 6	7 8	10 11	14 15	21 22	30 31	44 45	↑	↑	↑
F	20	↓	↓	↓	↓	↓	↓	↓	↓	↓	↓	↓	0 1	1 2	2 3	3 4	5 6	7 8	10 11	14 15	21 22	↑	↑	↑	↑	↑	↑
G	32	↓	↓	↓	↓	↓	↓	↓	↓	↓	↓	0 1	1 2	2 3	3 4	5 6	7 8	10 11	14 15	21 22	↑	↑	↑	↑	↑	↑	↑
H	50	↓	↓	↓	↓	↓	↓	↓	↓	↓	0 1	1 2	2 3	3 4	5 6	7 8	10 11	14 15	21 22	↑	↑	↑	↑	↑	↑	↑	↑
J	80	↓	↓	↓	↓	↓	↓	↓	↓	0 1	1 2	2 3	3 4	5 6	7 8	10 11	14 15	21 22	↑	↑	↑	↑	↑	↑	↑	↑	↑
K	125	↓	↓	↓	↓	↓	↓	↓	0 1	1 2	2 3	3 4	5 6	7 8	10 11	14 15	21 22	↑	↑	↑	↑	↑	↑	↑	↑	↑	↑
L	200	↓	↓	↓	↓	↓	↓	0 1	1 2	2 3	3 4	5 6	7 8	10 11	14 15	21 22	↑	↑	↑	↑	↑	↑	↑	↑	↑	↑	↑
M	315	↓	↓	↓	↓	↓	0 1	1 2	2 3	3 4	5 6	7 8	10 11	14 15	21 22	↑	↑	↑	↑	↑	↑	↑	↑	↑	↑	↑	↑
N	500	↓	↓	↓	↓	0 1	1 2	2 3	3 4	5 6	7 8	10 11	14 15	21 22	↑	↑	↑	↑	↑	↑	↑	↑	↑	↑	↑	↑	↑
P	800	↓	↓	↓	0 1	1 2	2 3	3 4	5 6	7 8	10 11	14 15	21 22	↑	↑	↑	↑	↑	↑	↑	↑	↑	↑	↑	↑	↑	↑
Q	1,250	↓	↓	0 1	1 2	2 3	3 4	5 6	7 8	10 11	14 15	21 22	↑	↑	↑	↑	↑	↑	↑	↑	↑	↑	↑	↑	↑	↑	↑
R	2,000	↓	0 1	1 2	2 3	3 4	5 6	7 8	10 11	14 15	21 22	↑	↑	↑	↑	↑	↑	↑	↑	↑	↑	↑	↑	↑	↑	↑	↑

↓ = Use the first sampling plan below the arrow. If the sample size is equal to or greater than the lot size, a 100% inspection is required.

↑ = Use the first sampling plan above the arrow.

Ac = Accept

Re = Reject

Quality of the presented lots ("*p*" as the defective units for an AQL ≤ 10; in defects per 100 units for AQLs of 1 to 1,000).

Source: Bureau de Normalisation du Québec, "Standard (S1)—Sampling Plans and Procedures for Inspection by Attributes," BNQ 9911-105, p. 12, Government of Quebec, 1980.

▼ **TABLE 4**
Random Numbers

83967	14924	89541	51612	74638	22887	01440	77044	88765	67919
84810	71607	28345	81501	01939	79269	48553	18277	72464	73678
49990	60102	81465	64575	29842	09931	07863	00794	03278	01746
02051	56587	00449	70323	12031	12667	59220	90638	63963	94213
65332	33393	55620	04433	42005	73246	93517	26453	01200	72848
16488	30109	68269	37990	47977	12554	18395	15333	63234	97025
42309	92592	36735	55291	19328	35287	96921	69836	47322	34173
04063	78232	58341	72165	29645	51112	53350	91169	81354	39908
84715	27421	44561	12085	53397	68175	91171	52015	47967	07223
41808	73356	81204	72525	26916	93035	09779	26854	74085	75577
63919	26528	31143	72416	36692	86316	74642	61419	82980	17560
83977	22550	87432	55450	25262	58739	01013	53986	62819	54189
97595	07664	26011	93502	95021	39467	19520	76784	15976	69282
17116	37954	73877	39252	29524	01604	78332	13434	37307	47707
78300	10752	90692	25847	17030	46309	16896	86861	66763	16917
42649	72929	11786	61052	09119	57481	15102	22645	64731	28369
34037	66495	15876	49914	81101	10242	18584	84838	84286	94905
84573	11233	57725	59688	69328	50492	53498	76395	52705	14914
08813	72506	89937	70437	39595	33439	69880	92733	85504	40482
14453	28524	00505	49093	49356	07906	99944	42915	90122	04254
67115	09713	53488	65453	28077	44302	35518	36525	28243	15801
41050	70270	37253	04510	15634	53906	88843	91204	80853	86163
14596	51852	42652	33009	93498	90782	34549	79647	84575	64270
62802	70782	19438	74095	44669	86482	76634	06821	35509	67491
70258	31460	97588	60863	18804	74258	58512	57562	81847	97537
26948	22222	32681	47666	00675	35037	91404	97932	56686	85710
83369	14328	23790	32429	04333	93470	00006	53143	41624	40254
81179	05024	30432	34781	04135	99768	65951	79207	30353	71102
83811	84002	07192	75171	32998	58893	70700	45538	07163	14252
49358	98073	99111	34768	05749	31856	76550	26164	79663	97378
68220	48443	96946	83149	49913	71387	50502	35754	95672	50840
09310	05061	71578	47096	48649	32532	39890	69737	63440	24573
24862	04020	10485	82977	83941	31261	30862	53123	79347	09247
72454	00111	70568	42384	55154	18424	61996	37536	67688	49846
45390	45974	38089	38894	03414	37582	71899	20677	56113	63450
89862	75158	88260	46611	56591	75549	05347	96258	11383	99200
95188	85863	23772	11654	60416	66254	53653	50801	51707	36900
15046	04962	80893	87145	43296	47451	42108	06018	67390	90423
42833	68672	70686	20934	79500	64409	47671	71747	92520	05383
64257	97486	50941	92047	97123	69116	18456	56066	91099	81875
73898	41586	87746	73523	63258	92394	84376	33867	60633	44127
80237	52241	92530	33681	85064	60636	49509	17121	08053	51371
12780	48192	84074	04194	19380	24737	00204	77861	46743	60925
44379	25266	52350	25797	80895	05521	58688	15989	35951	18886
78345	41277	29656	60400	70531	94918	43699	35663	06520	53678
79876	20477	15020	15908	36958	40144	25438	23046	90232	91098
35997	51080	06428	23261	45679	89549	13450	74163	30390	87346
07259	72771	17554	58133	94500	63308	50811	75108	54691	58679
47774	05905	05867	62842	49425	32541	76771	07999	35986	58221
75462	86471	27043	68089	39440	99419	02580	70821	22480	24456

AUTHOR INDEX

SUBJECT INDEX

O

operating system (definition of term), 23
operational objectives, 5
operations flow chart, 26-27
operations (definition of term), 5, 6
Optimized Production Technology (OPT), 282
OPT (Optimized Production Technology), 282
ordering costs, 64
    EOQ and, 66-67, 70-71, 73-75
    and inventory management, 57
    sensitivity analysis and, 72
order launching-expediting approach, 165
order point, 79. *See also* reorder point (Rop)
outputs, in manufacturing process, 23
output tables, 100, 102
overhead costs, 62

P

PAC. *See* production activity control
parent item, 173
Pareto analysis, 267, 268, 276, 277
pegging reports, 186
period order quantity (POQ), 188
PERT. *See* Project Evaluation and Review Technique
PESTE factors, 9, 19, 21
PIPC. *See* production and inventory planning and control
pipeline stock, 54
poka-yoke, 267, 277
Political, Economic, Social, Technological and Ecological (PESTE) factors, 9
    and product and process design, 19, 21
POM. *See* production/operations management
POQ (period order quantity), 188
PP. *See* production planning
PPC (production planning and control), 54
PP-MPS loop, 152
predecessors, immediate, 239, 248
predictive maintenance, 276
priority rules, 219-224
proactive inventory-management systems, 80, 84-86, 276
process
    (definition of term), 18
    manufacturing, 23
    type of flow, 32
process mass production system, 236
procurement, 170
    matrix organization and, 243-244
    and project management, 238
    and role of inventory, 53
    in value chain, 25

product
    (definition of term), 18
    flexibility, 30
    mix, 45
    and process design, 18-47
production
    (definition of term), 4-5
    matrix organization and, 243-244
    and rescheduling, 217. *See also* mass production system
production activity control (PAC), 153, 204, 205-217. *See also* production and inventory planning and control (PIPC); production control; production planning and control (PPC)
production and inventory planning and control (PIPC)
    JIT and, 271, 280-282
    and MPS, 151-153, 166
    PAC and, 204-206, 207, 209. *See also* production activity control (PAC); production control; production planning and control (PPC)
production control, 211. *See also* production activity control (PAC); production and inventory planning and control (PIPC); production planning and control (PPC)
production engineering, 22
production/operations management (POM), 2-13, 8-10, 98-99
    computers and, 121
    and design, 20, 21, 22
    forecasting needs, 103
    planning and, 116
    project management and, 238
    technology and, 39, 41
production planning and control (PPC), 54. *See also* production activity control (PAC); production and inventory planning and control (PIPC); production control
production planning (PP) (aggregate planning), 117, 151, 152
    conditions and restraints, 122-124
    detailed, 150-168
    and MPS, 150-153
    operations and, 116-141
production schedule, 120, 209. *See also* master production schedule (MPS)
production strategy, within company, 13
project control, 245-246. *See also* project management; project planning
project (definition of term), 236
Project Evaluation and Review Technique (PERT), 239-240, 255-257
project management, 236-259
    (definition of term), 236. *See also* project control; project planning